CW01276597

IBN KHALDŪN ON SUFISM

IBN KHALDŪN ON SUFISM:

REMEDY FOR THE QUESTIONER IN SEARCH OF ANSWERS

Shifā' al-Sā'il li-Tahdhīb al-Masā'il

Translated by Yumna Özer

THE ISLAMIC TEXTS SOCIETY

This first edition published 2017 by
The Islamic Texts Society
Miller's House
Kings Mill Lane
Great Shelford
Cambridge CB22 5EN, UK

British Library Cataloguing-in-Publication Data.
A catalogue record for this book is
available from the British Library.

ISBN: 978 1911141 28 0 paper

CONTENTS

Acknowledgements vii
Translator's Introduction ix

[Prologue 1]

CHAPTER ONE: On the Way of the Sufis, Its General Examination and Differentiation from the Other Lawful Paths. On the Meaning of This Name for the First Sufis 5

CHAPTER TWO: On the Aspirations of the Sufis Towards Spiritual Struggles and the Reasons Why They Engaged in Them 19

CHAPTER THREE: On Spiritual Struggle in General, Its Subdivisions and Its Conditions 35

CHAPTER FOUR: On How the Later Sufis Transposed the Name Sufism from Its Original Meaning and Our Refutation of Them on That Account 54

CHAPTER FIVE: On the Shaykh and When His Presence Is Required in the Spiritual Struggle 70

CHAPTER SIX: Arbitration between the Two Debaters: Ascertaining the Truth of Their Words and the Soundness of Their Arguments 79

CONCLUSION AND ASCERTAINMENT 109

Notes 111
Bibliography 143
Index 155

ACKNOWLEDGEMENTS

One of the issues handled by Ibn Khaldūn in *Shifā' al-sā'il li-tahdhīb al-masā'il* is the inadequacy of written communication to express deeper realities. In acknowledging all those who helped me with this project, I too feel this sense of inadequacy.

It is Safer Dal Efendi who taught me that the essence of Sufism was *ḥāl* (state) rather than *qāl* (word). His name is engraved in my memory and heart. As to Victor Danner, he was my *shaykh al-taʿlīm*, my teacher. He directed my PhD thesis with wisdom, patience and that dry humour of his that endeared him to his students and to all those who knew him. I will always remember him with respect and love.

How could I ever express my thanks to all the members of my family and to my husband Sami Özer? In particular, I would like to mention my youngest brother, Raja Adal, who was also my teacher. He taught me by patiently commenting, suggesting, editing, encouraging and advising me at every step. Thank you, Raja, from the bottom of my heart.

I would like to extend my thanks to William Chittick, who encouraged me to turn my thesis into a book, to Yousef Casewit and Mohammed Rustom for their comments and help, to our friends Cemil Aydın and Juliane Hammer from the University of North Carolina at Chapel Hill, for their care and support, and to Mustafa Demirci from the Ankara Yıldırım University for his kindness and help with many *ḥadīth* references.

I would also like to express my gratitude to all the members of my thesis committee at Indiana University. The late Wadie Jwaideh, whom we used to call 'a walking talking encyclopedia', will always be remembered with respect and fondness, as will Salih Altoma and Consuelo Lopez Morillas whom I thank for their interest in my work. Jean Louis Michon also helped me locate two manuscripts in

Rabat that were instrumental for my work, one of which had never been worked on by scholars of the *Shifāʾ*.

I could not end this note without mentioning how rewarding it was to work with Fatima Azzam from the Islamic Texts Society and with my editor Andrew Booso. Both helped me improve my manuscript through an interesting exchange of ideas and constructive dynamic communication. I am grateful to them and to the staff at the Islamic Texts Society for their professionalism, their engagement in the editorial process, and their commitment to and love of their work.

I hope that this annotated translation of Ibn Khaldūn's *Shifāʾ al-sāʾil li-tahdhīb al-masāʾil* will shed some light into Ibn Khaldūn's inner life and will be of interest to lovers of Sufism. May Ibn Khaldūn and the reader forgive me for the inevitable mistakes, which are mine alone.

Yumna Özer
Istanbul, May 2017

TRANSLATOR'S INTRODUCTION

1. A Sufi Debate and the Origins of the *Shifāʾ al-sāʾil li-tahdhīb al-masāʾil*

Towards the later part of the eighth/fourteenth century, a heated discussion arose among the mystics of Andalusia. These disputes were so intense that the verbal polemics often degenerated into 'fist and sandal fighting'.[1] The debate revolved around the following question: Can the wayfarer on the way to the Truth wholly depend upon the guidance of books on Sufism (*taṣawwuf*) or does he need the oral teachings of a master, a shaykh?[2]

The event was related by many later authors and Sufis, including Aḥmad Zarrūq (d. 899/1493),[3] Aḥmad al-Wansharīsī (d. 914/1508),[4] ʿAbd al-Qādir al-Fāsī (d. 1091/1680),[5] Abū ʿAbd Allāh al-Masnāwī (d. 1136/1724)[6] and Aḥmad b. ʿAjība (d. 1224/1809).[7] They tell us that the discussion was so drawn-out that the Sufis of Granada, unable to find an answer or agree on a solution, decided to appeal to the erudite and wise men in the Maghrib (the West). Abū Isḥāq al-Shāṭibī (d. 790/1388),[8] one of the renowned judges of Granada, addressed a letter to several scholars, including the Mālikī legist Abū al-ʿAbbās al-Qabbāb (d. 779/1377),[9] who was also one of Shāṭibī's teachers, and the famous Sufi Ibn ʿAbbād al-Rundī (d. 792/1390).[10] The texts of both answers are reported by Wansharīsī in his collection of legal opinions (*fatwās*), *Al-Miʿyār*.[11] We do not know whether Ibn Khaldūn (d. 808/1406), their contemporary, was involved in this controversy and asked to give his opinion in this matter, but he wrote a treatise in response to this controversy: the *Shifāʾ al-sāʾil li-tahdhīb al-masāʾil*.

Much has been written about Ibn Khaldūn the historian, politician and author, yet little is known about the man. Born in Tunis, his peregrinations stretched from Andalusia to the Maghrib and the

Mashriq (the East). He started his political life at the age of seventeen, holding several leading governmental posts in Granada, today's Morocco, Algeria, Tunisia and finally Egypt. His prolific writings include his seminal work the *Muqaddima*, in which he expounds his philosophy of history. Beyond the celebrated statesman and social theorist, however, there lies the man in his inner voyage, which is a subject that is seldom broached. I believe the *Shifā' al-sā'il li-tahdhīb al-masā'il* provides such a glimpse into the spiritual life of Ibn Khaldūn and, more broadly, into the world of legists (*fuqahā'*; singular *faqīh*) and Sufis in the fourteenth-century Maghrib and Mashriq.

II. Historical Overview

A. THE MAGHRIB (THE WEST)

Since the fifth/eleventh century, North Africa and Spain had been under the influence of dynasties that had greatly contributed to the religious and doctrinal unity of the Maghrib. The Almoravids and the Almohads, both Berber dynasties, repressed a number of incipient heresies and confirmed Western Islam's strong orthodox, Ashʿarī[12] and Mālikī heredity.[13] The reign of the Almoravids was also that of the legists. So great was their power that, in 503/1109, the state legists urged the sovereign ʿAlī b. Yūsuf b. Tashufīn (d. 538/1143)[14] to burn all the works of the Sufi Abū Ḥāmid al-Ghazālī (d. 505/1111),[15] including his seminal work, the *Iḥyā' ʿulūm al-dīn*. In the *Iḥyā'*, 'by bifurcating the Islamic sciences into worldly and otherworldly, Ghazālī contended that the politically connected legal scholars played second-fiddle to the mystics. The *Iḥyā'* thus equipped the latter with a set of arguments against the state-*fuqahā'* and gave them a basis for claims to a superior form of knowledge.'[16] The auto-da-fé of Ghazālī's books and the formalism of the powerful state legists were met with resistance. ʿAlī b. Ḥirzihim of Fez (d. 559/1164), a student of the famous Sevillian Qāḍī Abū Bakr b. al-ʿArabī (d. 543/1148),[17] who had introduced the *Iḥyā'* to the Maghrib, continued propagating Ghazālī's teachings.[18] Besides, the clash between the state legists and the Sufis or the opponents to the auto-da-fé was also intensified by the fact that 'the crackdown on the leading 6th/12th century mystics, in particular Ibn Barrajān (d. 536/1141)[19] and Ibn al-ʿArīf (d. 536/1141),[20] coincided with the book burning'.[21] In Portugal, Ibn Qasī (d. 545/1151) took advantage of the turmoil to rebel against the official stand and rule, organizing a pro-Ghazālian, syncretic-Sufi, anti-Almoravid uprising.[22] Nevertheless, beyond the sometimes politicized auto-da-fé crisis, 'the *Iḥyā'* served as a rallying point for alternative sources of religious authority and helped forge the self-identity of Sufism'.[23] Ultimately, while it drew inspiration from Ghazālī and Eastern ways, Western Sufism acquired a distinctive nature and would become integrated and widespread in the cities and rural areas of Andalusia and North Africa.[24]

The Almohad dynasty also epitomized, at least in its initial stages, another intense reaction against the excessive legalism that had prevailed during the reign of the Almoravids. The founder of the new dynasty, the self-proclaimed al-Mahdī b. Tūmart (d. 524/1130),[25] professed a return to Islam's origins and a less literalistic approach to the Qur'ān and Sunna, instead of the adherence to the canons and regulations of a formalized Mālikī juridical rite as understood by the state jurists.[26] Many opposed his views and reforms, and among the uncongenial were the legists. Ibn Tūmart's beliefs did not survive him; and ʿAbd al-Mu'min (d. 558/1163), his successor, re-embraced the doctrine of the legists.[27]

Yet again, despite the official line, the more mystically-oriented routes did not come to an end and Sufism flourished. One of the most eminent saints who lived during the reign of the Almohads is undoubtedly the Andalusian Abū Madyan of Tlemcen, called the Shaykh of Shaykhs (d. 594/1198).[28] Among his teachers were the above-mentioned Qāḍī Abū Bakr b. al-ʿArabī and Ibn Ḥirzihim of Fez, who introduced him to the teachings of Ghazālī, as well as the controversial Malāmatī Abū ʿAbd Allāh al-Daqqāq of Fez (d. end of 6th/12th or early 7th/13th)[29] and Abū Yaʿzzā al-Ḥazmīrī (d. 572/1177), the wandering ascetic of the Berber mountains.[30] The vast Shādhiliyya derives from Abū Madyan, through his follower ʿAbd al-Salām b. Mashīsh (d. 626/1228)[31] and the latter's only disciple Abū al-Ḥasan al-Shādhilī (d. 656/1258).[32] Ultimately, neither the Almoravids nor the Almohads were able to smother the amazing surge of spiritual life in the Maghrib or to suppress the influence of Ghazālī and the reassertion of Sufism as part of Islam, within the boundaries of Sunni Law. With time, Sufism became an integral part of Maghribi spiritual life, no longer disavowed by the legists.

It was under the Marinids, the main dynasty that dominated North Africa during Ibn Khaldūn's lifetime, that Maghribi rulers became the defenders of Sufism.[33] They were concerned with the tentative reforms of the Almohad al-Mahdī b. Tūmart, which they believed were laden with heresy, and they benefited from the experiences of their predecessors. The Marinid rule was a blend of orthodoxy and Sufism that gave free reign to the intense intellectual activity that had commenced with the Almohads; and their creed was pervaded with strong mystical tendencies which may have been the residue of the influence of Ibn Tūmart, but was more probably the direct consequence of the amazing proliferation of saints in the Maghrib.[34]

The Marinids venerated the great Sufis of the preceding era like Abū Madyan and Ḥalwī (d. 611/1214),[35] whose shrines were built by Abū al-Ḥasan ʿAlī b. ʿUthmān (d. 749/1348)[36] and Abū ʿInān Fāris (d. 758/1358),[37] respectively. They also honoured living saints such as Qāḍī al-Fishtālī of Fez (d. 779/1377)[38] and Ibn ʿĀshir of Salé (d. 764/1362).[39] The fact that Ibn ʿĀshir and Ibn ʿAbbād held teaching positions in the Marinid cities of Salé and Fez is illustrative of the flourishing of *taṣawwuf* in urban contexts. Sufism spread in the rural areas as well.[40] In his *Musnad*, Ibn Marzūq (d. 782/1380) confirms that one of the goals of the Marinid Abū al-Ḥasan was the building of state-controlled *madrasas*, as well as Sufi lodges (*zāwiya*), frontier outposts (*ribāṭ*) and hostels (*buyūt al-fuqarā'*).[41]

As for Ibn Qunfudh (d. 810/1407/8), who travelled throughout Morocco for some twenty years, he bequeathed to us in his *Uns al-faqīr wa-ʿizz al-ḥaqīr* one of the most precious extant documents on the fourteenth-century *ṭawā'if* (sing. *ṭā'ifa*) or *ṭuruq* (sing. *ṭariqa*), or Sufi orders, whose meeting places were these *zāwiyas*.[42] According to him, the numerous Sufi groups had many adherents, were closely connected to the lives of the tribes and often exerted a strong influence on the authorities, protecting and interceding for the population although never entering into direct conflict with the Marinid authorities.[43] It is difficult to ascertain the relationship between the more rural Sufi orders and the inhabitants of cities, where many individuals were not officially affiliated with any specific order or community. Yet, we know that there were masters in the cities, such as Ibn ᶜĀshir of Salé, around whom highly erudite city dwellers, like Ibn ᶜAbbād, would gather in a communal manner. These individuals may have had ties with the Shādhiliyya, which had its roots in urban Morocco and deeply influenced North African intellectual life,[44] particularly via the writings of Ibn ᶜAṭā' Allāh (d. 709/1309).[45] The Shādhilī approach emphasized the seeker's inward life over community rules, and its geneses and principles fit with the way of life of the more independent people in the Maghrib, as was the case for Ibn ᶜAbbād, for instance.[46]

In North Africa, many 'independent' eminent Sufis were also illustrious legists, and many a famous legist had a Sufi master.[47] The Marinid legists did not oppose Sufism provided it did not border on what they deemed to be heresy. In fact, the Sufi Path was not generally considered to constitute a rupture with the legal way; rather, it was simply the very natural consequence of a believer's deep inclination, the outcome of a burning need for self-purification and realization, and one that remained in conformity with orthodox traditional Islam. In the East, Ghazālī had attempted to reconcile the Law and the Sufi Path; but in the West, despite some demurrals and frictions—as in the *karāmāt al-awliyā'* polemic and the *Iḥyā'* crisis mentioned above—there was no dire need for such reconciliation because there was no conspicuous breach between the two. This phenomenon is particularly noticeable in the 'more independent' trend of Sufism described above, precisely the one that attracted and united legists and mystics, *fuqahā'* and Sufis. With this background, Ibn Khaldūn was an intellectual and legist who was first exposed to Sufism in the Marinid West before encountering it in the Mashriq, where he spent his last days.

B. THE MASHRIQ (THE EAST)

Unlike in the Mālikī West, Egypt saw no dominant school of Islamic law. Like the West, however, the instability of the Ayyubid[48] and

Mamluk[49] dynasties and the rapid turnover and corruption of the rulers drew more and more believers away from worldly fighting to the Path of Sufism. Since the beginning of Islam, the Nile Valley had seen some of the greatest Sufis in the history of *taṣawwuf*, starting with Dhū al-Nūn al-Miṣrī (d. 245/859), the physicians' patron saint and one of Cairo's legendary saints.[50] But of all eras, the seventh/thirteenth century was particularly prolific in saints. The most revered among them were Aḥmad al-Badawī (d. 676/1278),[51] his contemporary Ibrāhīm al-Dasūqī (d. 676/1277),[52] Abū al-Ḥasan al-Shādhilī, his disciple Abū al-ʿAbbās al-Mursī (d. 686/1287)[53] and Ibn ʿAtā' Allāh al-Iskandarī. The Badawiyya (or Aḥmadiyya) and Dasūqiyya (or Burhāniyya) *ṭarīqa*s were rustic orders that spread primarily in Egypt and drew most of their adherents from the rural population, although they also appealed to the less popular classes and attracted some members of the ruling Mamluk dynasty. Ibn Taghribirdī (d. 874/1469) tells us of the wife of Sultan Khushqadam, who was buried in 871/1466 with the red flag of the Badawiyya covering her coffin.[54]

As to the Shādhiliyya, its origins confirm the close connections between Eastern and Western Sufism. Abū al-Ḥasan al-Shādhilī was born in Ghumāra (today's Morocco), travelled to Tunisia and then Alexandria, where he taught. His initiatic chain binds him to the two great Maghribi shaykhs: ʿAbd al-Salām b. Mashīsh and, through the latter, to the patron saint of Tlemcen (in present-day Algeria), Abū Madyan. The origins of his successors, or *khalīfa*s—namely the Spanish Abū al-ʿAbbās al-Mursī and the Egyptian Ibn Atā' Allāh al-Iskandarī—also reflect the geographical and cultural inclusiveness of Shadhilī's teaching. They, too, followed his sober teaching method and often attracted more intellectually-inclined characters. Unlike the Badawiyya and Dasūqiyya orders, the adherents to the Shādhilī path were both Easterners and Westerners, as attested in Cairo, where the Shādhiliyya had many adepts of Maghribi origin.

The meeting place of Sufis in Egypt was the *khanaqa*.[55] It resembled its Western counterpart, the *zāwiya* or *ribāṭ*. Like the Marinid rulers of the Maghrib, the Ayyubid and Mamluk sultans encouraged the building of both *madrasa*s and *khanaqa*s.[56] Ibn Baṭṭūṭa (d.

778/1377), who visited Cairo in 726/1326, tells us that the Egyptian *khanaqa*s were meeting places 'assigned to a *ṭā'ifa* of dervishes, most of whom are men of culture trained in the way of Sufism'.[57] They were also houses where students, travellers, foreign Sufis and pilgrims on their way to Mecca could lodge, rest, pray and meet each other. Even more closely tied to the ruling dynasties than their Moroccan counterparts, the Cairo *khanaqa*s were officially sponsored and their head was appointed by the authorities. Qalqashandī (d. 820/1418) explains the rapport between the Egyptian *khanaqa*s and the Mamluk government with the following words: 'Since these institutions were in the gift of the Mamluk rulers and often very lucrative to their heads, anyone whom the ruler wished to provide with a sinecure without affecting his pocket was frequently given the appointment.'[58] The statements of Ibn Baṭṭūṭa and Qalqashandī imply that the heads of the *khanaqa*s were often high officials and intellectuals with knowledge of and possibly training in the Path of Sufism. This point is not lost on the reader who studies the *Shifā'* of Ibn Khaldūn, who was a judge (*qāḍī*) in Mamluk Cairo and the appointed head of its main *khanaqa*, as we shall soon see.

III. Sufism in the Life of Ibn Khaldūn

Little is known about Ibn Khaldūn's links to Sufism; he was rather reticent to expose personal feelings or spiritual ideals. Moreover, whenever religion is mentioned by him, some commentators have perceived sarcastic hints, stylistic subterfuges or political guile on the part of Ibn Khaldūn, while others have exonerated him from what they see as the inevitable reticence of a person in his position. In other words, 'whenever the links between Ibn Khaldūn and the Sufi Path are taken into consideration, it is generally to decry or deny them'.[59] These interpreters see in Sufism the hermetic speculations of some strange groups, a discipline that is the polar opposite of the one delineated by the religion of Islam and its substantive law (*fiqh*); and since they strived to associate Ibn Khaldūn with purely contemporary sciences and trends, they either disregard, or else dismiss, the elements of mysticism in his works and life as flashes of obscurantism.

To give here an exhaustive list of all of Ibn Khaldūn's reviewers in this regard is impossible, but perhaps a few examples will help illustrate the aforementioned propensity.[60] Even as early as the nineteenth century, Alfred von Kremer, orientalist and politician, believed that the religious references and formulae found in the *Muqaddima* were but an Islamic stylistic device that the reader should not heed. Around 1930, scholars such as F. Gabrieli, G. Bouthoul, J. Ritter and others analysed the works of Ibn Khaldūn in the light of positivism, determinism, sociology and nationalism, and wished to prove that, for Ibn Khaldūn, the driving forces behind history were such elements as the climate, standard of life, social milieu, tribal alliances or any other positivist element, insisting that the historian's thought was clearly separated from any sort of religious consideration. To the Egyptian writer and critic Ṭāhā Ḥusayn there was no religious influence in the thought of Ibn Khaldūn, and 'the arguments in the *Muqaddima*, that could lead to the belief that such a [religious] influence exists, only show Ibn Khaldūn's prudent desire to avoid blame for a purely historical analysis, one that is liberated from any theological background'.[61] As to the writer Kāmil ᶜAyyād, he believes that, for Ibn Khaldūn, the laws determining historical evolution were purely social and only these laws can justify history; Ibn Khaldūn's principles are, in ᶜAyyād's estimation, not theocentric at all since they oppose certain positions of Islamic theology and the traditional doctrine of causality and natural law. According to ᶜAyyād, religion is to Ibn Khaldūn a mere cultural and socio-psychological phenomenon, and the historian 'shows great adroitness in interpreting the Islamic law with his view, and so seeks to subordinate religion to his own scientific theories'.[62] For the social scientist Ali Wardi, there is no common ground between the theologians' use of logic and the logical social tools handled by Ibn Khaldūn.[63] Moreover, according to Wardi and his co-author Fuad Baali, 'Ibn Khaldūn took the Sufite dialectic, deprived it of its spiritualistic colouring, and fixed it anew upon a materialistic or sociological basis.'[64] As to Lacoste, one of the Marxist interpreters of Ibn Khaldūn's work, he also believes that Ibn Khaldūn's theories are precursory to historical materialism. For him, Ibn Khaldūn was unfortunately influenced by the bigotry prevailing in his time, by the religion of Islam, which had become a hindering ideology, and by the general preoccupation with theology and Sufism, which could only paralyse intellectual life. Furthermore, Lacoste argues that Sufism was a purely scholastic movement that burdened the teaching in the *madrasas* with illusionistic and anti-rationalistic speculations; it led to renunciation, escapism away from reality, and was therefore endorsed by the authorities since it could not represent a threat to the social establishment.[65]

Recently, many studies have insisted on the necessity for different approaches to Ibn Khaldūn's theories that rightly place him in his own intellectual and religious context.[66] The author grew and lived in a culture that was not secular but, on the contrary, spiritually oriented. His own personal formation was a solid juridical and religious one, and Sufism was omnipresent on the scene. There seems to be pertinent clues, for our purposes, in each phase of Ibn Khaldūn's personal biography: his early training; his sojourn in Andalusia, where his friendship with Ibn al-Khaṭīb developed and matured; and finally, his tenure in the Mashriq, where he was appointed as the head of a Cairo *khanaqa*. As to his textual legacy, our sources are the *Muqaddima*'s sixth chapter 'On Sufism' and his *Shifā'*, which is exclusively devoted to *taṣawwuf*.

A. SHAYKH ĀBILĪ IN THE MAGHRIB

Of Ibn Khaldūn's early cultural training, we have scant relevant details. In his *Taʿrīf*, or autobiography, the author states that his father was his first teacher and that both his father and grandfather had retired from the political and administrative world in order to lead a quiet religious life by joining one of the most respected *zāwiyas* in Tunis headed by Abū ʿAbd Allāh al-Zubaydī (d. 740/1340).[67] From the beginning, therefore, Ibn Khaldūn grew up in a religious enviroment and was taught the religious sciences by his family as well as by the most renowned teachers of the time. He recounts also that 'he learned the Qur'ān, reading it twenty-one times according to the seven [canonical] readings until he had memorized it, studied substantive law and Imam Mālik's *Muwaṭṭa*''.[68] To enumerate all his teachers would serve no purpose, but it is perhaps more relevant to deduce from the names and the subjects studied the nature of the author's elementary education, namely the reading of the Qur'ān, theology, religious Law and, as we shall see, Sufism.[69]

The name of one of his teachers, Shaykh Ābilī (d. 757/1356), is notable.[70] Ibn Khaldūn describes him as 'the greatest scholar in the Maghrib and the master of the sciences based on reason'. Ābilī was a guest in the family's home in Tunis for many consecutive years.[71] After his parents' death, Ibn Khaldūn followed his master from Tunis to Fez in order to pursue his studies. With Ābilī, Ibn Khaldūn studied mathematics, logic and 'those disciplines that come after logic: the fundamentals of religion, the Law and the philosophic sciences'.[72] In his teaching, Ābilī did not follow any particular philosophical school but relied mainly on the works of Ibn Sīnā (d. 428/1037), including, we are told, the sections dealing with mysticism in *Kitāb al-ishārāt* and *Kitāb al-shifā'* that the master studied with a few other privileged students only.[73] Interestingly enough, Ābilī himself had been taught by several teachers who were affiliated with Sufism, the most famous of whom was Ibn al-Bannā (d. 720/1320).[74]

That Ābilī not only taught rational sciences but also mystical ones, that he had Sufi masters and that he used to visit the tomb of Abū Madyan and teach in its *zāwiya*—all of this suggests that besides being a mathematician and a philosopher, he was a legist with an interest in the science of Sufism.[75] Furthermore, some of his disciples were recognized Sufis, like Ibn ʿAbbād al-Rundī (who is also believed to have been one of Ibn Khaldūn's friends) or Maqqarī (d. 758/1356).[76] From Ābilī's interest in Sufism, or possible connections to the Sufi Path, one cannot conclude that all of his students—including Ibn Khladūn—had official or non-official, theoretical or practical involvement in the practice of Sufism. Yet, it does confirm once more this all-important feature of Western Islam in the thirteenth and fourteenth centuries, namely that other than some inevitable clashes, official Islam did not see Sufism as a heterodox movement, as was often the case in the Mashriq despite Ghazālī's effort to reconcile the two. In the West, 'Sufism was not only tolerated but incorporated into the life of Maghribi Islam'.[77] Maghribi rulers as well as scholars seem to have been tinged with mysticism, even when not directly involved in the mystical Path.

Sufi works were read at the court, and we are even told that Ibn ᶜĀshir of Salé advised the Sultan Abū ᶜInān to read Muḥāsibī's *Kitāb al-riᶜāya*.[78] The learned here lived in a world where, for most of the time, there was no rupture between Islamic law and Sufism.

Besides their interest in the science of Sufism or their commitment to the Sufi way of life, Ābilī and many of his students also shared similar ideas about some of the burning issues at stake during the Marinid era. For example, Ābilī and his disciples were among the first to fear that, along with the successful blending of the legal and mystical sciences that gave rise to the intellectual renaissance of the Marinid era, there came a certain tendency towards standardization that would lead to an eventual passivity and rigidity in the search for knowledge. Towards the end of the eighth/fourteenth century, decadence seemed to threaten. Eminent scholars, such al-Sharīf al-Tilimsānī (d. 771/1369),[79] and Ābilī's own students, including Ibn Khaldūn, Ibn ᶜAbbād and Maqqarī, foresaw the dangers of an excessive systematization of learning. Not only did Ābilī oppose the building of *madrasas*—which he thought were a means to officialise and thus to control the intellectual activity in the country—but he also disapproved of the proliferation of books, treatises and abstracts that stifled personal effort and judgement, turning the students away from 'the holders of the true sciences'.[80] For him, the traditional master through whom knowledge was transmitted orally was being supplanted, which is precisely the subject matter of Ibn Khaldūn's *Shifā'*.[81] It is Ābilī who 'confronted Ibn Khaldūn with this question of knowledge, its sources, limits and transmission'.[82] Ibn Khaldūn reflected on this issue in the *Shifā'*, where he answered the question posed by the eighth/fourteenth century Andalusian Sufis, his contemporaries, namely the transmission of knowledge via books or masters.

B. IBN AL-KHAṬĪB IN ANDALUSIA

Andalusian and North African cultural lives were intertwined. If North Africa was the homeland of many a pious and saintly man, Andalusia was also immersed in a very intensive intellectual life. Yet, after the sixth/twelfth century, the political situation progressively deteriorated, the Spanish kingdoms surrendered to the Christian advance and the centres of intellectual life slowly shifted from Spain towards North Africa. Nonetheless, one of the last great cities of the Iberian Peninsula was the flourishing Granada, where political and literary life seemed to revolve around one man, Lisān al-Dīn b. al-Khaṭīb, Ibn Khaldūn's friend.

The many common patterns and similar experiences in the lives of the two friends captured our attention. Both had received a solid, vast and refined education with a strong emphasis on the Islamic sciences, participated in the political life of their time and faced the jealousies of their rivals. Both were recognized, in their time and today, as great writers and men of genius who evinced a solid faith, an interest in mysticism and, somewhere in their agitated, adventurous and worldly lives, a nostalgic yearning for solitude and peace.

More is known about Ibn al-Khaṭīb's links with Sufism than about Ibn Khaldūn's. Yet, we know that both were students of Maqqarī, who encouraged Ibn al-Khaṭīb to adhere to Sufism.[83] The name of another common teacher in mysticism deserves to be mentioned here as an additional link between Ibn al-Khaṭīb and Ibn Khaldūn: Abū Mahdī ʿIsā b. al-Zayyāt. There is little information about him besides the writings of Ibn Khaldūn, who devotes one of the sections of the *Muqaddima* to Ibn al-Zayyāt's commentary on ʿAbd Allāh al-Anṣārī's (d. 481/1089) *Manāzil al-sā'irīn*: 'I consider it appropriate to quote here a remark made by our master, the gnostic (*ʿārif*) and greatest saint in Spain, Abū Mahdī ʿIsā b. al-Zayyāt. He commented very often on [ʿAbd Allāh al-Anṣārī] Harawī's verse in his *Kitāb al-maqāmāt* [Book of Stations]. These verses seem to almost profess the theory of absolute oneness (*waḥda muṭlaqa*)'.[84] Ibn Khaldūn admits that he copied this commentary from his friend's treatise on divine love, *Rawḍat al-taʿrīf bi'l-ḥubb al-sharīf*, and he concludes this section with the following words: 'Here ends the quotation from Shaykh Abū Mahdī b. al-Zayyāt. I quoted it from the book on love by the *wazīr* Ibn al-Khaṭīb entitled *Al-Taʿrīf bi'l-ḥubb al-sharīf* [Information on the Noble Love of God]. I heard it from our Shaykh Abū Mahdī himself several times. However, I think that the written form, in Ibn al-Khaṭīb's work, preserves it better than my memory, because it has been a long time since I heard Abū Mahdī tell it.'[85] The influence of Abū Mahdī b. al-Zayyāt must have been profound on the two friends. Both Ibn al-Khaṭīb and Ibn Khaldūn adopted his explanation in justification of the *tawḥīd-waḥda* doctrine as put forward by many mystics, including Anṣārī and his school. Anṣārī had been attacked for refusing to profess divine unity (*tawḥīd*) when he in fact only objected to the profession of divine unity in the case of the wayfarer who has attained a higher station. At this advanced level, the wayfarer experiences absolute oneness (*waḥda*)—an intimate reality that can no longer allow for divine unity.[86]

A short distance south from Andalusia, across the strait of Gibraltar, the Moroccan city of Salé had become a Sufi gathering centre. There lived a great master, Ibn ᶜĀshir. Ibn al-Khaṭīb was able to meet with him during his forced exile to Morocco, whereas the Sultan Abū ᶜInān himself tried unsuccessfully to obtain an audience from the much-respected saint. The happiest, most fervent and peaceful days of Ibn al-Khaṭīb were those he spent in Salé during the year 762/1360. He withdrew there and, in his own words, 'lived in retirement in the Shellah necropolis, meditating and practising the litany (*wird*) and remembrance (*dhikr*) of the Sufis'.[87] Ibn Khaldūn shared with his friend Ibn al-Khaṭīb the same need for withdrawal from the world, away from their turbulent lives. He also fled several times the upheavals of political life and often retired to al-ᶜUbbād, the shrine of Abū Madyan in the city of Tlemcen.[88]

The correspondence between the two friends is our most precious source of information. When Ibn al-Khaṭīb writes to his friend telling him of his intention to renounce the world and worldly ambitions, Ibn Khaldūn answers, 'This is an admirable decision! Your soul has lofty aspirations; first its far-reaching desires were fulfilled and now it aspires to spiritual blessings.'[89] However, when Ibn al-Khaṭīb returns to Granada, he seems to relinquish his spiritual yearning for his previous worldly occupations. Again, he shares with Ibn Khaldūn his regrets and grief: 'Since you left, I have compiled many collections and writings concerning which one could say, "O Ibrāhīm! But there is no Ibrāhīm today!"'[90] In this rather cryptic interjection, Ibn al-Khaṭīb is actually referring to Ibrāhīm b. al-Adham (d. 159/776), prince of Balkh, who was summoned by a mysterious voice while hunting, and immediately abandoned his dissipated life, put on the frock of the dervishes and wandered about the world.[91] Ibn al-Khaṭīb laments his inward conflict between material and spiritual needs, his painful attachment to worldly vanities and his own vacillating spiritual state. Ibn Khaldūn will go through an analogous type of experience, although he did not express himself as openly as his friend. However, in his letters to Ibn al-Khaṭīb, he expresses his disillusions with the instability and the anarchy of life: 'We were the suns of glory, but they all disappeared and the horizon is lamenting.' He then reflects on uncontrollable human ambitions: '...[these] blind desires, this incurable disease, the perplexity that is about to take the soul...Is it of use, while my fortune is [leading me] down, to keep climbing after hopes?' He then concludes the letter with the following words: '...and in your useful admonition may there be the cure of this incurable disease, if God wills...For God alone is the saviour from the bondage of hopes and the guide to casting off these beguiling fortunes.'[92]

Unlike his friend Ibn al-Khaṭīb, however, Ibn Khaldūn does not give an explicit reason for aspiring towards withdrawal from worldly and political life. The cruel imprisonment and ignominious death of Ibn al-Khaṭīb (also named *dhū'l-mītatayn* for having been buried alive because he was condemned for holding heretical views) could more than account for our historian's excessive prudence in the verbalization of what could be used against him. Ibn Khaldūn made the final decision to abandon the world with its traps and deceptions more than twice.[93] Yet, in 776/1375, after his return from Granada, and like Ibn al-Khaṭīb, he was pressed into service by chieftains and monarchs who needed him to intercede and mediate for them. Again, in 784/1382, he departed for Egypt, once more aspiring to lead a less turbulent life, yet reluctantly acceding to the sovereign's request that he meet with Tamerlane in 803/1401.[94] It is only during the third and last phase of his life, in his Egyptian years, that Ibn Khaldūn's yearning for peace and solitude was answered.

C. SAᶜĪD AL-SUᶜADĀʾ IN THE MASHRIQ

The life of Ibn Khaldūn during this last Egyptian phase no longer reflects the conflict between the intriguing politician caught in the wheel of power and the religious scholar aspiring to solitude and devotion. Twice while in the East, Ibn Khaldūn performed the pilgrimage to Mecca. In 1384, he was appointed chief Mālikī judge (*qāḍī*) of Cairo, and in Rabīᶜ II 791/April 1389, he was appointed head of the Khanaqa al-Baybarsiyya in Cairo.[95]

Maqrīzī reports that the Khanaqa al-Baybarsiyya was the first *khanaqa* to be built in Egypt. It was named after its founder, al-Muẓaffir Rukn al-Dīn Baybars II al-Jashankīr (d. 709/1309), as al-Khanaqa al-Baybarsiyya al-Ṣalāḥiyya al-Muẓaffariyya al-Rukniyya. It is often more simply referred to as Saᶜīd al-Suᶜadāʾ.[96] According to Ibn Khaldūn, this establishment was 'the greatest and most successful [*khanaqa*], its profits were the largest, and its endowments [*awqāf*, singular *waqf*] the most numerous'.[97] We know, for instance, that the *wazīr* Ibn al-Khaṭīb had made several of his books an endowment for the *khanaqa*. In a letter to his friend Ibn Khaldūn, he writes, 'I sent the *Rawḍat al-taᶜrīf bi'l-ḥubb al-sharīf* to the East, along with my book on the history of Granada and other works I wrote, and it was declared a *waqf* at the *khanaqa* of Saᶜīd al-Suᶜadāʾ in Cairo and people rushed to read it.'[98]

The head of the Khanaqa al-Baybarsiyya was given the title of 'Shaykh of Shaykhs' (*shuyūkh*) by the Egyptian Mamluk sultans, 'which, however, was only honorific and did not imply any wider jurisdiction than that of his own establishment'.[99] In the year 791/1389, the Shaykh of Shaykhs Sharaf al-Dīn al-Ashqar died and Ibn Khaldūn was appointed to the directorship of the *khanaqa*[100] by Sultan al-Ẓāhir Sayf al-Dīn Barqūq.[101] We do not have many details concerning Ibn Khaldūn's activities and responsibilities while he held this position; however, we do know that in order to be able to hold this important and lucrative post, one had to be a member of the Khanaqa al-Baybarsiyya. Ibn al-Furāt testifies: 'Ibn Khaldūn spent one day in the *khanaqa*, and became a member because it was required that the shaykh of this *khanaqa* be one of its Sufi members.'[102] Nonetheless, he did not occupy this position for very long because

Barqūq was dethroned and Ibn Khaldūn was forced to resign.[103] We do not have more information on the subject but a final relevant fact concerning Ibn Khaldūn's death is telling. He was buried in a cemetery outside Bāb al-Naṣr, on the road to Raydāniyya (now ʿAbbāsiyya), in a cemetery that was established by the Khanaqa al-Baybarsiyya towards the end of the eighth/fourteenth century and was restricted to the burial of Sufis. The exact site of this tomb is unknown to us.[104]

The above-mentioned items bring to light some of Ibn Khaldūn's feelings and his links with religion and the Sufi Path, opening the way for new perspectives and validating efforts to reintegrate the historian into his century and milieu. We are not trying to turn Ibn Khaldūn into an eminent Sufi, but we would like to examine his attitude towards religion and Sufism, an unexplored and devalued area although an essential and determining one in the study of his thought. More important than the historical evidence about Ibn Khaldūn's links to Sufism is his textual legacy, and the study of Ibn Khaldūn's treatise on Sufism, the *Shifā'*, is the main source for such an investigation.

IV. The *Shifā'*, a Manuscript on Sufism

A mysterious halo seems to surround the *Shifā' al-sā'il lī-tahdhīb al-masā'il*. Not only do Khaldunian studies tend to slur over and slight the treatise, but Ibn Khaldūn himself forbears to mention it in his letters, works or autobiography. Why should the scholar shroud his own treatise in secrecy?

A. IBN KHALDŪN'S SILENCE

Ibn Khaldūn left no exhaustive, systematic list of his works and did not even mention the early ones.[105] If we postulate that the *Shifā'* is one of Ibn Khaldūn's early works—a question that will be discussed later on—his silence is interpreted as follows by some Khaldunian scholars. Ibn Khaldūn recounts in the *Taʿrīf* that some of Ābilī's advanced students 'used to meet alone with the master in his house' when studying works on mysticism.[106] Besides, the fact that mysticism is by essence a secretive and well-guarded discipline that intimates a personal innermost search and a thorough bond with the spiritual guide, and in spite of the rather generalized recognition of moderate Sufism in the Maghrib, it seems that a certain discretion was deemed to be necessary when a student was reading works on mysticism with his teacher. Most likely, discretion was all the more essential when an author was writing a treatise on the same subject.[107] We must also bear in mind the torture and death of the *wazīr* Lisān al-Dīn b. al-Khaṭīb, accused of heresy (*zandaqa*) by his enemies in 776/1374. We do know that Ibn Khaldūn wrote the *Shifā'*[108] after his friend had completed the *Rawḍat al-taʿrīf bi'l-ḥubb al-sharīf* (probably in 768/1367), and it was four years later, in 772/1371, that the *wazīr*'s 'heretical views' were denounced. Ibn Khaldūn, who seems to have had the nature of a prudent diplomat who was aware of the dangers of certain views on religion, became all the more cautious not to flaunt his ideas and beliefs about mysticism. As to Ṭanjī, one of the greatest Khaldunian scholars, he simply construes this silence as very normal for a historian and a courtier who was proud to mention his works only when these were dedicated to royalty. This is why, according to him, Ibn Khaldūn only referred to, quoted from and taught his two major works, namely the *Muqaddima* and the *ʿIbar*, and ignored all of his other works.[109] Ibn Khaldūn's silence concerning the *Shifā'* should not raise doubts about its authenticity, as his lack of allusion to his other so-called minor works (like the *Lubāb*, for instance) has never called their legitimacy into question.

B. AUTHORSHIP

Despite our last assertions, it is legitimate to ask whether the author of this book could be other than Ibn Khaldūn. Ṭanjī and Badawī demonstrate that some statements of the historian himself and those of his commentators provide the proofs for the attribution of the *Shifā'* to Ibn Khaldūn. After the conventional opening phrases, two manuscripts specify the name of the author as 'Abū Zayd ʿAbd al-Raḥmān, son of the accomplished and versatile legist, the pious and saintly late shaykh, Abū Bakr Muḥammad b. Khaldūn al-Ḥaḍramī (may God have mercy upon his soul)'. This is the first substantial element identifying the author of the treatise as Ibn Khaldūn. Ṭanjī, in his introduction to his edition of the *Shifā'*, stresses that one of the manuscripts (our Ms.B) had belonged to a well-known Moroccan erudite named al-Ḥasan b. Masʿūd al-Yūsī (d. 1111/1699),[110] 'a very trustworthy scholar according to the sources'.[111] Ṭanjī asserts that had Yūsī doubted the authenticity of the manuscript, he would certainly have questioned its attribution to Ibn Khaldūn.[112] Therefore, not only do the manuscripts provide us with clear evidence as to the name of the author of the treatise, but several subsequent writers refer to Ibn Khaldūn in connection with the *Shifāʾ* and the debate that took place in eighth-/fourteenth-century Andalusia.

Aḥmad Zarrūq refers to the treatise in three instances: he summarizes the debate in *Qawāʿid al-taṣawwuf*, tells us in *ʿIddat al-murīd* that Ibn Khaldūn wrote a treatise concerning this specific question, and refers to our author in his commentary on *Al-Qaṣīda al-nūniyya* by Abū al-Ḥasan al-Shushtarī,[113] saying, 'Ibn Khaldūn tells us in the *Shifāʾ al-sāʾil* that Plato was one of the Sufi masters and this is an unsettled question.'[114] Finally, he also alludes to the treatise and its author, although implicitly this time, in *Al-Naṣīḥa al-kāfiya*, when he discusses the question of the one attracted to God (*majdhūb*) and their sanctity, and quotes a rather lengthy passage from the conclusion of the *Shifāʾ*, telling the reader, 'This was dealt with by one of the scholars.'[115] One of Zarrūq's commentators later clarified this latter statement, confirming that 'the scholar' is none other than 'Abū Zayd b. Khaldūn'.[116] As to ʿAbd al-Qādir al-Fāsī, he brings up the debate that took place between the later Andalusian Sufis concerning guidance through books rather than through a shaykh, and adds that 'they wrote down their questions and these were answered by Shaykh Ibn ʿAbbād [al-Rundī], Abū Zayd b. Khaldūn, and others, with each one answering according to his knowledge'.[117] Finally, Masnāwī states in *Juhd al-muqill al-qāṣir*: 'Ibn Khaldūn said in his comprehensive answer concerning the need for a shaykh in the Sufi Path that the great Sufis must not divulge their knowledge in books, or in words, because their knowledge is a secret between the servant and his Lord...and he [Ibn Khaldūn] adds...al-Ḥusayn b. al-Ḥallāj was killed because of an order issued both by the people of the Law and the people of the Path', a comment that indeed pertains to the *Shifāʾ*.[118] Masnāwī cites Ibn Khaldūn a second time when he mentions Shushtarī and his shaykh Ibn Sabʿīn. He explains that Ibn Khaldūn referred to them as the partisans of absolute oneness, 'in the answer we mentioned earlier [namely the *Shifā'*]...So consult it if you wish!'[119]

Yet, along with these valid and convincing references, there are two somewhat puzzling cases where Ibn Khaldūn is alluded to, again in connection with the *Shifā'*, but under an altered name. In the first instance, Abū al-ʿAbbās Aḥmad al-Fāsī (d. 1021/1612),[120] in his commentary on the poem *Al-Rā'iyya fī al-sulūk* by Abū Bakr Muḥammad b. Aḥmad al-Sharīshī (d. 7th/13th),[121] twice refers to 'Abū Bakr Muḥammad b. Khaldūn' as author of a treatise entitled *Shifā' al-sā'il.*[122] In the second instance, Ibn ʿAjība (d. 1224/1809), in his commentary on Ibn al-Bannā's *Al-Mabāḥith al-aṣliyya*, ascribes to the historian a new agnomen (*kunya*), that of Abū ʿAbd Allāh.[123] These two cases caused the critics to question and doubt the attribution of this treatise to ʿAbd al-Raḥmān b. Khaldūn. But the historian Ṭanjī solves this dilemma by considering both the names and agnomens of all the family members of Ibn Khaldūn who could possibly have been the authors of the treatise and by matching the date of their death with the date of composition of the *Shifā'*. Although Ibn Khaldūn's father was named Muḥammad and had Abū Bakr as an agnomen, he died in 749/1348, the year of the plague. His brother was also named after his father, although we ignore his agnomen, but he died in 735/1352. As to the agnomen Abū ʿAbd Allāh, it was never mentioned by the biographers and Ṭanjī reaches the cogent conclusion that Abū al-ʿAbbās Aḥmad al-Fāsī and Ibn ʿAjība simply made an inadvertent mistake. Since the debate between the Andalusian Sufis took place during the third quarter of the eighth/fourteenth century, none other than ʿAbd al-Raḥmān b. Khaldūn could possibly have written the *Shifā'*.[124] Thus, Ibn Khaldūn refers to himself as the author of the treatise, and the subsequent Sufis and their commentators refer to it or quote from it as a work by him. If Ibn Khaldūn was the author, the next question is when and where did he write his treatise on Sufism?

C. DATE OF COMPOSITION

It is around 768/1367 that Lisān al-Dīn b. al-Khaṭīb wrote his *Rawḍat al-taʿrīf bi'l-ḥubb al-sharīf*; and since, as we mentioned earlier,

Ibn Khaldūn admits having borrowed several passages from his friend's treatise on divine love, the *Shifā'* could not possibly antedate the *Rawḍa*. We also know that the debate between the Sufis of Andalusia took place during the third quarter of the eighth/fourteenth century. We know, too, the death dates of the scholars involved, which considerably narrows down the rather vague period called 'the end of the century'. Ibn ʿAbbād died in 792/1390, Shāṭibī in 790/1388 and Qabbāb in 778/1386. The debate in Andalusia obviously could not have taken place after 778/1386, death date of Qabbāb, who took part in it by writing a *fatwā* in answer to the question that so agitated these Sufis. Ibn Khaldūn's life also helps determining the date of composition. The author went twice to Fez, the city where Shātibī sent letters on behalf of the Andalusian Sufis, asking Qabbāb and Rundī for their opinion. Ibn Khaldūn's first visit to Fez took place in 755/1354, a date that is cancelled by the first argument (date of composition of the *Rawḍa*). He went there for a second time in 774/1372, this time for a period of two full years. It seems more than likely that Ibn Khaldūn composed the *Shifā'* in Fez between 774/1372 and 776/1374, a time on which both scholars Badawī and Ṭanjī agree.[125]

D. ASSESSMENT OF THE MANUSCRIPTS

To our knowledge, there are three extant manuscripts of the *Shifā'*. The first one (hereinafter referred to as Ms.A) was copied in 816/1413, that is, seven years after the death of Ibn Khaldūn. It is catalogued at the Moroccan Royal Library in Rabat under the number 5522. The second one (hereinafter referred to as Ms.B) was copied much later, in the year 890/1485, eighty-two years after its author's death and seventy-four years after Ms.A. It belonged successively to the well-known Moroccan scholar Abū ʿAlī al-Ḥasan b. Masʿūd al-Yūsī, his son ʿAbd al-Karīm, and ultimately the historian ʿAbd al-Raḥmān b. Zaydān (d. 1365/1946).[126] In 1949, the librarian Abū Bakr al-Taṭwānī took the *Shifā'* to Cairo, where it was copied and kept in the Dār al-Kutub al-Miṣriyya under the number 24299b. In 1967, he gave it to the Royal Library of Rabat where it is now catalogued under the number 12143. There is a third manuscript still extant (hereinafter referred to as Ms.C); it was copied in 1075/1664 in Morocco and belongs to the private library of Aḥmad b. al-Mallīḥ al-Fāsī.[127]

We were able to obtain copies of Ms.A and Ms.B. we did not have a copy of Ms.C, so we did not consult it; however, according to Ṭanjī, this third manuscript is not critical to this study.[128] Of the two manuscripts we consulted, it is undoubtedly Ms.B that presents the most problems. Ms.B is 173 pages long and each page has twenty lines. It is written in a relatively clear and legible Moroccan script although the copyist has misvowelised some words and made many grammatical mistakes, which seems to indicate, as Ṭanjī suggests, that he was not very well educated.[129] Furthermore, three pages (pages 10 to 12) are missing and the order is disturbed (pages 75 to 84 in the numbering of Ms.B should actually be placed after page 9 of the same manuscript). The writing in Ms.B is small, tight and sometimes difficult to decipher. Ms.A seems to be by far the best manuscript. It is forty-three pages long, with thirty-one lines per page; the order of the pages is undisturbed, unlike Ms.B, and no pages are missing. There are fewer mistakes in Ms.A than in Ms.B and very probably than in Ms. C since Ṭanjī and Badawī tell us that in this respect Ms. C is actually worse than Ms.B.

E. THE PRINTED EDITIONS AND THE TRANSLATIONS

There are three printed editions available of the *Shifā'*. The first one was published in Istanbul in 1984 by Muḥammad b. Tāwīt al-Ṭanjī, one of the most famous Khaldunian scholars. He had published in 1951 Ibn Khaldūn's *Taʿrīf* and was preparing an edition of the *Muqaddima*, on which he had spent more than thirty years, but unfortunately he died with his work still unpublished. His edition of the *Shifā'* is a critical one based on Ms.B and Ms.C. It is an extremely thorough work which shows not only his knowledge of Ibn Khaldūn but also his understanding of Sufism. The second edition by Ignace-Abdo Khalifé appeared in Beirut in 1959, about nine months after Ṭanjī's edition. It is based only on a microfilm of Ms.B and reflects all the errors of this manuscript. Some pages are missing, others are misplaced and many words were not read correctly. ʿAbd al-Raḥmān al-Badawī harshly criticizes this edition for its deficiencies.[130]

The third more recent edition, edited by Muḥammad Muṭīᶜ al-Ḥāfiẓ and published in Damascus in 1996, is based on the two manuscripts that we consulted and provides the reader with a well-structured, meticulously edited and reader-friendly text. Finally, one should mention a Turkish translation of the *Shifā'* by Suleyman Uludağ, published in Istanbul in 1977 and again in 1984; this translation is based on Ṭanjī's edition and the commentary reflects the editor's knowledge of Islamic and mystical literature. The *Shifā'* was translated into French by René Perez and published in Paris in 1991, under the title *La Voie et la Loi ou le Maître et le Juriste*. It is a very thorough work that shows a deep knowledge of Ibn Khaldūn, the Maghrib and Sufism. René Pérez (like Ṭanjī and Khalifé) was not aware of the existence of Ms.A, by far the best of the three existing manuscripts.

F. NATURE AND PURPOSE

The *Shifā'* is a written treatise born out of an oral debate around the question of orality or writing, which in the Middle Ages refers to the debate between the need for a master's oral transmission or the sufficiency of a book's written testament.[131] According to Ibn Khaldūn, every science can be compiled. Scientific technical terms and logical arguments are tools that help convey meanings, but these tools become hazardous when dealing with the mystical domain. In the *Shifā'*, Ibn Khaldūn denounces the Sufis who compiled books in which they tried to describe with technical words some mystical truths that no book could possibly contain and no word could possibly express because spiritual realities go beyond the limits of conventional language. This is especially true for the mystic who has reached the more advanced stages of development in the wayfaring. Yet, Ibn Khaldūn wrote a treatise on Sufism, the orally-transmitted science par excellence.

According to Ibn Khaldūn, communication takes place through verbal expression or written form.[132] The *ᶜibra*, or spoken word, is a medium between the speaker and the listener. The recorded word is inferior to direct conversation but is necessary when the purpose is urgent and when the need can only be met in this way. It is needed when an author wishes to communicate his thoughts 'to persons who are out of sight or physically distant, or to persons who live later and whom one has not met, since they are not contemporaries'.[133] Indeed, this was the only way Ibn Khaldūn could communicate with the distant-in-space Sufis of Granada, effectively tackle a present-day issue and leave a message for present and future generations.

v. Ibn Khaldūn's Understanding of Sufism

A. 'SUFISM' AND THE 'SCIENCE OF SUFISM'

For Ibn Khaldūn, Sufism always existed. It was an abiding reality and an integral and immutable part of Islam. Thus, it was born with Islam; or, rather, it was Islam since the first Sufis were the Prophet and his Companions. However, Ibn Khaldūn makes a distinction between 'Sufism' (*taṣawwuf*) and the 'science of Sufism' (*ʿilm al-taṣawwuf*) that appeared subsequently.

The pious earlier generations of Muslims led virtuous lives that largely accorded with the Law (*sharīʿa*) and the teachings of the Sufi Path. This was a period in which Sufism had not yet become a formal science, as it was a lived reality. After this initial wholesome period of widespread unity, there came a second age when more disagreements appeared among the members of the Islamic community. These disagreements caused breeches between the Law and the Path; this led to splits within the individual himself that, consequently, roused dichotomies among the members of the community as well. Many people forgot the importance of inward deeds and neglected the actions stemming from the heart. The signs of aging and decline were already visible but Sufism was still alive. Nevertheless, it became necessary for the legists to standardize ritual observances and codify laws, and for a number of Sufis to put into writing some of the recordable aspects of the Path. This was a sign of growth and maturity perhaps, but also a precursor to the somewhat inevitable ultimate third age that Ibn Khaldūn considered to be defined by heretical and distorted doctrines. Around the year 200 AH, 'the elect among the Sunnis were those who valued the actions stemming from the heart, and isolated themselves, following the steps of their worthy predecessors both in their inward and outward deeds. They were called Sufis.'[134]

Already by the fourth/tenth century, ʿAli b. Aḥmad al-Būshanjī had described the fundamental transformation in Sufism with a few words that epitomize Ibn Khaldūn's historical theory for the development of mystical science in Islam: 'Today Sufism is a name without a reality, while it used to be a reality without a name.'[135] Nascent Islam had no need for a label or a codified science of *taṣawwuf*, but the subsequent schools of Sufism developed their own separate legal systems, and the 'reality without a name' slid down towards the level of any other scientific endeavour in Ibn Khaldūn's epistemological structure, to become a category of science, 'the science of Sufism'.

B. IBN KHALDŪN'S EPISTEMOLOGY

Ibn Khaldūn's epistemological system is one of the issues that has puzzled many a scholar who came to believe the historian was torn between two tendencies: 'the most sublime rationalistic transports...and the most obvious mystical obscurantist propensity'.[136] Some detected contradictions in Ibn Khaldūn's theory of knowledge because they wished to see in him an early representative of materialistic dialectic or positivism.[137] These misunderstandings and misinterpretations of his epistemological methodology stem partly from a secular critical interpretation that has tended to forget that Ibn Khaldūn's work was produced in an intellectual context in which belief in a spiritual world was prevalent and divine agency was held to be omnipresent.[138]

Ibn Khaldūn defines knowledge according to its object and the object of Sufism is knowledge of the ultimate Truth. His epistemological system is a hierarchical one with three ways of knowing: the scientific or acquired learning (*ʿilm kasbī*) by scholars; inspired knowledge (*ʿilm ilhāmī*) or intimate finding (*wijdānī*) open to saints and Sufis; and prophetic knowledge, which is only accessible to prophets through revelation (*waḥy*). In this epistemological structure the science of history belongs to the first level, as it uses scientific methods of inquiry, whereas Sufism, which fits in the second category, does not. If facts can be observed and measured and their causes perused in a purely deductive, methodical and objective way, the inscrutability of revelation and the Laws of God cannot and should not be probed with the same tools. So long as this hierarchical view of knowledge is respected, so long as the gap between the rational sciences of the scholars, philosophers and theologians (*ahl al-naẓar* or *aṣḥāb al-dalīl*) and the intuitive way of the Sufis (*ahl al-kashf wa'l-mushāhada*) is maintained, each method is sound and reliable. As soon as any confusion appears between the methods of the two ways, their validity is to be questioned.

The rational is the key element to the philosophical and a tool in the theological sciences. Philosophy is essentially a search, and therefore a step from ignorance to knowledge. It is not the science of philosophy as such that Ibn Khaldūn attacks, but the philosophers, or rather 'the pretenders to philosophy' who believe that ultimate Truth can be reached through speculation.[139] And as to the positive, transmitted, legal sciences (*al-ʿulūm al-waḍʿiyya al-naqliyya wa'l-sharʿiyya*), reason has some role to play in their verification or application, although a very restricted role; for it is one that is limited to relating 'subsidiary problems to the fundamental'.[140] Thus, reason is not completely disqualified, but is given a limited role. As such, reason is but a tool of the mind: it differentiates true from false, but is also the source of many illusions. Its shortcomings become apparent when it tries to deal with that which is beyond our own being and our human perception.[141] For Ibn Khaldūn, when the rational infiltrated the spiritual domain, mysticism deviated from its original course and was no longer a way of life, or a gradual inward wayfaring, or a harmonious balance between the Law and the Path.

C. THE LAW AND THE PATH

Despite the overall cordial relationship between the legists and the Sufis in the period under discussion, some Sufis held that their Path and the way of the legists had diverged.[142] Ibn Khaldūn's position is here noteworthy. Not only was he a legist, a Māliki judge, and therefore an eminent supporter of the state religion, but he was also a man with an interest in and ties to Sufism. If there are some critical references to Sufism in Ibn Khaldūn's writings, 'none pertain to the Sufi theory of knowledge'.[143] Indeed, Ibn Khaldūn did denounce some later mystical systems that he thought were strange and harmful.

His critique and objections focused on two groups, the first that believed in [Self] disclosure (*aṣḥāb al-tajallī*) and the second in Oneness (*aṣḥāb al-waḥda*). Nonetheless, in other instances, he actually defends Sufism against the attacks of the legists.

Ibn Khaldūn does not believe, like Ibn ʿAbbād, that the solution for the wayfarer on the mystical Path lies in the outright shunning of the representatives of the Law. But he believed that the legists lacked the intuitive experience of the Sufis and were unable to understand what lay beyond demonstration (*burhān*) and proof (*dalīl*).[144] Neither does Ibn Khaldūn fully endorse Ghazālī's theory of reconciliation between the Law and the Path. But he does agree with Ghazālī (and Ibn ʿAbbād) that the legist concentrates on the actions related to the physical body and worldly needs, whereas the Sufi deals with the deeds of the heart and struggles in view of the Hereafter. Yet, the distinction between the legist and the Sufi is not so trenchant in Ibn Khaldūn's thought. For Ibn Khaldūn, by trying to reconcile the people of the outward (*ahl al-ẓāhir*) and the people of the inward (*ahl al-bāṭin*), Ghazālī only succeeded in further widening the gap that separated the two factions. While acknowledging the rift, Ibn Khaldūn the historian ascribes this rift to historical factors and not to any inherent difference between the two ways.[145] After the second/eighth century, one unified and unique science was split into two, namely the knowledge of the outward (*fiqh al-ẓāhir*) and the knowledge of the inward (*fiqh al-bāṭin*) or Sufism. Therefore, the original synergy that had existed between the outward and inward facets of life faded away, leaving the legist only in charge of the laws regulating worldly matters. For Ibn Khaldūn, the *shifā'*, or cure, is neither reconciliation (as exemplified by the thought of Ghazālī) nor eschewal (like Ibn ʿAbbād). Instead he argues for a voyage back in time, a return to an earlier Islam when there was an 'absolute complementarity' or harmony between inward and outward, because the Legislator did not set two separate ways, one for the outward and one for the inward life.[146]

Accordingly, the upholders of the Law should be able to help guide the individual to salvation. This is possible, he writes, unless the 'particular *muftī*'s knowledge is limited to the first half of the

Law, namely the one related to the outward only, and therefore he can only pass judgement on the validity or invalidity of the actions in view of this worldly life. Then this is a different problem'.[147] Ideally, however, the wisdom of the legists and the Sufis should be all-inclusive. As a Mālikī, Ibn Khaldūn follows in the way of Imam Mālik who is reported to have said, 'He who studies the Law (*tafaqqaha*) and does not study Sufism is perverse (*fāsiq*); he who studies Sufism and does not study the Law is a heretic (*zindīq*); and finally, he who studies both, will reach the truth.'[148] So spiritual perfection lies in the knowledge of and fidelity to the Law, whereby the legal structure absorbs the teaching of Sufism and Sufism conforms to orthodoxy. Ibn Khaldūn agrees with Ibn ʿAbbād when the latter insists that 'he who transgresses the Law goes against the Truth (*ḥaqīqa*), and he who goes against the Truth transgresses the Law'.[149] But for Ibn Khaldūn there should be no conflict because the Law and the Path are one. The legists should understand that the Law applies to the believer's outward life as well as to his inward life. As to the Sufis, they should return to the Sufism of the Companions of the Prophet and the early masters, for in that time *taṣawwuf* was Islam.

D. BOOKS OR MASTER?

Time had altered Sufism and its transmission methods. It was meant to be a reality attained through mystical tasting (*dhawq*) and insight (*baṣīra*), and passed on from master to disciple. When decline loomed and its transmitters, the Sufi shaykhs, became rare and difficult to find, some scholars strived to compile Sufi teachings in books or manuals. Can books replace the master? This is the question that so agitated the Sufis in Andalusia and the debate that is at the root of Qabbāb's *fatwā*, Ibn ʿAbbād's letter and Ibn Khaldūn's *Shifāʾ*.

Abū al-ʿAbbās Aḥmad Qabbāb was a Mālikī legist who taught substantive law in Gibraltar and Fez and followed for some time the Sufi Path with Ibn ʿĀshir in Salé. In his *fatwā*, Qabbāb humbly and cautiously starts by apologizing for his lack of both theoretical and practical knowledge about Sufism.[150] He then proceeds with the argument, insisting on the need for a guide as a general rule in whichever discipline is sought, because no art, whether it be grammar, law, medicine or any other science, can be mastered from books alone. This rule is even more rigorous in the particular case of Sufism since it is a discipline whose adherents often convey perceived realities through symbols or allusions. Qabbāb takes a firm position in favour of the need for a living master by telling us that the seat of knowledge used to be the hearts of men but when it was transferred to books, the keys to these books moved to the hands of men. Besides, he adds: 'As far as I know, it is not enough to learn about the science of Sufism—one has to taste it; it is no use studying the doctrine or the written material without assuming the qualities, or realizing its spiritual states.'[151] Sufism has two aspects: an inward mystical side dealing with the knowledge of the states and stations, for which the presence of a shaykh is indispensable; and an ethical facet involving the awareness of the flaws and blemishes in the self, and the learning about their appropriate cures. Knowing this second part of the science of Sufism is the duty of all believers and it is a much easier task that could perhaps be achieved by way of books, but only in case the novice cannot find a master, although again following a guide would be preferable. As to the works that dwell on the ecstatic experiences of the Sufis, Qabbāb describes them as unessential and even dangerous, as they can lead the reader astray. This is why a Sufi like Fishtālī sought to erase from works like Ghazālī's *Iḥyā'* and Qushayrī's *Risāla* all the cryptic passages devoted to the world of the Unseen (*ᶜilm al-ghayb*), and leave only the sections dealing with the Law.[152] Indeed, adds Qabbāb, these explanations are usually more confusing than enlightening to the average reader. As to those who contend that a shaykh can also lead his disciple to error, Qabbāb concludes that is true, but so can books.

As to Ibn ᶜAbbād al-Rundī's letter, it is a long and interesting essay in which the renowned Sufi refuses to get involved in the Granada quarrels and chooses to concentrate on the role of the spiritual guide.[153] There are two types of spiritual guides: the teaching shaykhs (*shuyūkh al-taᶜlīm*) and the educating shaykhs or spiritual guides (*shuyūkh al-tarbiya*). Not all wayfarers need a *shaykh al-taᶜlīm*, but those 'who have a banal mind and rebellious lower self' definitely need one, just like the chronically ill need a competent physician.[154] As to those 'who have expansive minds and who have their lower selves under control', they need a *shaykh al-tarbiya* who will direct every individual according to his specific needs.

On the question of books, Ibn ʿAbbād recommended that the wayfarer read the writings of the Sufis, provided the authors have sufficient learning and intimate knowledge; but the writings must be by Sufis with a genuine spiritual genealogy and their writings must be perfectly consistent with the demands of the Law. Yet, in order to gauge all these criteria, the disciple might need the help of a teaching shaykh. Therefore, books do not altogether dispense with teachers who, anyhow, are very difficult to find these days. Instead of siding with either of the two Granada factions, Ibn ʿAbbād offers his advice: rather than depending on either books or masters, the wayfarer should rely on God. It is no use waiting for a shaykh because a spiritual master and the Sufi Path are but gifts from God, signs of divine grace, and it is equally pointless for the aspiring wayfarer to relinquish his goal. The final object in the quest is neither books nor masters, but inheres in the attitude of the believer who must concentrate on his spiritual activity while also hoping and praying for a guide.

But the question that seems to preoccupy Ibn ʿAbbād most is the change in Sufism that not only led to the excessive reliance on other than God, but also to the excessive need for a teaching shaykh. Ibn ʿAbbād relates the increased demand for teaching shaykhs to a deep change in the nature of the wayfarers: 'I do not know which of the two calamities is greater: the disappearance of the spiritual guide with profound understanding, or the lack of sincere disciples.'[155] Ibn Khaldūn, like Ibn ʿAbbād, deplores the change that has occurred in the Sufi way. Ibn ʿAbbād the *Sufi* regrets the excessive need of an increasing coarser-minded majority for the teaching shaykh and disapproves of the developing dichotomy between the teaching shaykh and shaykh of spiritual direction.[156] Ibn Khaldūn the *legist* deplores the failure of the majority to value the deeds of the heart and the life of the spirit and hence disapproves of the dichotomy between legist and Sufi.

Ibn Khaldūn views the question of teaching or guiding in terms of spiritual struggles (*mujāhadāt*). The first struggle, God-wariness (*taqwā*), is incumbent upon all Muslims; and Ibn Khaldūn—like Ibn ʿAbbād—affirms that the novice must not wait for a master in order to start working on himself. At this stage, books such as Muhāsibī's *Riʿāya* are sufficient and 'the shaykh will not add anything to the writings of scholars who transmit the teachings of the Book and the Sunna'.[157] Yet, collaborating, emulating and learning from a teacher cannot harm the novice; on the contrary, it would perfect his struggle.

In the second struggle, the wayfarer strives to walk on the straight path and cure his heart of its imperfections. This step is not an obligation on every individual subject to the Law, nor is the presence of a shaykh required because the foundation of this path is the Qur'ān and the Sunna, and these are thoroughly and openly expounded in books such as Qushayrī's *Risāla* and *ʿAwārif al-maʿārif* by Suhrawardī (d. 631/1234).[158] Nevertheless, since it is difficult to know the self, the wayfarer may need a teaching shaykh to guide him, correct him and help him in his study of such writings and laws.

As to the struggle towards the third combat of unveiling (*kashf*) and witnessing (*mushāhada*), its aim is to uncover and witness the realities of the spiritual world. In it, the guidance of a shaykh is imperative. The shaykh must not only be a teacher (*muʿallim*) but he must also be a guide in spiritual training (*murabbī*).[159] Four givens render the shaykh indispensable in this last combat. Firstly, unlike the Sufis who see in this struggle the ultimate essential goal of the spiritual search, Ibn Khaldūn the legist thinks it has become a special path with its own laws and rules different from the common way of the Law to which all Muslims are subjected. Secondly, the wayfarer will go through spiritual states (*aḥwāl*) for which he needs to be watched over by a shaykh who can correct his conduct and modify his behaviour. Thirdly, the essence of this Path is premeditated death, which implies 'the extinction (*ikhmād*) of all human forces until the wayfarer is dead in body but alive in spirit',[160] and man cannot grasp this phenomenon by himself. Fourthly and lastly, the nature of this search is one that has to do with mystical tasting and secret realities rather than with conventional ideas and scientific rules; and these cannot be contained in words or summarized in books. Nonetheless, quite remarkably for one who was to all intents and purposes a 'friend' of Sufism, Ibn Khaldūn considers this 'third spiritual struggle' to be 'utterly reprehensible to the point of being prohibited, or even more'. However, he then quickly steps back from this stance and concedes that the wayfarer 'can still seek unveiling and progress a little on its path', but 'it is a difficult and dangerous path strewn with dangers and obstacles, so he must heed and avoid'. Yet if he pursues it, Ibn Khaldūn stresses that he must travel the Path under the guidance of a spiritual master and educating shaykh.

Like Ibn Khaldūn, most Sufis have always urged the seeker to follow a shaykh in wayfaring (*sulūk*), often adducing the following Qur'ānic verse: 'O believers, fear God, and seek the means to come to Him, and struggle in His way; haply you will prosper' (5:35). The 'means' (*wasīla*) is understood as being the spiritual guide who can in no way be replaced by books. As the Sufi-aspirant (*mutaṣawwif*) progresses in his wayfaring, books prove inadequate and the need for a guide is no longer a favoured option but becomes an urgent need. When the Sufi, with God's help, reaches towards the ultimate stages in the Path to become the receptacle of ephemeral inrushes (*wāridāt*) or Self-disclosures (*tajalliyāt*), then the need becomes vital. Certainly, 'seduced, deceived and outwitted on this path is he who imagines himself able to traverse the limitless desert and attain the Kaᶜba of union with the strength of his mere human footsteps, without guide or escort', warns Najm al-Dīn al-Rāzī.[161] Therefore, the advanced stages in the spiritual struggle are safe inasmuch as they are fought under the direction of an educating master who has knowledge of the Path and of men. There are two exceptions to the general rule: some will follow an initiatic path without the guidance of a living master but guided by his spiritual essence (*rūḥāniyya*), as in the case of the Uwaysīs, for instance; and the ones attracted to God who have lost their mind and are not accountable for legal observance, as discussed by Ibn Khaldūn in the appendix to the *Shifā'*.[162]

For the Sufis, it is the presence of the beloved guide that validates the third struggle, which for Ibn Khaldūn is a debatable endeavour. Ibn Khaldūn the legist does not dwell on the bond of love, which is the sole catalyst in the initiatic chain binding the wayfarer onto his Lord and authenticating the mystical wayfaring to its utmost stages. Unlike foremost Sufi works by realized Sufis, one word is remarkably absent from the *Shifā'*: *ʿishq*, at best translated perhaps with the hackneyed English 'love'.[163] Had *ʿishq* been alluded to in the *Shifā'*, even if hastily, the intellectual argument put forward by the Sufis of Granada would have crumbled and the questioner would have found its cure. The intellect overthrown, the lover would have trampled on books in his burning journey to the Beloved, and 'whilst the pen was making haste in writing, it split upon itself as soon as it came to Love', cries out Jalāl al-Dīn al-Rūmī.[164] For the Sufi lover, meanings evade their wordy prisons, questions are not posed and answers are not needed. The lover is deprived of personal will, with no possible choice but one. So the wise bondsman submits to the guidance of a loved master leading him onto the Beloved.

The *Shifā'* does not touch upon this vital quintessence of Sufism. Ibn Khaldūn does point his finger at the differences and complementarities between the teacher (*shaykh al-taʿlīm*) and the educator or shaykh of spiritual education (*shaykh al-tarbiya*), or between the legist and the Sufi. He informs us of the gap between imitation (*taqlīd*) and realization (*taḥqīq*), and the difference between the three levels of realization: the science of certainty (*ʿilm al-yaqīn*), the vision of certainty (*ʿayn al-yaqīn*) and the truth of certainty (*ḥaqq al-yaqīn*). In addition, he deals with the issue of the spoken word (*qāl*) and spiritual state (*ḥāl*), the harmonies and dichotomies between the written book (*kitāb*) and the spiritual guide (*shaykh*), oral and written transmission of knowledge, and conveyed report (*khabar*) and direct vision (*naẓar*). He throws light on the difference between the outward science enclosed in the written treatise (*maqāl*), acquired through the mind, and the orally-transmitted knowledge, transferred by the recognized spiritual master, which leads to the realization or mystical tasting of the spiritual states (*aḥwāl*), the seat of which is the heart. In all this, Ibn Khaldūn was an 'intellectual [who] handles an intellectual issue that he patiently examines from all its facets'.[165] He was first and foremost a legist 'who could not possibly have understood *tasawwuf* in the same way as the disciples of a more contemplative mind did...'.[166]

Ibn Khaldūn was a man of action and a pragmatic scholar, but with lofty ideals; and his life fluctuated between adventurous journeys and yearning for peace. His works voice lucid rationalism in matters pertaining to this world and echo the recognition of a believer's limitations in the face of spiritual realities. Ibn Khaldūn is first and foremost a child of his time, a Muslim who lived in the fourteenth-century Maghrib and Mashriq. He was a Mālikī legist, an advocate of some aspects of Sufism, and we can now say, after reading the *Shifā' al-sā'il li-tahdhīb al-masā'il*, a historian of Sufism, a Sufi 'sympathizer' and, even if very prudent, one who was nevertheless involved in the Granada debate among his contemporary Sufis.

Note on Chapter headings and Sub-headings

The original Arabic text of the *Shifā'* contained descriptions of the content of sections of the text that could be considered as chapter headings. These descriptions are too long to be included as actual chapter headings in an English text. We have therefore taken from the original what is suitable for chapter headings in a translation. We have done the same for the sub-headings and in places added new sub-headings in order to clarify the text.

REMEDY FOR THE QUESTIONER IN SEARCH OF ANSWERS

[Prologue]

In the Name of God, Most Compassionate and Merciful
May God bless and grant peace to our lord and master
Muḥammad, his family and Companions.

Said the shaykh, the leader, the venerable legist and accomplished teacher, the skilled scholar, whose versatile knowledge embraces many fields, the most learned and unique master, the pole of the religious sciences, the bearer of the standard thereof, he who unlocks and solves all obscure intellectual questions and the precursor to the ultimate object thereof, Abū Zayd ʿAbd al-Raḥmān, son of the accomplished and versatile legist, the pious and saintly late shaykh, Abū Bakr Muḥammad b. Khaldūn al-Ḥaḍramī (may God have mercy upon his soul).

Praise be to God who, by His grace, bestowed inspiration upon us that we may glorify Him; and may His blessings and benedictions be upon our lord and master Muḥammad, His servant and noble messenger, and may His approval be upon the members of his family and his Companions!

To proceed: certain brethren (may God protect them) made me aware of a document that arrived from the Andalusian region, the homeland at the frontiers (*ribāṭ*) of the holy war (*jihād*), the shelter of the righteous (*ṣāliḥūn*), ascetics (*zuhhād*), legists and worshippers (*ʿubbād*). This document was addressed to some of the eminent people of the city of Fez, a city where royal power is in effervescence, where the seas of science and religion are overflowing, and where God's promised rewards are secured to the supporters of His religion and caliphate. The document hoped to shed light on the Path of the Sufis, the people who seek self-realization (*taḥaqquq*) through the mystical tasting of divine unity (*al-tawḥīd al-dhawqī*) and intimate finding of gnosis (*al-maʿrifa al-wijdāniyya*). The question raised by the brethren was the following.

Is it possible to travel this very way, taste this knowledge and see the veil lifted from the spiritual world by studying the books written by the Sufis and conforming to their counsels which describe the nature of the Path? Is it sufficient to study the written tradition, to peruse these sciences and to rely upon books of guidance, such as the *Iḥyā'* and the *Riʿāya*, which offer ample knowledge concerning the beginning and arrival in this Path?[1] Or is it indispensable for the disciple (*murīd*) to have also a spiritual master (*shaykh*), who would point out to him the signs along the Path, caution him against its dangers and differentiate for him between an ephemeral inrush (*wārid*) and a true state (*ḥāl*) in instances when confusion occurs? In this way, the shaykh would assume the role of a physician to the ailing or the just guide to the unruly community.

This same document told of a debate that took place between two students, one of whom had a negative attitude and the other a positive one. The discussion encompassed arguments deriving from rational reasoning (*maʿqūl*) on the one hand, and the inherited tradition (*manqūl*) on the other. One student believed that the way could be followed without a shaykh whom the wayfarer could emulate, without a leader's method to follow. As to the other student, he held that a shaykh was indispensable for he would train the wayfarer on this path (*sālik*), caution him about the dangers he perceived and give him the enabling strength to sustain the ensuing spiritual visions (*maṭlaʿ*)[2]. The shaykh would also distinguish between lawful spiritual states and heretical innovations (*bidaʿ*); and consequently, as a result of his guidance, the disciple's life becomes filled with spiritual joy and he is protected from the errors that could separate him from God or cause His wrath. The debate was long and many saints (*abdāl*)[3] and learned men (*ʿulamā'*) took part in it. Finally, all moderation and temperance disappeared between the two disputants.

Yet, even though they had deviated from the correct answer, they were closer to it than they thought.

I have therefore decided to clarify this issue and to answer these questions. Can one arrive to the goal or not in this Path? Can the novice attain it with books and compiled material alone, or is it necessary for him to follow carefully a guide, to listen to him and act upon his words? I have relied upon God in this, inasmuch as all help, protection and sustenance come from Him. God sufficeth me! What a wonderful Provider!

Discussion of this issue requires us to examine the Sufi way closely and distinguish it from the other ways. Why was Sufism, in its beginning, known as an expression of worship (*ʿibāda*) and spiritual struggle (*mujāhada*) and referred to in these terms? How did the name Sufism (*taṣawwuf*) become the common appellation when subsequently the Sufis started practising other forms of inward struggle? Why did some of the later Sufis use this appellation when referring only to the results of these combats, rather than to the combats themselves, and how can their theory be refuted? Defining all these terms will help greatly in clarifying this issue. And God is the guide to the Truth!

CHAPTER ONE

On the Way of the Sufis, Its General Examination and Differentiation from the Other Lawful Paths. On the Meaning of This Name for the First Sufis

The Individual's Legal Obligations Prescribed by the Law Divide into Two Groups

Know that God—glory be to Him, and may our hearts be filled with the light of His guidance—has imposed upon our hearts certain acts of belief (*aʿmālan min al-iʿtiqādāt*) and upon our limbs some acts of obedience (*aʿmālan min al-ṭāʿāt*). The individual's legal obligations regarding the worship of God, as prescribed by the Law, divide into two groups.

Firstly, there are principles of behaviour (*aḥkām*) which relate to external actions (*al-aʿmāl al-ẓāhira*), namely worship (*ʿibādāt*), customs (*ʿādāt*) and daily affairs (*mutanāwalāt*).

Secondly, there are principles of behaviour which relate to inward deeds (*al-aʿmāl al-bāṭina*), namely faith (*īmān*) and the various qualities (*ṣifāt*) involving the heart and colouring it. Some of these qualities are praiseworthy, such as chastity (*ʿiffa*), justice (*ʿadl*), courage (*shajāʿa*), generosity (*karam*), modesty (*ḥayā'*) and patience (*ṣabr*); others are blameworthy, such as conceit (*ʿujb*), dissemblance (*riyā'*), jealousy (*ḥasad*) and hatred (*ḥaqd*). Although all actions are important for the Legislator (*shāriʿ*), the deeds of the inward (*bāṭin*) are even more consequential than outward actions (*ẓāhir*); and this is because the inward always rules the outward, and conditions it. Inward actions are the principle of outward ones, which are their mere effects. If the principle is good, then its effects are too, whereas if the principle is corrupt, so are its effects. The Prophet (may God bless him and grant him peace) said, 'There is a piece of flesh in the body which, if healthy, renders the whole body so, and if corrupted, corrupts the whole body. This piece of flesh is the heart.'[1]

God Created Instincts and Forces within the Heart

This means that God (may He be glorified) has created instincts (*gharā'iz*) and forces (*quwā*) within the heart. Each one of these instincts or forces was created with its own specific need, the fulfilment of which gives it satisfaction and brings it to completion. Thus, the instinct of anger finds satisfaction and fulfilment in reprisal and revenge, whereas the instinct of appetite finds pleasure in the edible and the carnal. In short, the instinct demands what befits its own nature. Similarly, the instinct of the intellect (*ʿaql*) naturally seeks learning (*ʿilm*) and gnosis (*maʿrifa*). Moreover, since God has put in the intellect the love of perfection (*kamāl*), it is constantly operating in order to perfect itself by utilizing discursive thinking (*fikr*) as its servant in all of this, to link, analyse, synthesize and differentiate. For instance, the intellect will envision the enmity that a particular person has for it, and so will provoke the bodily members to seek to avenge upon this very person. It can also see perfection and beauty in another person, and so will urge the bodily members to find its pleasure in that person. When in a state of hunger, it can fancy a dish as being agreeable and therefore stimulate the bodily members to obtain this food. It can also become convinced that it has found perfection in another human being, hence its desire and anxiety to win over and possess this being exclusively. It might be irritated with some other person and will devise a way to avenge itself upon this person. The instinct can also imagine that perfection resides in itself, so it consequently becomes self-conceited and disdainful of others, deeming them to be inferior to itself.

In this manner, also, the instinct of the intellect demands the fulfilment of its own nature in knowledge and learning and incites discursive thinking to pursue them. Thinking yearns for the highest perfection (*al-kamāl al-aʿlā*) through the knowledge of its Creator, for it does not see any being more perfect than Him.[2] To achieve this end, thinking contends with the chains of thoughts and concepts that succeed each other in it, separating and intertwining them together and then scattering and re-examining them again. All this activity is aimed towards drawing nearer its Creator. It proceeds in an uninterrupted, unceasing fashion without the slackening or sloth that is common to the rest of the body. Discursive thinking moves faster than lightening and faster than a burning wick in the wind. In his supplications, the Prophet (may God bless him and grant him peace) often pleaded, 'O Director of the hearts!'[3] When taking an oath, he would say, 'No, by the Director of the hearts!'[4] He (may God bless him and grant him peace) also said, 'The Merciful holds the believer's heart between His two fingers.'[5]

Nevertheless, not everything the heart imagines to be perfection and pleasure for these instincts is indeed so when viewed against the Hereafter and eternal life, the felicity or wretchedness of which has been described to us by the Legislator. On the contrary, the derivation of pleasure in the satisfaction of these instincts is only experienced through that which is immediate and temporal. What remains are only the effects these actions leave upon the heart and the dispositions that colour it, leading in the Hereafter to either goodness and bliss or to evil and chastisement. This applies also to the instinct of the intellect for even when its beliefs and concepts are related to its Creator, some of these very beliefs and concepts lead to felicity while others lead to wretchedness. It is only by means of the Law (*sharʿ*) that one can come to know which deeds, of both the spirit and the body, will lead to eternal felicity.

The Prophet (may God bless him and grant him peace) has differentiated between the praiseworthy (*maḥmūd*) and the blameworthy (*madhmūm*), separating the good (*ṭayyib*) from the evil (*khabīth*). He also insisted upon the greater importance of the inward deeds, for it is the inward that leads to walking on the straight path and is the source of goodness or corruption in all actions, as shown in the tradition cited above. This tradition is interpreted as follows: rectitude must be observed in the actions of the external body members (*istiqāmat al-jawāriḥ*) in order to leave its effect on the soul (*nafs*).

With constant reiteration, the soul becomes the guide; and without any constraint, it leads the wayfarer in all his deeds towards walking on the straight path.

The Prophet (may God bless him and grant him peace) said, 'God does not reckon with your external aspects or possessions, but with your hearts and deeds.'[6] This is why faith (*īmān*) is the source of all action and the highest level of felicity, being the loftiest among all the inward deeds; and worth how much more than the outward ones! When God opened the hearts of the Prophet's Companions (may God be pleased with them), they embraced Islam and accepted, with the light of their Lord's guidance, clear evidence of Him.[7] They concentrated their efforts mainly on inward deeds, much more so than on outward ones. They examined themselves and scrutinized their thoughts, well-aware of their hearts' deceiving tendencies. It is this issue that they discussed most of the time, warning and seeking each other's help against their hearts' errings.

Listen to ʿUmar b. al-Khaṭṭāb's[8] question to Ḥudhayfa[9] (may God be pleased with them both) and meditate upon it. One day Ḥudhayfa brought up the subject of the Hypocrites (*munāfiqūn*) and repeated what the Prophet (may God bless him and grant him peace) had said concerning them. ʿUmar asked, 'I implore you by God who permitted the heaven and earth to be, do you know if the Prophet (may God bless him and grant him peace) included me among them?' Ḥudhayfa answered, 'No, although apart from you, I cannot exonerate anyone else.'[10] Look at how vigilant ʿUmar was (may God be pleased with Him) with respect to this hypocrisy (*nifāq*), and reflect upon its nature. You will therefore understand that you need to beware of the hidden aspects of inward actions and what is to be blamed and avoided therein. This will make you realize how important and dangerous they are in religion. For if by hypocrisy Ḥudhayfa or ʿUmar were referring to that which is generally implied—namely the action of displaying Islam while actually hiding misbelief (*kufr*), like the Hypocrites of Medina, or others—ʿUmar, well aware of his innocence in this, would not have been alarmed and would not have asked Ḥudhayfa this question. Indeed, any man knows that which he discloses and that which he conceals, so how could ʿUmar possibly be unaware of this? What ʿUmar feared was another type of hypocrisy: the hidden dangerous fault that lies in the inward deed and that strikes suddenly without man being aware of it.

As God had granted him the ability to see through the hearts (*iṭṭilāʿ ʿalā al-qulūb*), the Prophet was able to penetrate their secrets and read them. The word hypocrisy came to designate this type of action, in which the inward reality is in contradiction with the observable outward claim. Now the believer claims and displays rectitude, but errors hide in his inward self. And despite the fact that errors happen against his will, these do nonetheless vilify rectitude because they are concealed in the heart and, consequently, resemble hypocrisy in that they reflect a contradiction between the outward and the inward. Therefore, in spite of the difference in meaning with hypocrisy as commonly understood, the word has also been used metaphorically and by extension to designate this particular type of blameworthy act that can elude the man subject to the Law (*mukallaf*). The believer is to watch over the states of the inward, exerting it to go straight, so that the outward in its totality is guided to felicity. If a man is ever heedless or slack in this duty, he becomes a hypocrite.

In a similar way, the word associationism (*shirk*) has become interchangeable with dissemblance (*riyā'*) since many objects become the target of worship. The dissembler's prayers are not directed solely to God, but partly also to the object of his dissemblance. In this, he is like the associationist who worships two gods, which explains why the word associationism has been used in lieu of dissemblance. The Prophet (may God bless him and grant him peace) said, 'Dissemblance is a lesser associationism (*al-shirk al-aṣghar*).'[11] All this clearly proves that the inward is of the greatest significance. To concern oneself with curing it is the wayfarer's most important duty.

Intention Is the Principle of All Actions

Let us go further in our explanation. Outward actions are all subjected to free choice and man's power, whereas most inward actions are not governed by free choice and rebel against human rule. The human rule has no control over the inward while the outward is liable to free choice, since it is governed by it and operates under its authority, command and instruction. This is why intention (*niyya*) is the principle (*mabda'*) of all actions, the foundation of (*aṣl*) and the spirit (*rūḥ*) behind all acts of worship. So much so that, if an action is devoid of good intention, it is considered null and is not counted as an act of obedience for the man subject to the Law. The Prophet (may God bless him and grant him peace) said, 'It is the good intention that counts in an action. Every man is granted that which he longs for: if he yearns for God and His Prophet, he is led to them; if he aspires to the world, he obtains it; if he desires a woman, he will marry her. Thus, he reaches the object of his migration (*hijra*).'[12]

Those Who Value Actions Stemming from the Heart Are Called 'Sufis'

When the Companions (may God be pleased with them) passed away, and the second generation of Muslims came upon the scene, those who had been guided by the Companions themselves, through oral teaching and instruction, were called the Followers (*tābiʿūn*). The generation after them was called the Followers of the Followers (*atbāʿ al-tābiʿīn*). But thereafter people divided into different opposing groups and many deviated from the main road and the straight path. The actions stemming from the heart were forgotten and neglected. The majority engaged in the betterment of physical actions and conformity to religious rites, while totally disregarding the inward. The legists worked on what had become a generalized need: the standardization of outward worship (*al-ʿibādāt al-ẓāhira*) and the codification of the principles dealing with human interaction (*aḥkām al-muʿāmalāt*). They dealt with both fields either according to the people's need for guidance, or as doctors of the Law dealing with a collectivity in need of formal legal pronouncements (*futyā*). Those who were endowed with hearts (*arbāb al-qulūb*) were then referred to as ascetics, worshippers, seekers of the Hereafter, or those dedicated to God. They held on to their religion 'like those who grip live coal between their palms', according to the reported tradition.[13]

Then an era of calamitous innovative beliefs followed. The Muʿtazila,[14] Rāfiḍīs[15] and Khārijīs[16] arrogated worship and renunciation. Since their belief—and belief is always the root of all things—was distorted, their attempts to improve their deeds, whether inward or outward, was in vain. The elect among the Sunnis were those who valued the actions stemming from the heart and isolated themselves, following the steps of their worthy predecessors both in their inward and outward deeds.[17] They were called Sufis. The teacher Abū al-Qāsim al-Qushayrī said, 'The name "Sufi" became widespread around the year 200 AH.'[18] Generation followed generation and nation followed nation. The predecessors guided their successors, who in turn transmitted the knowledge of God (*fiqh Allāh*) that they had inherited from their elders to those God led to their Path.

The Law Is Divided into Two Branches

In the period after the Followers of the Followers, the knowledge of the Law (*fiqh al-sharīʿa*) was divided into two branches.

The first branch is the knowledge of the outward (*fiqh al-ẓāhir*), which either applied to the actions of the physical members (*afʿāl al-jawāriḥ*) and concerned the person subject to the Law as an individual, or else applied to worship, customs or other outward actions and therefore concerned the individual as a part of the community. This body of rules is generally called substantive law (*fiqh*); the specialist in it is the legist, who issues formal legal pronouncements and is the guardian of religion.

The second branch is the knowledge of the inward (*fiqh al-bāṭin*), and it is the knowledge of the actions stemming from the heart (*afʿāl al-qulūb*). It concerns the individual subject to the Law on a personal level as it applies to his worship and to the necessities of life.[19] It is called variously the knowledge of the heart (*fiqh al-qulūb*), the knowledge of the inward, the knowledge of moral care (*fiqh al-waraʿ*), the knowledge of the Hereafter (*fiqh al-ākhira*), and Sufism (*taṣawwuf*).

The first—the knowledge of the outward—was dealt with extensively because it simultaneously fulfils the needs of the majority and answers a ruler's need for changes in formal legal pronouncements.

With every new era, its transmitters increased and its subjects multiplied.[20] The second—the knowledge of the inward, and the most essential for the individual on a personal level—was scarcely dealt with at all. At times, some learned men feared that this knowledge (*fiqh*) would fall into oblivion and its upholders would disappear; they feared that God's decrees governing the acts of the heart and the movements of the inward would be ignored. Indeed, these are more important for the believer subject to the Law and more likely to bring him salvation. For this reason, works of great benefit, even though not too numerous, were written by some men of wisdom like Ibn ʿAtā',[21] Muḥāsibī with his *Riʿāya* and Ghazālī with his *Iḥyā'*.

In view of the two explanations mentioned above, the Sufi-aspirant (*mutaṣawwif*) and the legist converge concerning the actions related to the physical members and the way an individual subject to the Law is to deal with his needs. However, the Sufi-aspirant and the man concerned with moral care (*mutawarriʿ*) insist on the importance of the deeds of the heart, its beliefs and colourations. They differentiate between praiseworthy and blameworthy, salutary and pernicious. They distinguish the ailment from the remedy. As to the legist, he discusses the general need of all men subject to the Law with respect to social interaction, marriages, buying and selling, legal limits and other aspects of substantive law.

Ghazālī compared the attitudes of the legist and Sufi-aspirant with regards to worship and daily affairs.[22] The legist views them with the benefits of this life in mind, the Sufi-aspirant with those of the Hereafter. Ghazālī says:

> The legist considers the religious practices—the root of which is Islam—and determines the following. Are these practices valid, and therefore deserving of reward, as they do comply [with the Law] and do not draw on a binding juridical sentence [forbidding them]? Or, are these practices corrupt and therefore do not deserve reward, as they do not comply [with the Law] and will bring about a binding juridical sentence [prohibiting them]? The legist must judge when the blood of a man is licit because he refuses to perform his duty, or when a man is to be protected because

> he does perform his duty. In a similar fashion, he sets apart the lawful from the unlawful, as in the case of a man who has disposed of someone's property: should this property be restituted to its legitimate owner or not? In view of that, should justice be put into effect or not? All these matters are of a worldly nature.

Ghazālī also says that for the Sufi-aspirant all this can be explained in terms of wounds in the heart, affecting his walking on the straight path, which is the foundation of salvation (*najāt*). The Sufi-aspirant sees ritual prayer as an act of worship, the essence of which is the heart's focus on divine unity (*al-tawḥīd bi'l-qalb*).[23] Yet, ritual prayer will only supply provisions in the Hereafter when performed with a conscious heart. The Prophet (may God bless him and grant him peace) said, 'A man is only rewarded for the moments during which he performed his prayers in a state of consciousness.' Also, 'A man might perform his prayers and not be rewarded with a half, a third, a fourth, not even a tenth of it.'[24] Islam is both [inward] affirmation (*iqrār*) and [outward, verbal] confession (*iʿtirāf*). If this is not mirrored in the heart—so that, in turn, the effects of this confession can be reflected in the physical members' obedient subjection—then it bears no consequence whatsoever in the Hereafter. Likewise, the Sufi-aspirant only looks at the lawful and the unlawful in as much as they constitute wounds in the soul or illnesses that must be uprooted. The Prophet (may God bless him and grant him peace) said, 'Leave that which is doubtful and reach for that which is sure.'[25] He said (may God bless him and grant him peace), 'A man is not among the God-wary (*muttaqīn*) until he has forsaken that wherein there is no evil out of fear of an evil therein.'[26] Ghazālī adds: 'The legist does not investigate the wounds that mark the heart and the way to avoid them. Everything he deals with is tied to this world, since it contains a valid road that leads to the Hereafter. If the legist is to ponder about sin, the attributes of the heart and the rulings of the Hereafter as such, he would be going beyond the limits of his own science.'[27]

As for me, I believe these words must not be taken in an absolute sense. The legist's viewpoint is not limited to this world as such because it is a worldly point of view, but for other reasons related to his position. Indeed, as explained earlier, those who were charged to impart the Law split into two groups. The first group gathered for deliberations and issued formal legal pronouncements. The ruler and the community relied on them to implement God's rulings in their external aspects for all His people. The second group, namely the worshippers and the ascetics, stressed the aspects in God's laws that concerned them as individuals. Besides, some legists might indeed uphold both laws at once.

The prophets guide men to God. They drag them by the belts to protect them from Hellfire. They lead them to felicity and safeguard them from torment by reprimanding, beating or killing them, depending on how harmful their actions could be with regards to their future life. From the prophets, we learn that the most perfect level in salvation is attained by submitting to the prescriptions of the Law and implementing them in the best and most complete way, through ensuring that the inward and the outward are in harmony. The inward should be guarded and examined until no heedlessness or slackness permeates it.

But there is also another level inferior to the preceding, at which religious prescriptions are sometimes kept; and that is where the outward and the inward will still agree, but while the outward is perfect, the inward has been infiltrated with heedlessness and slackness. This level differs from the first; but even there, salvation might be granted since it is but a grace and mercy from God.

Then, there is the lowest level of performance of the religious prescriptions which are observed to perfection outwardly, but are totally neglected inwardly. In this case, man is not rewarded for his obedience and this does not lead to salvation. However, the Legislator's pronouncements that befall those who completely neglect the Law's prescriptions inwardly, namely sanctions, trials or even death, do not apply to this last group because He did not give right of access to the inward. Every man subject to the Law is answerable to himself, since he is best aware of his own ailment. This being the case, one can only hope that the amended inward will match the outward. The Prophet (may God bless him and grant him peace) said, 'Did you split his heart open?'[28] He also said, 'You come to me with your quarrels and one of you might be more convincing in his arguments. If I pronounce any judgement in that man's favour at the expense of his brother's right, then I have only allotted him a share in Hellfire.'[29]

The difference between the three levels at which the Law can be kept corresponds to the three stations: submission (*islām*), faith (*īmān*) and excellence (*iḥsān*). In the station of submission, the deed is performed outwardly and the religious prescription is either accepted or rejected. In the station of faith, there is agreement between the outward and the inward in the fulfilment of the worship, albeit with some heedlessness. There is hope for salvation at this level. At the level of excellence, there is harmony between the inward and the outward; and constant self-examination is sustained so that no heedlessness can ever infiltrate the actions. This is the most perfect level for the one who seeks salvation. Every act of worship or religious prescription is performed within one of these three levels. Indeed, when some eminent scholars say that the Law has both aspects—the outward and the inward—they mean that it concerns the individual who is subject to it, not only in his outward actions, [but also in his inward actions].[30] This does not imply, as some Bāṭinīs[31] claim in trivial statements contradicting the foundation of the Law, that the Legislator has divulged some laws while He has concealed others. And God is above their words!

Accordingly, the expert legist (*al-faqīh al-muftī*) is the one to understand all of this. If he is consulted in reference to the believers' actions in view of the Law, and has to judge whether these are good or corrupt, valid or invalid, his judgement (*fatwā*) is passed according to this worldly life, a matter wherein he is competent, as Ghazālī says. If an individual seeks advice concerning his own salvation, the *muftī* will set forth a judgement that will guide the individual in question to salvation. This will be so, unless this particular *muftī*'s knowledge is limited to the first half of the Law, namely the one related to the outward only, and therefore he can only pass judgement on the validity or invalidity of the actions in view of this worldly life. Then this is a different problem.

As to the few capable of observing both the states of the inward (*aḥwāl al-bāṭin*) and the knowledge of the heart, they kept decreasing with every new age; and remained hidden in every district where the Law was transgressed and the souls had degenerated, [whereby they were] busy pursuing their desires and being slaves of their lower thoughts. [This latter state of affairs was] so much so that the Path of these few had become a burden to most men's hearts, for it went against their nature's innate dispositions, their instinctive propensity to yield to passions and the delusive ambition [of thinking] that salvation can be reached by means of outward actions only.

Nevertheless, in their innermost hearts, people regarded the few with reverence and longed for the qualities that only this minority possessed: the knowledge of the Islamic dogma (*ʿaqāʾid islāmiyya*) they had studied and were taught, and their natural love for purity and good. Indeed, had he shown determination, one single thought would have animated the soul of the Muslim who had truly comprehended his parents' religious practices: only by walking the Path that this minority had followed would he be led to the Truth;[32] and only by imitating them would he be ensured of right guidance.

Yet, the scarce number of supporters and the lack of assistance induce laziness and is a step towards idleness. Even though a man might be certain that felicity lays in the path followed by the elite (*khawwāṣ*), he will tend to follow the majority and blindly conform to the fathers and teachers of the time, in words and actions. Man is wrapped up in the life of this world, which he cherishes more than anything else. His soul is attached to that which is familiar to him and to others and will indulge in the hope of going straight in future times to secure divine mercy and salvation. May God Most High make his dreams come true and lead wretched souls to His mercy! The Prophet (may God bless him and grant him peace) conveyed [in a sacred tradition (*ḥadīth qudsī*)], 'I am of the same thinking as My servant is towards Me. So let him think of Me as he wills.'[33] ʿĀʾisha (may God be pleased with her) said, 'On the Last Day, people will be judged by their intentions.'[34] Those who lived a life of bliss in this world might also enjoy His mercy in the next. '*Say: O my people who have been prodigal against yourselves, do not despair of God's mercy; surely God forgives sins altogether; surely He is the All-forgiving, the All-compassionate*' (Q.XXXIX.53).[35]

Thus, the elite gave precedence to the deeds of the heart over the actions of the bodily members in both the prescriptions of the Law and customs. Junayd (may God be pleased with him) said, 'If you see a Sufi concerned with his outward, then know that his inner is in a state of ruin.'[36] This group was then referred to by the name and appellation Sufi.

The Etymology of the Name 'Sufi'

Some people took upon themselves to find the etymology of this name, but their analogies did not help them much.[37] *Ṣūfī* was said to be an appellation for the man clothed in wool (*ṣūf*), but Sufis did not use wool exclusively.[38] Only their imitators wore wool, thinking that the Sufis' occasional wearing of a woollen garment as a token of austerity (*taqallul*) and asceticism (*zuhd*) was a distinguishing feature. This thought was pleasing to the imitators and this is how they became the instigators of this derivation. Actually, the Sufis who wore wool did it to emphasize austerity and asceticism, since they preferred to be clothed in the habit of poverty like those whose primary attachment is not this world. The Prophet (may God bless him and grant him peace) said, 'Let not this world be your main concern for it will destroy you as it destroyed those before you.'[39] The Prophet (may God bless him and grant him peace) also said in a sacred tradition that conveys His Lord's words, 'Be in this world like a stranger or like a passer-by.'[40] It is also said that ʿUmar b. al-Khaṭṭāb (may God be pleased with him) used to patch his clothes with pieces of leather.[41]

Some claim that the name *Ṣūfī* derives from *ṣuffa*, which they think explains the origin of this Path.[42] Some of the Emigrants abided by the veranda of the Messenger of God's mosque (may God bless him and grant him peace) and they were called the People of the Veranda (*ahl al-ṣuffa*). Among them were Abū Hurayra al-Dawsī,[43] Abū Dharr al-Ghifārī,[44] Bilāl al-Ḥabashī,[45] Ṣuhayb al-Rūmī,[46] Salmān al-Fārisī[47] and others. Know that, during the life of the Prophet (may God bless him and grant him peace), the People of the Veranda were not singled out by any kind of worship peculiar to them, but because they resembled the Companions, both in their acts of worship and in their performance of the legal duties.[48] The People of the Veranda were distinguished only because they were poor, strangers and abided by the mosque. The Prophet (may God bless him and grant him peace) made the Emigrants of Quraysh brothers with their hosts from the neighbouring tribes of Aws and Khazraj.[49] But since the People of the Veranda remained strangers, the Prophet gave them shelter with himself. He shared his mosque with them and ordered that they should be helped. He would seek their company and they would accompany him when he was invited to a meal. Bukhārī[50] cites Abū Hurayra (may God be pleased with him) who said in a long tradition, 'The People of the Veranda are the guests of Islam. They did not seek refuge with a family, in wealth, or with anyone. If the Prophet (may God bless him and grant him peace) was given alms, he would send it to them without retaining anything from it. If he received a gift, he would call for them, keep a portion of it for himself and share the rest with them.'[51] In spite of all this, it is an etymological mistake to derive the world *Ṣūfī* from *ṣuffa*.[52]

Similarly, others argue that *Ṣūfī* comes from *ṣafā'* (purity), but etymologically this is also incorrect.[53] There remains that the name *Ṣūfī* is merely a name to designate this group and to differentiate it from others. It is only later that various forms were derived from it, such as Sufi-aspirant or Sufi, their path being called Sufism, and their people the Sufi-aspirants (*mutaṣawwifūn*) or the Sufis (*ṣūfiyyūn*).[54]

Since we have agreed that the name Sufi is used to refer to the people on this specific Path, let us now elucidate its meaning by defining and describing it. We say that Sufism is the observation of the rules of proper conduct vis-à-vis God in both inward and outward deeds, respecting the limits He has imposed upon us, giving precedence to the deeds of the hearts, watching its secret recesses, while aspiring therewith to salvation. This is what characterizes this Path as such. This will also explain the way of the last among the Predecessors (*salaf*) as well as the earlier Sufi generation, and how, after them, the name Sufi came to designate one of the spiritual struggles only: the one leading to the lifting of the veil (*rafʿ al-ḥijāb*). We will now elucidate and clarify this.

CHAPTER TWO

On the Aspirations of the Sufis Towards Spiritual Struggles and the Reasons Why They Engaged in Them

Let us first go through some preliminary definitions in order to clarify the nature of the Sufi Path.

Preliminary I

On the Meaning of the Spirit, the Soul, the Intellect and the Heart
On the State of Perfection and What Befits It

Know that God (glory be to Him) created man of two substances: the first is a visible corporeal mass with a tangible frame, namely the body (*jasad*); and the second, a subtle reality (*laṭīfa rabbāniyya*) that He bestowed upon man and deposited in the body, its seat. The subtle reality is to the body what the horseman is to his mount or the sultan to his people. The body yields to its authority and submits to its will. The body has no power over the subtle reality and is incapable, even for one moment, of rebelling against it since God gave the subtle reality mastery and diffused in it power over the body. The Law refers to it as spirit, heart, intellect or soul. At the same time, these terms denote other concepts; if the reader wishes to know more concerning this point, he can consult Ghazālī's book.[1]

By subtle reality, the Legislator might designate the trust (*amāna*). God Most High said, '*We offered the trust to the heavens and the earth and the mountains, but they refused to carry it and were afraid of it; and man carried it. Surely he is sinful, very foolish*' (Q.xxxiii.72). According to one of the interpretations of trust, man is sinful for he dared to carry it, despite the immense dangers it entailed for either his future felicity or wretchedness. May God protect us and shower us with His kindness! The word 'carrying' (*ḥaml*) is only a metaphorical approximation because, in reality, man is helpless, capable of neither bearing nor shedding this burden or trust. His carrying of the burden, and his acceptance to carry it, actually refers to that which has been preordained in the Mother of the Book, namely a 'carrying' that will lead either to his felicity or to his wretchedness.

God has created the subtle reality. It originated in the World of Divine Command; and its essence was still incomplete when God granted it an innate disposition that aspires to perfection. The Prophet (may God bless him and grant him peace) said, 'Every child is born according to his primordial nature (*fiṭra*); it is his parents who lead him to Judaism, Mazdeism or Christianity.'[2] The reality was then brought into this world in order to obtain the perfection that befits its essence and conforms to its nature (*ṭabʿ*). Since this subtle reality emanates from the Spiritual World (*al-ʿālam al-rūḥānī*), wherein knowledge is intrinsic and does not need to be acquired by the essences, the perfection of the subtle reality's essence lies in its acquisition of the science and knowledge related to the reality of existents (*mawjūdāt*). With this knowledge and science, the reality is then able to envision its own original world and to know the Attributes of its Creator and His effects. In order to attain this stage of perfection, the subtle reality has to be brought into a world that was created for it and is a gift from God to the individuals subject to the Law (*mukallafūn*). As it is repeatedly said in the Qur'ān, '*God has subjected to you what is in the heavens and earth*' (Q.XLV.31); He '*assigned to you... heaven*' (Q.II.22); '*He who made the earth [submissive to] you*' (Q.LXVII.15); '*He who has appointed for you the stars*' (Q.VI.97), and many other verses. Accordingly, in this world the body acts, animated by the forces suffused in it by the subtle reality. The effects of the body's actions, in turn, redound to the subtle reality. In so doing, the subtle reality's aspiration towards perfection increases and its incentive to acquire knowledge intensifies. And thus it is until this knowledge is disclosed and its essence partially or fully completed.

Actions (*aʿmāl*) and learning (*ʿilm*) are, then, to the subtle reality what sustenance is to the body. With nutrition, the body increases in strength, its frame is completed, and it develops naturally for the young man who reaches maturity. Actions and learning have the same function for the subtle reality. When it first comes into the world, the subtle reality is like a young child who is just starting to grow up; yet, it is in this world that it reaches perfection as it is affected by the imprint that learning and actions leave upon it.

Because the world is in essence a world of opposites (*ʿālam al-mutaḍāddāt*), the actions with their effects redounding on the subtle reality are of two kinds. Some, such as good deeds and virtues, help it advance towards perfection, while others, such as evil deeds and vices, are obstacles that divert it from perfection.

If the effects attained promote goodness and purity, then the subtle reality's aspiration for perfection increases, and so does its yearning and longing for good; it also becomes easier for the subtle reality to lean towards and perform such actions. If the good action is repeated, the effects that permeate the subtle reality are multiplied; and with reiteration, this process continues and increases until the virtues that secure perfection become firmly rooted in the subtle reality, overwhelming it and preparing it for its eternal felicity.

If, however, the deeds further evils and vices, the subtle reality is diverted from its aspiration to perfection and becomes incapable of reaching it. This, in turn, paves the way for other vices and more evils to beset the reality, finally leading it to ultimate wretchedness, unless God in His compassion and mercy saves it. God Most High said, '*As for him who gives and is God-wary and confirms the reward most fair, We shall surely ease him to the Easing. But as for him who is a miser, and self-sufficient, and cries lies to the reward most fair, We shall surely ease him to the Hardship*' (Q.XCII.5–10); '*Whoso does righteousness, it is to his own gain, and whoso does evil, it is to his own loss*' (Q.XLI.38); '*Every soul shall be pledged for what it has earned*' (Q.LXXIV.40); and '*God charges no soul save to its capacity, standing to its account is what it has earned, and against its account what it has merited*' (Q.II.286). The Prophet (may God bless him and grant him peace) said, '[On Judgement Day], your actions will be given back to you.'[3] If God illuminates the subtle reality with the light of faith, purifies it through good deeds, and keeps it from the foulness of vile ones, then it can return to

God liberated from the impediments of this world and its obstacles. The subtle reality will have then captured the perfection for which it was created and brought forth into this world. God Most High said, '*I created the jinn and humankind only that they might worship Me*' (Q.LI.56); and, according to Ibn ʿAbbās,[4] 'to worship means to know'.[5] God Most High said, '*Then unto Us you shall return, then We shall tell you what you were doing*' (Q.X.23).

Preliminary II

On the Difference between Acquired Science (al-ʿilm al-kasbī), *Inspired Science* (ilhām) *and Revelation* (waḥy)

Know that, when the body became the seat of the subtle reality, the latter diffused in it a strength emanating from itself and aiming at reaching perfection in this worldly existence. Because the reality emanates from the World of Divine Command (*ʿālam al-amr*) and the Dominion (*malakūt*),[6] two possible ways were determined for it to perfect itself through sciences and knowledge.

The first way lay within the world that was created for the subtle reality, and where everything is subjected to it. The second way is through the subtle reality's own world, from where it originates and with which it partakes of the same essence. Through the way of life in this lower world, the subtle reality acquires sciences and learning in the following manner: it apprehends the objects of perception with the external senses; with the help of the imagination, it draws out the forms these objects, and from these forms it abstracts their intelligible meaning; finally, discursive thinking deals with these concepts through synthesis, analysis and the setting of analogies. This continues until the subtle reality attains its goal. This type of knowledge is called acquired learning (*al-ʿilm al-kasbī*).

The other way is that of the higher realms: the World of Divine Command and the World of Spiritual Entities (*ʿālam al-rūḥāniyyāt*), wherefrom the subtle reality draws its knowledge by way of cleansing itself from the impurities engendered by vile deeds and freeing itself from the darkness of the human condition. Then it becomes receptive to the breezes of compassion and flows of perfection and felicity emanating from the higher realms. Thus the light of learning and gnosis can shine in the heart.

The subtle reality is cleansed and liberated from impurities through spiritual combat in two ways. The first is whereby the reality is purified by way of an instinct (*gharīza*) settled in its innate disposition from the moment it was created. This instinct is called preservation (*ʿiṣma*) since its role is to prevent the reality from yielding to what could involve any wrongdoing (*mukhālafa*). If the opaqueness of the human condition is obliterated, and the lot of the devil in the human heart extirpated by the light of prophethood, God will bring about the knowledge shining forth from that higher realm and cast it along with the contemplation of the transmitter of this knowledge, who is an angel. This is revelation (*waḥy*), the knowledge of the prophets (may God's blessings be upon them). It is the highest level of knowledge.

On the other hand, if the process of purification (*taṣfiya*) and liberation (*takhlīṣ*) of the subtle reality is undertaken through a matter of acquisition (*iktisāb*) and artificial labour (*ṭarīq ṣināʿī*), the resulting knowledge imparts neither consciousness of its cause nor of its transmitter; it is but a breath in the innermost heart. This type of knowledge is inferior to the first and characterizes the saints (*awliyā'*) and the sincere believers (*ṣiddīqūn*). It is called inspiration (*ilhām*), unveiling (*kashf*), or God-given learning (*ladunī*). God Most High said, '*We had taught him knowledge proceeding from Us*' (Q.xviii.65).

Revelation and acquired learning are two obvious matters: acquired learning is obtained through the senses, whereas revelation comes necessarily through religion. As for inspired knowledge (*al-ʿilm al-ilhāmī*), it is almost agreed that it is a finding of an intimate nature (*wijdānī*). Its clearest and most truthful proof is the station of dreams (*ḥāl al-ru'yā*), when the veil of slumber is removed, the burden of the external senses is lifted from the heart and its powers concentrate on the inward. The subtle reality seizes a perception pertaining to its own world in a straightforward manner, through an image or by way of a similitude. The veracity of this type of perception is confirmed in the states of wakefulness. These states result from a lessening of many factors that normally impede this perception, such as the numbness of the external senses. And what if the corporeal obstacles were to be lifted and all the other traits peculiar to the human condition erased! The Prophet (may God bless him and grant him peace) said, 'A true vision (*al-ru'yā al-ṣāliḥa*) is one of the forty-six gifts of prophethood';[7] and 'A vision is a heralding sign (*mubashshirāt*).'[8] Revelation (*waḥy*) from and spiritual perception (*iṭṭilāʿ*) into the Dominion (*ʿālam al-malakūt*) always start with a vision. ʿĀ'isha (may God be pleased with her) said, 'The revelations of the Prophet began with a veridical vision (*al-ru'yā al-ṣādiqa*). All his visions arose like the breaking of dawn in the morning.'[9]

Ghazālī illustrates these two different sources of knowledge for the soul with two examples.[10] In the first example, there is a pond, the water of which flows in from outside springs or from a spring located in the pond's bottom that has been silted up with mud. What the outside springs are to the pond, the senses (*ḥawās*, sing. *ḥiss*) and discursive thinking (*fikr*) are to those who work to acquire knowledge. What the removal of the mud at the bottom is to the pond, purification and spiritual struggle are to those who are endowed with inspiration. The second example tells the story of Indian and Chinese artisans. They were ordered to engrave two walls that faced each other in the king's palace. The Indians toiled in order to create masterly images, creative sculptures and unprecedented inscriptions. As for the Chinese artisans, they polished the wall facing the Indians. A lowered curtain separated the two walls. When the artisans' task was over, the Chinese were told, 'What did you achieve?' They answered, 'We perfected our work.' They were asked, 'Prove it to us.' The curtain was lifted and the engravings of the Indian artisans, with all their statues, were reflected on the polished surface of the facing wall: more perfect in beauty and more truthful in its reflection. These two examples might not constitute a proof for all. Yet, he who is endowed with a healthy nature, a penetrating insight and a sound taste will find them helpful. For the Sufi, no proof can better testify to the validity of inspired learning (*ʿilm al-ilhām*) than vision (*ru'yā*).

Let us go further in our explanations. When God (praise be to Him) created the world, He did not immediately thrust it into sensory existence (*al-wujūd al-ḥissī*), but did so gradually and in phases. First, God deposited all of its realities (*ḥaqā'iq*) and essences (*dhawāt*)—great or small, collectively or individually—in a Book He named the Tablet. He called the Creative Principle (*ibdā*ʿ) the Pen (*qalam*), as attested to in the Qur'ān. On this Tablet are recorded the realities that have been, are and will be until the Day of Resurrection. Then, from this Tablet, and according to a gradual progression in the created universe, God brought out His creation into sensory existence. All of this is well known and we will not linger on this point.

When God brought forth the subtle reality, He created it with a desire to perfect itself, through knowledge of and learning about the realities of the existents and the Attributes of its Creator. For this purpose, He created it with two facets. One side of the subtle reality is turned towards sensory existence wherefrom it draws the forms of the existents, which are then brought by the senses to the intellect where their abstract meanings are disengaged. Finally, the imagination and discursive thinking arrange them in a significant order. The other facet of the reality is turned towards the Tablet and the forms of the existents are impressed therein. However, the human condition and the corporeal state can prevent and hinder this imprint, as they are a veil between the Tablet and the reality. If the veil is lifted through purification and deliverance from impurities, then perception (*idrāk*) is achieved in its most perfect aspect; more perfectly so than by means of the first facet. Indeed the senses and the imagination cannot always be relied upon to transmit faithfully the forms and realities of the existents to the subtle reality, nor can discursive thinking as it disengages and orders them to allow their conceptualization (*taṣawwur*).

Senses and imagination as well as discursive thinking are only means and tools used by the subtle reality to grasp what it can of its own essence. Actually, the subtle reality could faithfully imprint these forms in itself, because they are part of 'its' self. Therefore, to reach the subtle reality's essence through itself is safer than reaching it through something other than itself; and reliance on itself is safer than reliance on other than itself. The perception one can attain through the second possibility, the way of the spiritual world, is clearer than the one attained through the first one, the way of sensory existence. Plato, the greatest Sufi amongst the ancients, did not believe that peripheral perception of the spiritual world through acquired learning constitutes an irrefutable certainty.[11] According to him, such learning only grasps what is most probable and most suitable. He thought that the difference between acquired and inspired knowledge is comparable to the difference between opinion (*ẓann*) and knowledge (*ʿilm*).

The Qur'ān and the Sunna affirm that God-wariness is the key to guidance and unveiling. It is knowledge obtained without a learning process. God Most High said, '*And [in] what God has created in the heavens and the earth, surely there are signs for a God-wary people*' (Q.x.6); '*This is an exposition for mankind, and a guidance, and an admonition for such as are God-wary*' (Q.III.138); and '*O ye who believe! If ye keep your duty to God, He will give you discrimination (between right and wrong)*' (Q.VIII.29).[12] Discrimination (*furqān*) is described as a light with which man can differentiate between truth and falsehood and with which he will avoid uncertainties. The Prophet (may God bless him and grant him peace) often prayed for light in His supplications: 'O God, enlighten me; increase the light in me; and fill my heart, my hearing, my sight, my hair, my skin, my blood and my flesh with light.'[13]

God Most High said, '*But those who struggle in Our cause, surely We shall guide them in Our ways*' (Q.XXIX.69); '*And fear God; God teaches you*' (Q.II.282). The Prophet (may God bless him and grant him peace) was asked about the meaning of the words of God Most High, '*Is he whose breast has expanded unto Islam, so he walks in a light from his Lord...?*' (Q.XXXIX.22). He explained that expansion results from the light cast into the heart, and the chest expands and lies receptive to it. The Prophet (may God bless him and grant him peace) also said, 'He who acts according to what he knows, God will grant him the knowledge of what he does not know';[14] 'He who has sincerely worshipped God for forty mornings will see sources of wisdom gush forth from his heart unto his tongue';[15] and 'Beware of the believer's perspicacity (*firāsa*) for he does see with the light of God.'[16] He also affirmed, 'There are inspired people in my community, and ʿUmar is one of them.'[17] As to Abū Yazīd, he said, 'The learned man is not the one who has memorized part of God's Book by heart—indeed if he forgets, he will become an ignorant man—rather, the learned man is the one who draws his knowledge directly from his Lord: whenever He wishes to He bestows it upon him, without any need for memory or study.'[18] Let us also quote the words of God Most High, '*And We had taught him knowledge proceeding from Us*' (Q.xviii.64).

As we have mentioned earlier, knowledge is imparted directly from God. If it is acquired through learning, it is not God-given (*ʿilm ladunī*). God-given knowledge will blossom in the innermost heart without any external habitual cause. There are innumerable examples of it, especially among the followers of the Prophet, their followers and those who came after them. Abū Bakr told ʿĀ'isha (and may God be pleased with both of them), 'They are your [two brothers and] two sisters'; his wife was then with child and she indeed gave birth to a girl.[19] Similarly, the famous story of ʿUmar (may God be pleased with him) who said during his sermon, 'O Sāriya, the mountain, the mountain!'[20] Many other examples could be given if we wanted to examine this aspect in depth. This, however, would lengthen our explanation and distract us from our study.

Preliminary iii

On the Meaning of Felicity and Its Degrees

Know that felicity lies in attaining the bliss and pleasure that are obtained through the satisfaction of the instinct, when granted what it longs for and what fulfils its nature. Therein lies perfection for the instinct. The pleasure of the instinct of anger lies in revenge, that of concupiscence in food and coupling, and that of sight in vision. The pleasure that fulfils the subtle reality lies in learning and gnosis since, as we said earlier, it is through them that it is able to fulfil its nature.[21] Thus, the degrees in pleasure vary with the degrees of the different instincts themselves.

It was made evident that the subtle reality is the most perfect among the faculties of perception. Consequently, the pleasure that it derives from perception is also the most complete and most intense.

Here, also, pleasure varies according to the levels of the object of knowledge. For example, the sciences of grammar, poetry and substantive law are not the knowledge of God, His Attributes and His acts. Learning about subjects and peasants is different from knowing the secrets of kings and the ruling of their kingdoms.[22] As we mentioned earlier, this knowledge and acquired learning are different from each other.

If the object to be known is more sublime and noble, if a science is more complete and clear, if the longing to know this object is more intense, then learning about this object is undoubtedly most pleasurable. Since there is nothing loftier, nobler and more perfect than the Creator of all entities, the Giver of existence and order, how could there be a supreme presence more sublime, perfect and beautiful than the Lord whose Majesty none can even attempt to describe. It is through God-given and inspired learning, spiritual perception and unveiling that one can grasp the secrets and know the order encompassing all the existents. This is the highest type of knowledge, the most perfect, clearest and pleasurable. This learning fosters delight, joy and awareness of perfection.[23]

It was made clear that learning is pleasure, and that the most pleasurable type of learning is the knowledge of God, His Attributes, His acts and the ruling of His kingdom. This is inspired God-given knowledge (*al-ʿilm al-ilhāmī al-ladunī*), as we explained earlier. He who perseveres in his pondering and wishes to grasp the secrets of the Dominion will experience an even greater joy when the veils are removed. He will then be beside himself with joy. This can only be understood when experienced through mystical tasting, so trying to describe it with words is useless. The students in some acquirable science will have a foretaste of this pleasure when, after a long and fervent perseverance, they finally solve an ambiguous question.

There are two types of pleasure. The first relates to the corporeal instincts and lies in the satisfaction of their needs; the second relates to the heart and is attained when its essential nature and need for knowledge are fulfilled. The highest pleasure is the knowledge of God Most High and His Attributes. The Prophet (may God bless him and grant him peace) describes the pleasure resulting from the perception of Beauty in the presence of the Lord, 'I have prepared for My good servants what no eye has ever seen, no ear ever heard and no heart ever witnessed.'[24] After death, the process of perception and knowledge that had been impeded by the body is further unveiled and clarified, whereby the object of perception and knowledge is then seen. This is called a vision (*ru'yā*).[25]

The explanation is the following: if an observer looks at another man and then lowers his eyelids, the image of this man remains in the imagination. When he opens his eyes again, the object will be perceived as it was perceived the first time; yet, the second perception differs from the first one in intensity of evidence and clarity; in every other respect, however, the observed object has not undergone any change. Similarly, if a man perceives a human silhouette in the dark, at dusk or at night, he is unable to distinguish the person and he can only imagine it; when morning comes, daylight renders his perception clearer and he can then see the object from all perspectives; yet, the observed object has still undergone no change.[26]

These are two levels of perception: the object when imagined and the object when seen. Thus, it is not too far-fetched to say that there are also two degrees in the knowledge of non-illusory existents, such as the Creator (*al-Bārī*) and His acts. One perception is clearer and the other dimmer, the latter being clarified after death occurs, when corporeal veils and hindrances are removed. The body—like the eyelids, dusk or darkness—prevented the perfectly clear perception of the object and only allowed it to register in the imagination. Since clarity depends on perception, what is to prevent God from giving the eye, an organ or any other bodily member He chooses the ability to perceive? When the veil is lifted after death, the seat of vision is freed of all corporeal uncleanness and moral impurities and brought to perfection by God. It is then that the Truth manifests Himself. The Self-disclosure (*tajallī*) of the Truth and the removal of the veil (*inkishāf*) perfect man's prior perception, just as the vision of the observed object in full light completes the work the imagination did beforehand.

The vision is without shape or substance; however, it is a real image. It adds clarity and further unveils the knowledge gathered in this world. Knowledge is a seed to the vision that will turn into unveiling (*mukāshafa*), just like the seed grows to be a tree or a harvest. He who does not have a date pit will not grow a palm tree. Hence, he who has not enjoyed some knowledge in this life will not enjoy any vision in the Hereafter, because no one will ever be granted what he did not pursue in this world. The Hereafter is the abode of recompense (*jazā'*), not the abode of prescriptions (*taklīf*). The Prophet (may God bless him and grant him peace) said, 'Man dies in keeping with how he lived. He will be raised [on the Judgement Day] in the state he was in when he died.'[27] Thus, gnosis must lead to direct vision and witnessing. The pleasure will then intensify, just as the lover's does when he beholds the object of his love.

The knowledge that can be gathered in this world has countless degrees. Likewise, there are different levels of Self-disclosure. As we explained earlier, there are different stages in the visual perception of the observer who looks at an object in the darkness of the night. This also applies to the disclosure of essences (*dhawāt*) when unshackled by the imagination. The Prophet (may God bless him and grant him peace) said, 'Verily, God manifests Himself to the people in general and to Abū Bakr in a special way.'[28] This was due to Abū Bakr's perfect knowledge. The Prophet (may God bless him and grant him peace) said, 'Abū Bakr was not superior to you because of his frequent praying and fasting but because of something which had settled in his heart.'[29] This connotes knowledge, as shown previously.

It is evident that, for the individual subject to the Law, felicity in the Hereafter is two-fold: firstly, corporeal felicity related to the pleasure of the instincts and their forces; secondly, felicity pertaining to the heart, which lies in the vision of God's Face. Even though the visual faculties are a corporeal vehicle, the pleasure resulting from the knowledge initiated by this perception [of God's Face] lies in the heart. This type of knowledge is more important to and loftier for the gnostics (*ʿārifūn*), who give it priority. Thawrī[30] asked Rābiʿa,[31] 'What is the true nature of your faith?' She answered, 'I did not worship Him for fear of His Hellfire or out of ambition for His Paradise, for then I would have been like the vile mercenary;

rather, I worshipped Him out of love and desire for Him.'[32] She was also asked, 'What do you say about Paradise?' Her answer was, 'The neighbour has precedence over the house.'[33] There are many stories in this vein.[34]

Preliminary IV

On the Pleasure Resulting from Knowledge Obtained through Unveiling in This Life and on Its Different Levels

Know that, if the subtle reality that is in us reaches the level of inspired knowledge (*ʿilm ilhāmī*)—also called unveiling (*kashf*) and spiritual perception (*iṭṭilāʿ*)—through purification and spiritual struggle, as explained earlier, knowledge is granted according to different levels, which vary with the degree of purification and cleansing the soul has achieved. Its initial point is the state of presence with God (*muḥāḍara*), which constitutes the last level after the removal of the veil and the first level in the unveiling; then comes [the fullness of] unveiling (*mukāshafa*), followed by witnessing. This last stage only occurs if all the traces of the individual existence (*aniyya*) are erased. Al-Junayd (may God be pleased with him) said, 'He who is in the state of presence with God is still tied to his individual existence; he who has reached unveiling is drawn closer [to God] by his knowledge; as to him who has attained witnessing, he is obliterated by his gnosis.'[35]

The teacher Abū al-Qāsim al-Qushayrī said, '"Presence with God" can be reached by means of a chain of arguments. It is the presence of the heart which is overwhelmed with the power of remembrance, yet it is still behind the veil. "Unveiling" is the presence with clear evidence of His Attributes (*ḥuḍūruhu bi-naʿt al-bayān*); in it there is no need to reflect upon established proof (*dalīl*), or to search for the way or to protect oneself from the allegations of doubts; and in it there is no veil that would prevent ascribing an attribute to the Unseen (*ghayb*). Finally, "witnessing" is the presence with the Truth without any trace of doubt left (*ḥuḍūr al-Ḥaqq min ghayr baqāʾi tuhma*).'[36] The difference between the three degrees in evidence is illustrated by the following example. If one sees Zayd in the house from a close distance or in the courtyard at noon, this perception of Zayd in the radiant sun will be perfect and total. If another person sees Zayd from a room, from afar or at sunset, he will know from the shape that it is Zayd, yet he cannot picture the details of the concealed facets of his shape. This is similar to the difference between the degrees of unveiling in the religious sciences. The highest level of unveiling is that of witnessing; it is the most perfect knowledge of God, His Attributes, His acts and the secrets of the Dominion.

We explained that knowledge is like a seed within the subtle reality, leading it in the Hereafter to ultimate felicity (*al-saʿāda al-kubrā*): the vision of God's Face. In the other world, felicity, which is Self-disclosure, varies according to the degree of knowledge attained in this world. Witnessing is its highest level; it is most precious and noble, rare and evanescent. It will overwhelm him whose heart has been purified to the most perfect degree possible.

After these introductory points, let us now clarify the position of the Sufis with regard to this spiritual struggle and purification; the preconditions, principles and rules of proper conduct they stipulate for the attainment of the station of unveiling; what they set down as technical terms; and how the word Sufism came to prevail as a name and a surname for the Path. We will elucidate all of this, as we promised earlier.

Know that we have explained the meaning of this Path for the first generation among this group, and how it required the observance of the rules of proper conduct (*riʿāyat al-ādāb*), inwardly as well as outwardly. Inasmuch as the Sufis started watching their inner selves (*bawāṭin*) and concentrated on liberating their hearts, heedful of their secrets, then purification was achieved and the lights of inspired knowledge could shine forth. This knowledge, as we explained before, resulted from purification and the removal of the veil and led them to experience pleasure. With perseverance, the Sufi who had steadily progressed on the Path and whose heart was in a perfect state of purity reached unveiling and witnessing. Many Sufis were eager to pass beyond all these steps to attain witnessing, the elixir of ultimate felicity in the Hereafter and the vision of God's noble Face. They set conditions for this spiritual struggle and for the purification leading to inspired knowledge, but we shall be talking about them later.

The observance of the rules of proper conduct defined by the Law (*al-ādāb al-sharʿiyya*) in both the inward and the outward became the first step in the ascensions (*maʿārij*) towards witnessing. However, the experienced Sufis did not prompt to the seeking of this station because of its dangers and due to the fact that human forces are unable to sustain the spiritual vision. They see that a slight lifting of the veil and a bit of inspired knowledge are like seeds in the heart for obtaining vision in the Hereafter, even though the seeds be few in number. Fewer seeds are safer than many that carry with them great perils and grave dangers. What follows proves this. Many of the Sufis, whose purification was completed and perfected after the veils were removed, have been suddenly bewildered by the light of Self-disclosure and witnessing. They were obliterated and drowned in an ocean of annihilation (*fanā'*). Some died on the spot, like the disciple who said repeatedly, 'I saw God,' to which Abū Yazīd replied, 'Should he see me, he would die.' The disciple was brought to his presence and as soon as his eyes fell on Abū Yazīd, he died.[37] This is a well-known story and there are many others. Some were struck with madness, drawn into a state of rapture and divine attraction (*jadhb*), and they lost their minds and abandoned the religious prescriptions; among them are the madmen and the lunatics, like the famous Bahlūl.[38] Other Sufis remained staring fixedly, motionless until they died. Finally, there are those who are able to withstand the lights of witnessing and Self-disclosure (*anwār al-tajallī wa'l-mushāhada*); but they are few. The Prophet (may God bless him and grant him peace) said, 'God has seventy veils of light. If He were to remove them from His Face, the sublimity of His Face would burn whatever He would glance at.'[39]

He who has reached witnessing and progresses beyond it becomes firmly rooted therein and is obviously stronger and more able to withstand Self-disclosure. When the disciple gains control over a particular station, then, so long as he has control over it, he has even more mastery over the previous ones. In a chapter on sudden inspirations (*bawādih*), the teacher Abū al-Qāsim says, 'Some people can withstand what can strike them unexpectedly because of their station and strength; they are the masters of the moment (*abnā' al-waqt*).'[40]

He who does actually return from this journey victorious, having reached the goal, will caution those who risk this path and warn them about its dangers and even its goal, which seldom brings about salvation. May God protect us! What a great victory for the one who is protected from all this!

The shaykh of the gnostics said, 'Do not seek witnessing, because when man witnesses the Truth (*shuhūd al-Ḥaqq*), he perishes.'[41] Abū ʿAlī al-Jūzajānī said, 'Be a man who walks on the straight path and not one who solicits miracles; it is your soul that urges you to perform charismatic acts (*karāma*) and your Lord who calls upon you to walk on the straight path.'[42] Another Sufi master said, after having defined spiritual struggle and clarified the Path of Sufism, 'We have mentioned this to caution the one who hastens to attain the pleasure of witnessing and longs to be in a state of annihilation before he has firm roots and before its due place. Our masters reject this.'[43] He added, 'You would be seeking that which should be deferred to its proper abode, namely the Hereafter, where there is no action anymore. It would have been preferable for you had you spent your time trying to perform outward actions while searching for some inward knowledge, rather than reaching out for witnessing...The beauty and virtue would then have increased in your soul, which longs for its Lord, and in your self, which longs for its Paradise. If you renounce the world of religious prescriptions, which is the ground for ascensions and advancement, then you will reap only what you have sown.'[44] (This is the extent of his words).[45]

Listen how these words forbid seeking witnessing. In truth, more inward knowledge is necessary for reaching witnessing after death. It is safer indeed, because more plants will harvest more fruits.

CHAPTER THREE

On Spiritual Struggle in General, Its Subdivisions and Its Conditions

To recapitulate briefly what we have come across while examining the doctrines and the statements [of the Sufis], we say that spiritual struggle divides into three distinct, gradually-ascending kinds.

The First Spiritual Struggle

As we said in the beginning of this book, God-wariness signifies cautiously observing the limits imposed by God, because the aim of this struggle is salvation and fear of His punishment. Outwardly, all transgression [of the Law] is to be avoided; if any transgression occurs, repentance (*tawba*) is necessary. It is also imperative to forsake that which would lead to a transgression, like the pursuit of fame, excessive riches, an unrestrained way of life or fanatical religious opinions. Inwardly, the deeds of the heart must be watched because they are the source and principle of all actions, lest the forbidden is yielded to or an incumbent duty neglected. Ibn ʿAṭā' said, 'God-wariness consists of both the outward and the inward. Outwardly it is to abide by the divine limits, and inwardly it is to have the right intention and sincerity (*ikhlāṣ*).'[1] This struggle is essentially based on moral care (*waraʿ*). The Prophet (may God bless him and grant him peace) said, 'That which is lawful is evident, and so is that which is unlawful; yet between the two lies uncertainty. He who is wary of the uncertain is cleared from blame in his honour and religion; but he who is drawn to the land of ambiguity is like the grazing animal on the verge of a forbidden area, about to fall in it. Indeed every king has some forbidden lands and God's forbidden lands are His interdictions.'[2] The Prophet (may God bless him and grant him peace) also said, 'Leave that which is doubtful and reach for that which is not.'[3] As to Ibn ʿUmar, he said, 'God-wariness is to discard the acceptable for fear of the unacceptable'; and 'The servant of God is not fully wary of Him until he is able to ignore that which generates doubt in his heart.'[4] Finally, Abū Bakr al-Ṣiddīq said, 'We used to leave seventy kinds of lawful things for fear we would fall into the unlawful.'[5]

The Second Spiritual Struggle

The struggle of walking on the straight path is that of the soul striving for rectitude and moderation in all its natural traits until it is polished and realized. Then, good deeds emanate from the soul with ease. Thereafter ascetic discipline (*riyāḍa*), spiritual education (*tahdhīb*) and the teachings of the Qur'ān and the prophets become natural as if they were part of the soul's innate disposition. The incentive behind this struggle is the pursuit of the higher degrees of '*those whom God has blessed, the prophets, sincere believers*' (Q.IV.69). Going straight is the path to these levels. God Most High said, '*Guide us in the straight path, the path of those whom Thou hast blessed*' (Q.I.7). If God has urged man to pray for rectitude seventeen times a day during the seventeen obligatory prayer units, when the believer recites the opening chapter of the Qur'ān, it is precisely because going straight is arduous, its goal is lofty and its fruit noble.[6] The Prophet (may God bless him and grant him peace) said, 'Go straight and no charge will be held against you.'[7]

In order to go straight, the soul's character traits (*khuluq*) must be cured and healed by opposing passion (*shahwa*) and caprice (*hawā*), and resisting the traits' urges, inclinations or predispositions. This is carried out through opposite action: miserliness is cured with generosity, arrogance with humbleness, covetousness through the renouncing of the coveted object, and anger with gentleness. God Most High said, '[*Those*] *who when they expend are neither prodigal nor parsimonious, but between that is a just stand*' (Q.XXV.67); '*And eat and drink, but be you not prodigal*' (Q.VII.31); '*And keep not thy hand chained to thy neck, nor outspread it widespread altogether*' (Q.XVII.29); '[*And those who are with him*] *are hard against the unbelievers, merciful one to another*' (Q.XLVIII.28).

[While he is trying to amend his soul], the wayfarer must show forbearance because the remedy is bitter. Shaykh Abū al-Qāsim al-Junayd said, 'Know that only great men can withstand walking on the straight path, because it implies departing from the habitual and parting with the conventional and customary. A man must stand between God's hands with total sincerity.'[8] When the Prophet (may God bless him and grant him peace) said, 'Hūd and its sisters made me turn grey',[9] he was referring to the imposition of walking on the straight path in the words of the Most High, '*So go thou straight as thou hast been commanded*' (Q.XI.112). Initially, performing right actions is unnatural, difficult and arduous, but with repetition the effects of these actions slowly penetrate the soul until they become deeply rooted qualities and innate dispositions. The man who is learning to write goes through a similar experience: at first he finds it difficult, but gradually the traces of the act of writing rise to his inward self, the quality of writing becomes part of him as if it were a natural disposition, and fine writing originates with utmost ease.

As the wayfarer is struggling to walk on the straight path, the therapy does not imply the stifling or total renunciation of his human traits; these are natural dispositions and each one of them is created for a purpose: if the appetite in man were suppressed, the human race would either die out from hunger, or become extinct out of abstinence. If anger were extirpated, man would perish due to being unable to defend himself against the oppressor. The purpose of this therapy is to establish rectitude firmly in the soul. Then, the soul can govern its instincts naturally, according to the laws of conduct set by God. In so doing, the soul becomes accustomed to life after death, when it will sever its ties with this world and meet its Creator with a heart freed of anything that would keep it from walking on the straight path. Indeed, with every deviation, one of the soul's natural traits will cling to it and alienate it from God. This is what is meant by erasing the blameworthy dispositions in the heart, and purifying it through praiseworthy virtues. Any departure from the middle course and moderation is reprehensible.

Know that striving to walk on the straight path is an individual obligation (*farḍ ʿayn*) with respect to the prophets (may God's blessings be upon them). God Most High said, '*So go thou straight as thou hast been commanded*' (Q.xi.113); and '*Thou art truly among the Envoys on a straight path*' (Q.xxxvi.3). He also told Moses and Aaron (peace be upon them both), '*So go you straight, and follow not the way of those that know not*' (Q.x.89). When ʿĀ'isha (may God be pleased with her) was asked to describe the nature of the Prophet (may God bless him and grant him peace), she said, 'Have you not read the Qur'ān? His nature (*khuluq*) was the Qur'ān.'[10] The Prophet (may God bless him and grant him peace) was taught what to do and what to avoid by the Qur'ānic verses. He (may God bless him and grant him peace) was the first to be taught and educated thus; and from him, light shone unto the rest of humankind. First he was taught by the Qur'ān and then he taught men. The Prophet (may God bless him and grant him peace) said, 'I was sent to bring to perfection the noble character traits (*makārim al-akhlāq*).'[11]

Will (*irāda*) is the first condition in this struggle and ascetic discipline is the second one. By will, the Sufis do not refer to that which is commonly implied, namely fancying an object and then striving for it; this is the way of the soul. Rather, for the Sufis, will is a state of absolute certainty (*ḥāl al-yaqīn*) that overcomes the heart to the point whereat an act is determined upon so fully that the disciple seems compelled rather than free in his purpose. The teacher Abū al-Qāsim says:

> Will is the initial step on the Path of the wayfarers and it is called will because it is the first station for the travellers on their way to God. The attribute of will is the premise of every action, because if a man does not will, he does not act. Since this is the first station for the wayfarers, it is called 'the will' by analogy with 'the purpose' (*qaṣd*) that sets off an action. According to the rules of etymology, the 'willer' (*murīd*) is he who has a will (*irāda*), just as the learned (*ʿālim*) is he who has knowledge (*ʿilm*). Nevertheless, in this particular Path, the wayfarer or 'willer' has no will. In the mystical Path, he who has not stripped himself of his own

> will is not a 'willer', just as in a grammatical sense, he who does not have a will is not a 'willer'.[12] Essentially, will is the awakening of the heart to the quest for the Truth. It has been called 'a burning desire that dispels all fear.'[13]

As for ascetic training, it consists in cleansing the heart from all vices and blameworthy faults and purifying it through praiseworthy virtues, namely through rectitude and moderation in all of its traits, instincts and natural dispositions.

The therapy concerns the outward first: the wayfarers must ignore that towards which men tend to lean and with which the Devil can tempt the believers' hearts, such as the seductions and lures of this worldly life, honours, riches, social involvement, the cravings of the flesh, lust and the luxury of sleep. God Most High said, '*Decked out fair to men is the love of lusts—women, children, piled-up heaps of gold and silver, horses of mark, cattle and tillage. That is the enjoyment of the present life; but God—with Him is the fairest resort*' (Q.III.13). So long as he is likely to deviate from the straight path, and until he masters it and firmly establishes himself in this station, the wayfarer must avoid and renounce [these worldly pleasures] and keep away from them as he would from a deadly snake.

Then, the wayfarer has to remedy his inward by liberating it from the traces left by these faults, just as he had severed the outward from the causes behind the traces. The struggle is a long one and varies with the different factors, age, character and the predominant blameworthy traits [of each wayfarer]. This is an abstruse science except to the one whose path God has eased—'*We shall surely ease him to the Easing*' (Q.XCII.7). A shaykh might be the one sent by God to guide and ease the way [of the wayfarer] to his Lord.

As we said above, in this spiritual struggle and healing process, the general rule consists in resisting caprice and curbing passion as well as all the motives behind the traits likely to dominate the wayfarer's soul. The disciple must do so until his soul reaches moderation and rectitude, and until the desire and leaning of the instincts—towards one direction or another—disappear. The wayfarer is to become indifferent to action (*fiʿil*) or non-action (*tark*), prosperity (*wajd*) or poverty (*faqr*). He concentrates with all his strength on submitting to the Truth and the Just (*al-ʿAdl*), and devotes himself exclusively to God Most High. He no longer shows any preference for renunciation over enrichment (*tamawwul*), or for monasticism (*rahbāniyya*) over a life of enjoyment (*tamattuʿ*). The Prophet (may God bless him and grant him peace) said, 'I fast and break my fast; I sleep and I stay awake; and I also marry women. Whoever does not follow my tradition is not amongst my followers.'[14] The disciple must apply these spiritual exercises gradually, not too rigorously, for then, as the Prophet (may God bless him and grant him peace) said, he will be 'like the rider who overloads his mount and neither travels far nor spares the back of his mount'.[15] He (may God bless him and grant him peace) also said, 'The effort that is most pleasing to God is the one that is most persistent';[16] and 'Undertake only what you are able to accomplish.'[17] There are many similar statements. If the heart is given the quality of rectitude, if it is modelled on the Qur'ān and guided by its rules of conduct, then this means that [the wayfarer] respects the Sunna and follows in the straight path of '*those whom God has blessed, prophets, sincere believers, martyrs, the righteous; and how excellent are those companions!*' (Q.IV.69).

The Third Spiritual Struggle

This is the struggle towards unveiling and spiritual perception. In this struggle, the human qualities (*al-ṣifāt al-bashariyya*) are obliterated, and the corporeal forces (*al-quwā al-badaniyya*) in man are neutralized, the way they are after death or virtually so.[18] This is achieved through ascetic discipline and spiritual struggle. Then the subtle reality faces the Truth, the veil is lifted and the secrets of the universes and the sciences are made transparent to the witnessing soul. This is inspired knowledge, a knowledge which is attained through purification, as we explained earlier. According to the Sufis, there are several conditions to this struggle.

The first condition is to have realized the first stage described earlier: God-wariness. Indeed, this is the foundation of worship; its goal is the first level of bliss, namely salvation. Jarīrī said, 'He who has not fully achieved God-wariness and fully examined his self (*muḥāsaba*) has not reached unveiling and witnessing.'[19]

The second condition is to have secured the aforementioned second struggle: going straight. Wāṣiṭī said, 'Walking on the straight path is the quality through which beautiful virtues (*maḥāsin*) are perfected.'[20] The reason going straight is indispensable before the wayfarer can devote himself to the third struggle bears upon the substance of the term unveiling. The heart, through purification, unveiling and Self-disclosure of the realities in it, becomes like a polished body that mirrors the images facing it. Yet, the images are not unconditionally reflected in the mirror. They are reflected faithfully if the polished surface has a spherical shape with equal radii from its centre to its periphery. Only then are images mirrored as they are in their reality. If the polished surface is rectangular, quadrangular, concave or convex, the images are not mirrored as they are in their reality, but according to the reflecting surface and its shape. So it is with the heart: if it has acquired the quality of going straight, if the deeds emanating from it—whether action or non-action—are in equal proportion, then it resembles the circle's surface. The forms of the existents and the realities of the objects of knowledge (*ḥaqā'iq al-maʿlūmāt*) are disclosed in it as they are. Then perception is true and knowledge complete.

On the contrary, if the heart has not acquired the quality of going straight, if the deeds emanating from it—whether action or non-action—are in uneven proportion, so that it tilts away from the straight path by leaning towards it with some deeds and moving away from it just as much with other deeds, then the heart resembles the rectangular, quadrangular, concave or convex-shaped polished surface on which perfect reflection is impossible. The realities are disclosed according to the heart as it is, not according to what they are. In this case, the heart harvests nothing but weariness and deprivation. This is why many wayfarers, longing for unveiling, pursue it before they have even firmly settled themselves in the previous station, i.e. going straight. Sometimes erroneous ideas can infiltrate their hearts; then, the realities are reflected according to what is in their hearts and in no way according to what they are. These wayfarers turn into freethinkers; they ignore the revealed Laws and become outright atheists. May God protect us from such a fate! Walking on the straight path, then, is a precondition for this unveiling, which is the key to inspired knowledge and to the flawless and faithful disclosure in the heart of these realities as they are indeed.

Yet, some can experience unveiling—namely the lifting of the heart's veil (*rafᶜ ḥijāb al-qalb*)—by purifying their selves of that which is not God (*aghyār*), and polishing their hearts through hunger, fasting and sleepless nights without having fulfilled the pre-condition of walking on the straight path. This is why many people, followers of different religions as well as adepts of the magical sciences, labour towards unveiling by calling upon the power of celestial spirits (*rūḥāniyyat al-aflāk*); and with their help, they exercise free disposal (*taṣarruf*) over the natural world. To them, the realities of the objects of knowledge are not revealed as they are, but rather as they are in their selves. They can only reap '*the manifest loss*' (Q.xxxix.15).

The third condition is to follow a shaykh who is a wayfarer, has experienced the spiritual struggles and travelled the Path to God. To him, the veil has been lifted and the lights have radiated. He has gone through the different states and can lead the disciple step by step on the ascending paths until the latter is bestowed divine mercy (*al-raḥma al-rabbāniyya*) and attains the station of unveiling and spiritual perception. If the disciple succeeds in finding such a shaykh, he should imitate him, be guided by his words and deeds and hold on to him like the blind man on the seashore holds on to his guide.[21] He should submit to him and be in his hands like the corpse in the hands of the mortician.[22] He should know that it is more to his benefit to follow in his master's footsteps, even in his mistakes, rather than rely on his own personal opinion albeit sound.[23]

The fourth condition is to sever all the ties binding the wayfarer's soul through the practice of asceticism, isolation (*infirād*), spiritual retreat in obscure places, by covering the head with one's robe, or wrapping the body in a tunic or heavy cloth, as well as by total silence, days of fasting and sleepless nights. As he struggles to walk on the straight path (*mujāhadat al-istiqāma*), the disciple aims at realizing all this within the limits of moderation until the even proportion between action and non-action becomes an innate disposition to the heart. However, in this particular struggle, the wayfarer is asked to avoid all action, as well as numbing and mortifying all other human forces, including discursive thinking. He must become dead to his flesh and awaken in his spirit.[24] His heart must be void of all things but Him, as though his corporeal side were obliterated, extinct the way it is for the dead man. The Prophet (may God bless him and grant him peace) referring to this state says, 'Die before you die.'[25]

The fifth condition is sincerity of intention (*ṣidq al-irāda*). This is where the love of God overwhelms the wayfarer's heart, and he becomes like the fervent lover with only one desire. If these conditions are fulfilled, the course of the struggle is the following: the shaykh asks the disciple to devote himself to the constant remembrance of God and to avoid excessive outward litanies (*al-awrād al-ẓāhira*) and Qurānic recitation; he limits the disciple's prayers to the obligatory (*furūḍ*) and supererogatory acts of devotion (*rawātib*). The disciple's litany consists in the incessant remembrance of God in a heart that has been emptied of anything else. Shiblī[26] told Ḥuṣarī, 'If, from one Friday to the next, anything other than God crosses your mind, then do not even come to see me.'[27] The shaykh instructs the disciple to withdraw for a spiritual retreat in a secluded place away from people (*zāwiya*) and asks someone to give him the necessary amount of lawful food; indeed lawful food is essential in all religions. The shaykh gives the disciple a specific [formula of] remembrance with which he will occupy his tongue and heart. The disciple will sit and repeat, '*Allāh, Allāh, Allāh*!' or 'There is no god but God, there is no god but God' (*lā ilāha illā Allāh, lā ilāha illā Allāh*)![28] He must persevere until the tongue's movements subside and the imagination of the movements remains. Then the trace of the imagination disappears from the tongue and the word's image remains in the heart.[29] Ultimately, the image of the word is erased from the heart—that has become void of everything—and only the word's meaning (*maʿnā*) remains in it, present and permanent. It is at this stage that the wayfarer must be most wary of the Devil's whispers and worldly thoughts. He must watch his inward states unremittingly and inform his shaykh if he detects any indifference or ardour, laziness or sincere effort. The wayfarer must discuss his state with none but his shaykh for he knows how to best nurture him.

The shaykh, too, must be cautious because this phase is very dangerous for the wayfarer as his mind might be invaded by some [distracting] imagining, whereby the disciple might become lax and his efforts will be invalidated. Even him whose heart is solely occupied with the remembrance of God is threatened by the dangers of conceit, joy and self-satisfaction (*qunūʿ*) at the first charismatic acts (*karāmāt*) or spiritual states he experiences, which could bring about a feeling of indifference in him and become an obstacle in his wayfaring. The wayfarer must sustain his effort all his life as if he were a man whose thirst even the seas cannot quench. Withdrawal from the world (*inqiṭāʿ*) and spiritual retreat are his capital wealth. If the wayfarer escapes all these dangers and if his heart concentrates on his Lord, the supreme presence unveils and the Truth discloses Himself to him. The wayfarer is then transported with joy and pleasure; and divine subtle realities, that no word can possibly describe, are manifested.

After the lifting of the veil, the greatest danger for the wayfarer lies in divulging all this and occupying himself with counselling and advising other people. The soul finds pleasure in leadership by means of teaching, referring to the Sunna and being listened to wholeheartedly and intently. The wayfarer will think he is a guide to God. Nonetheless, there is yet another danger for him, namely relinquishing work and efforts, which are the means to Self-disclosure. The disciple will here think that he has reached the goal and thenceforth does not need the means to reach it; so, consequently, the state of Self-disclosure abates and the veil is lowered again. These obstacles can drown him in a shoreless ocean of destruction. His plight is such because he has simply aspired to the level of witnessing. If he had sincerely restricted himself to the struggle of walking on the straight path and waited for the witnessing until its proper time—namely in the Hereafter, the abode of recompense (*dār al-jazāʾ*), as He promised—then the wayfarer would have escaped such mortal dangers. May God, in His bounty, protect us![30]

These are the spiritual struggles of the Sufis. As we mentioned earlier, the first struggle used to be called Sufism. Then, when the aspirations of the wayfarers led them to the levels of the just (*abrār*) and to the stations of the sincere believers, they devoted themselves to going straight. Some of them longed for the ultimate felicity and sought the struggle leading to unveiling. This is how the name Sufism came to refer to the two later struggles. Subsequently, the followers of this path taught about a new kind of personal struggle, different from the one fought by the majority. In their teaching, they began to use a nomenclature and specific words that referred to their own endeavours, like the following: station (*maqām*); state (*ḥāl*); annihilation (*fanā'*) or abiding in God (*baqā'*); obliteration (*maḥū*) or affirmation (*ithbāt*); soul (*nafs*); spirit (*rūḥ*); the innermost consciousness (*sirr*); unexpected impulses (*bawādih*); spontaneous intuitions (*hawājim*); incoming suggestions (*khāwāṭir*) and ephemeral inrush (*wārid*); glimmers (*lawā'iḥ*); flashes (*lawāmiʿ*) and divine rays (*ṭawāliʿ*); colouration (*talwīn*) and stabilization (*tamkīn*); separation (*farq*); unification (*jamʿ*) and ultimate unification (*jamʿ al-jamʿ*); mystical tasting (*dhawq*) or drinking (*shurb*); absence (*ghayba*) or presence (*ḥuḍūr*); sobriety (*ṣaḥw*) or intoxication (*sukr*); the science of certainty (*ʿilm al-yaqīn*); the vision of certainty (*ʿayn al-yaqīn*) and the reality of certainty (*ḥaqq al-yaqīn*); the presence of the heart with God (*muḥāḍara*); unveiling (*mukāshafa*) and witnessing (*mushāhada*); interaction with God (*muʿāmala*); union with God (*muwāṣala*) and descent of the divine graces (*munāzala*); the science of interaction (*ʿilm al-muʿāmala*); and the science of unveiling (*ʿilm al-mukāshafa*).

Let us explain these terms. As we said earlier, the essence of the spiritual struggle is the soul's gradual sequential acquisition of and colouration with praiseworthy virtues, namely will (*irāda*); repentance (*tawba*); God-wariness (*taqwā*); moral care (*waraʿ*); renunciation (*zuhd*); spiritual struggle (*mujāhada*); contentment (*qanāʿa*); trust in Him (*tawakkul*); reverence (*khushūʿ*); humbleness (*tawāḍuʿ*); gratitude (*shukr*); certainty (*yaqīn*); patience (*ṣabr*); self-examination (*murāqaba*); satisfaction with God's decree (*riḍā'*); servanthood (*ʿubūdiyya*); going straight (*istiqāma*); sincerity (*ikhlāṣ*); truthfulness (*ṣidq*); the profession of divine unity (*tawḥīd*); gnosis (*maʿrifa*); love (*maḥabba*); and yearning towards the Beloved (*shawq*).

The first among these qualities is will, which, as explained earlier, is not submitted to the power of choice. The last, the ultimate pursuit and noblest goal, is gnosis, Self-disclosure or witnessing. While the soul is struggling in order to acquire these virtues, it is at the same time overtaken by and coloured with other qualities that are not acquired or submitted to any choice but are divine gifts (*mawāhib*). Among these gifts are joy (*surūr*) and sadness (*ḥuzn*), delight (*ṭarab*) and turmoil (*ihtiyāj*), yearning (*shawq*) and uneasiness (*inziʿāj*), hope (*rajāʾ*) and fear (*khawf*), expansion (*basṭ*) and contraction (*qabḍ*), reverence (*hayba*) and intimacy (*uns*).

The virtues that depend on choice or acquisition are called 'station'; and among these are trust in Him, patience, satisfaction with God's decree and so forth. As to the virtues that cannot be acquired, they are called 'state'; and they include joy, sadness, hope, fear and so on. Nevertheless, the praiseworthy virtues only penetrate the heart after the blameworthy ones have been extirpated from it. The removal of that which is blameworthy is called annihilation and obliteration, and the gaining of that which is praiseworthy is called affirmation or abiding in God.

To the Sufis, the heart has three facets: it is the soul, insofar as it is a place wherein vice gathers; it is the spirit, insofar as it the place wherein virtue gathers; and it is the innermost secret, insofar as it is the place wherein the lights of witnessing and gnosis gather. Sometimes, the heart is suddenly overtaken by feelings of sadness or joy; these feelings come from the world of the Unseen, and they are known as unexpected impulses or spontaneous intuitions. As to what befalls the conscience (*ḍamīr*), if it happens in the manner of an address (*khiṭāb*), it is an incoming suggestion (*khāṭir*) originating from an angel, a devil or the soul. If it is not in the manner of an address, it is called an inrush. When the struggle comes to its end, when the stages of development are over and while the veil is being lifted, lights intermittently flare through the soul like lightening. These illuminations are called divine glimmers, flashes and rays. When the lifting of the veil as such occurs—namely [full] unveiling—these illuminations become radiantly revealing and are known as gnosis, witnessing and Self-disclosure.

As long as the disciple is progressing on the Path from one spiritual state to the next, he is said to be going through different colourations. When the goal is attained and the quest fulfilled, he is in a state of stabilization. Similarly, as long as he sees objects as entities emanating from God, he is in a station of separation (*maqām farq*), for indeed, although he sees God, he still sees the existents as well. If he sees the existents in God, he is in a station of unification (*maqām jamᶜ*). Finally, if he sees God only, he has reached the station of ultimate unification (*maqām jamᶜ al-jamᶜ*).

After the Self-disclosures, the wayfarer experiences other spiritual states that are described in terms of mystical tasting or drinking, and that derive from Self-disclosure also. Sometimes the witness can lose consciousness and find himself in a state of absence or intoxication; and when the vision fades away, he awakens in a state of presence and sobriety. The Sufis believe that, as long as a science is based on demonstration (*ᶜilm burhānī*), it is 'the science of certainty' (*ᶜilm al-yaqīn*). When the wayfarer's knowledge results from evidence (*ḥukm al-bayān*), it is called 'the eye of certainty' or 'the vision of certainty' (*ᶜayn al-yaqīn*). Finally, when the Sufi realizes the evidence (*naᶜt al-bayān*), it is called 'the truth of certainty' (*ḥaqq al-yaqīn*). These three stages are also known as presence, unveiling and witnessing. These are the levels of the wayfarer in relation to the degrees of the science aforementioned, or rather in relation to the levels of the knowledge within him.

The Sufis speak about interaction with God, descent of divine graces and union with God. By interaction, they mean wayfaring and spiritual struggle; by graces, the lifting of the veil and the unveiling; finally, union is gnosis and witnessing. Within the spiritual struggle, various stations need to be acquired; and these include repentance, trust in God, moral care, asceticism and so forth; the explanation of these terms varies depending on the motive underlying the spiritual struggle, such as God-wariness, walking on the straight path or gnosis (*ᶜirfān*). Indeed, the repentance of the beginner is different from the repentance of the realized wayfarer. Dhū al-Nūn said, 'Common people repent for their sins, the elite repent their heedlessness of God (*ghafla*) and the gnostics repent for all that which is not God.'[31]

The Prophet (may God bless him and grant him peace) says in a tradition, 'O my people, repent! For, I do repent one hundred times a day.'[32] The same rule applies to trust in God: 'The believers rely on God's promise, the elite are content with His knowledge and the gnostics are satisfied with His judgement.'[33] For the common people, moral care is withdrawal from that which is uncertain; for the elite, it is the relinquishing of all personal undertakings; and for the gnostics, it is not allowing anything other than God infiltrate the heart. So it is with asceticism: the common people shun the unlawful, the elite disregard that which is unnecessary even in the lawful, and the gnostics forsake that which deters their attention from God.

In the same way, the explanation of the words divine unity, gratitude, certainty, patience and other qualities varies according to the motives behind each struggle, as we determined from the Sufis' books. Sufis follow different rules and methods in their struggles. They keep their distance with people, and even more so when discord and deviation from the straight path becomes widespread.

It is possible that the gnostic might express a truth that the masses hasten to disavow because it is beyond their capacity to comprehend it. Some have been condemned for statements which should have been clarified, such as the following, 'I say, "O God, O Lord," and find it heavier upon me than mountains.'[34] In this instance, the Sufi cries out because he is behind a screen. Have you ever heard of a man calling out to someone sitting right next to him?[35] Without this explanation, this saying is criticized and the speaker condemned. This also applies to the rule defining retreat and the remembrance of God for the aspirant to witnessing: the wayfarer must refrain from litanies and from Qur'ānic recitation and concentrate on the obligatory prayers and the remembrance of God. This is because Qur'ānic recitation comprises rules and stories, and the heart becomes dispersed while trying to understand them, whereas the aim [of the spiritual retreat] is to concentrate on the One remembered in order to behold the light of witnessing (*nūr al-mushāhada*). Without this interpretation, the rule stating that litanies and Qur'ānic recitation must be relinquished could be objected to. However, if we take into consideration the incentive behind the struggle, this rule means giving up one incumbent duty for a worthier one and abandoning one obligation for one more deserving.

All of this required the Sufis to develop a nomenclature so that they could communicate with each other and explain the rules and laws regulating their struggles, their various stations and teaching methods. Furthermore, some of their obscure statements and utterances also had to be clarified. All this is a special science called the 'science of Sufism' (*ʿilm al-taṣawwuf*).

To reiterate, there are three levels to the spiritual struggle. The first struggle towards God-wariness (*mujāhadat al-taqwā*) consists in abiding by God's rules, in both the outward and the inward: respecting the limits set by Him while watching inward states as well. Its incentive is the above-mentioned search for salvation. This was the Path for the first generations among the Sufis. The second struggle of walking on the straight path concentrates on the amendment of the soul as it strives towards the straight path. With training and spiritual education, the soul is able to conform to the rules laid down by the Qur'ān and the prophets until they become its innate disposition. In this struggle, the wayfarer longs for the levels of '*those whom God has blessed, prophets, sincere believers, martyrs, the righteous*' (Q.IV.69). In the third struggle for unveiling and spiritual perception (*mujāhadat al-kashf wa'l-iṭṭilāʿ*) all human forces, including reflective thoughts, must become extinct. The goal is to be in the lordly presence (*al-ḥaḍra al-rabbāniyya*); and the aim is the lifting of the veil and witnessing the Divine lights in this life. In so doing, the vision of God's Face in the next life is obtained. This is the highest level for the blessed ones (*suʿadā'*).

The name Sufism refers to all three struggles separately and jointly. This label, however, has come to designate the last two levels only. The first level was described as knowledge of moral care, with the knowledge of moral care and the knowledge of the heart as its sciences. As to God-given learning (*al-ʿilm al-ladunī*), that is called 'the science of Sufism' (*ʿilm al-taṣawwuf*), it is the knowledge of the last two struggles, their laws, paths and rules. It also consists in understanding what impairs or obstructs the wayfarer on his Path. This science, in addition, includes the explication of the terms used by the Sufis in their discussion of these matters.

Varying Definitions for the Sufi Path

Many have tried to define Sufism in one comprehensive sentence, but no statement has ever been complete. Some have described the Sufi Path in terms of its initial stages. Jarīrī said, 'Sufism is the acquisition of elevated virtues and the abandoning of vile traits.'[36] Qassāb said, 'It is noble virtues coming from a noble man in a noble era.'[37]

Others spoke of the Path in terms of its last stages. Junayd said, 'The Truth makes you die to yourself and live by Him.'[38] As to Ruwaym, he declared that Sufism is 'to abide with God as He wills, possessing nothing and possessed by nothing'.[39] Finally, for Samnūn, it was 'to be with God, unattached to anything other than God'.[40]

Some Sufis spoke of one characteristic of the Path. For Baghdādī, 'The sincere Sufi is the one who experiences poverty after having lived a wealthy life, the one who is disgraced after having been honoured, and the one who is forgotten after having been celebrated; the pretender is the one who follows the reverse route.'[41]

Others defined the Path according to its principles and foundations. Ruwaym said, 'Sufism is based on three qualities: holding fast to poverty (*faqr*) and deprivation (*iftiqār*); realizing the qualities of bounty (*badhl*) and altruism (*īthār*); and finally, renouncing all claim (*taʿarruḍ*) and free choice.'[42] Sometimes principle and foundation were not separated; Kattānī said, 'Sufism is having good character traits; the one who increases in goodness will increase in Sufism.'[43]

There are many such definitions. Every Sufi describes what he has achieved and his definition reflects his state. Actually, Sufism cannot be confined in one phrase. Indeed, in the mystical Path, the wayfarer first assumes the traits of the struggle that are suitable for walking on the straight path, at which point his wayfaring may come to an end. If, subsequently, he assumes the traits of the struggle for unveiling, he will take on the qualities of both struggles at once because going straight is one of the pre-requisites for unveiling. The outcome reflects the underlying motive. Behind the struggle for going straight lies the desire for felicity in the Hereafter without any aspiration for unveiling in this life, while behind the other struggle lies the desire to lift the veil in this life. Therefore, the two spiritual struggles differ and it is difficult to contain them in one single definition. Here we have dealt with each separately, but both are part of Sufism. The reader who wishes to have more detailed and comprehensive explanations concerning this subject can consult the books of the Sufis. We have only touched upon the difference between this Path and the others; and '*had not God guided us, we had surely never been guided*' (Q.VII.43).

Concluding Remarks on the Sufi Path and the Law

We have described the spiritual struggles, their characteristics in general as well as the differences between them; let us now talk about their statutes with regards to the Law.

The first inward struggle is an individual obligation upon everyone subject to the Law since the duty of every Muslim is to fear God's chastisement. He must, therefore, observe the limits set by Him (*ḥudūd*) and know that '*Whosoever transgresses the bounds of God—those are the evildoers*' (Q.II.229), the unbelievers and the ungodly.

The second inward struggle is legally permissible for the community and an individual obligation for the prophets (God's blessings be upon them). Its source is evidently the Law. The Legislator, inasmuch as He was intent upon saving mankind—and because both legal and customary wisdom prescribe the elimination of wrongs before benefits can accrue—urged men to enter the path to salvation and to be safe from perdition and Hellfire. These are the general rules for those subject to the Law. The Legislator spelled out the various degrees of salvation and damnation and the different degrees in felicity. Indeed, the sincere believers, the martyrs and the righteous reach a level of felicity higher than salvation. The second struggle is walking on the straight path, '*the path of those whom Thou hast blessed*' (Q.I.5). In it, the most sublime felicity is the vision of God's Face.

As for the third inward struggle, [namely] unveiling, it is, in our view, utterly reprehensible (*maḥẓūra*) to the point of being prohibited (*ḥaẓr al-karāhiyya*), or even more. God Most High said, '*And We set in the hearts of those who followed him tenderness and mercy. And monasticism they invented—We did not prescribe it for them—[whereby they] only sought the good pleasure of God; but they observed it not as it should be observed. So We gave those of them who believed their wage; and many of them are ungodly'* (Q.LVII.27).[44] This inward struggle is monastic since the meaning of monasticism (*rahbāniyya*) for the past generations implies celibacy and seclusion in hermitages. God Most High has shown that monasticism was not an imposition on those who practised it, but they did it to seek His pleasure and did not observe it the way they should have. God Most High said that '*many of them were ungodly*'. Indeed, it is deplorable and blameworthy to follow monasticism and not observe it rightly. Qāḍī Abū Muḥammad b. ʿAṭiyya explains, 'It follows, from the interpretation of this verse, that everyone who begins a voluntary or supererogatory act of devotion must do so to perfection, must persevere therein and observe it with proper care.'[45] Notice God Most High's words, '*as it should be observed*'. It is difficult to persevere in this particular struggle, because it is difficult to observe it.

The degree of observance varies because, as we explained earlier, the states that befall the wayfarer in this struggle are not subject to the will. This can lead to sinfulness and loss of faith. The Prophet (may God bless him and grant him peace) said, 'I fast and break my fast, I sleep and I stay awake, and I also marry women. Whoever does not follow my tradition is not amongst my followers.'[46] When the Prophet learned that ʿAbd Allāh b. ʿAmr had sworn he would fast every day and stay up all nights in prayer, he forbade him from doing so and told him to fast three times a month only; to this ʿAbd Allāh answered, 'But, O Messenger of God, I can endure more than this!' The Prophet replied, 'The fast kept by the Prophet David was most beneficent; he would fast every other day, pray half the night, sleep one third of it, and then wake up and pray for one sixth of the same night.'[47] The Prophet (may God bless him and grant him peace) also forbade ʿUthmān b. Maẓʿūn from leading a life of celibacy.[48] He said, 'Walk on the right path; and if not, walk as well as you can, early in the morning, in the evening and also a little towards the end of the night.'[49]

Furthermore, ʿĀ'isha said, 'The Messenger of God (may God bless him and grant him peace) fasted in such a way that we thought he would never break his fast, and he broke his fast in such a way that we thought that he would not fast.'[50] The Prophet (may God bless him and grant him peace) forbade uninterrupted fasting: 'I am not like you: I remain awake all night long and my sustenance comes from my Lord.'[51] This means the following: since knowledge of the spiritual world and witnessing of the divine presence are both an innate gift to and an inborn quality of the prophets, the preservation (*ʿiṣma*) manifested in their hearts is a spontaneous characteristic. God made them travel their path guided and inspired by their own primordial nature and good character. To them, the path is easy and obvious. They are like the baby who knows the way to his mother's breast and like the bee who knows how to build its hexagonal hive: '*Our Lord is He who gave everything its creation, then guided it*' (Q.xx.50). God Most High sustains the Messenger with food and drink and whatsoever He wills from His provisions.

As for the helpless man, for whom witnessing is neither part of his primordial nature nor of his innate disposition, he faces many obstacles that block his way. He can still seek unveiling and progress a little on its path, even though he is incapable of reaching the stations of the prophets (may God bless them). But as we mentioned earlier, it is a difficult and dangerous path, strewn with dangers and obstacles, so he must heed and avoid.

CHAPTER FOUR

On How the Later Sufis Transposed the Name Sufism from Its Original Meaning and Our Refutation of Them on That Account

Know that, as we explained earlier, the struggle for unveiling encompasses the two prior struggles, namely walking on the straight path and God-wariness, and both are pre-requisites to the third. Therefore, the last combat consists in spiritual struggle and ascetic discipline, followed by unveiling and witnessing. Consequently, this particular science divides into two sections: firstly, the study of the science of interaction, or the rules and conditions of ascetic discipline and spiritual struggles. Secondly, the science of unveiling and knowledge of the inward, or the science of the lifting of the veil, with its ensuing states.

Indeed, when the heart is purified and cleansed from the reprehensible and when human forces have been subdued therein, it can then face the Truth. The veil is lifted and divine light irradiates the heart, as we explained earlier. The secrets of both lower and higher existence as well as earthly and celestial realms are thus disclosed and the meanings of sciences and arts are elucidated. As a result, all doubts and uncertainties are dissolved; the secrets of the hearts and existence are clarified; and the ambiguities of the Law are understood. The heart proceeds in this way until it knows all the realities of the existence intrinsically, from the Divine Essence (*dhāt Allāh*) to His Attributes (*ṣifāṭ*), Acts (*afʿāl*), Principles (*aḥkām*), Decree (*qaḍā'*), Destiny (*qadar*), Throne (*ʿarsh*), Footstool (*kursī*), Preserved Tablet (*lawḥ*) and Pen (*qalam*). The heart grasps the wisdom behind the creation of this world and the next, and understands how life in the Hereafter is contingent upon life in this world. The heart discovers the meaning of prophethood, revelation, the Night of Destiny (*laylat al-qadr*) and the ascension of the Prophet (*miʿrāj*). It learns about angels and devils, comprehends the enmity of the devils towards humankind, the meeting between angels and prophets and their apparition to them, the descent of revelation to the Prophet, the charismatic acts bestowed upon the saint (*walī*), the Path and its struggles, and the cleansing and purification of the heart. The meanings of heart and spirit are here made manifest. The heart sees through the Hereafter and the circumstances of the Resurrection; and all things [pertinent to those events] become transparent to it: the Bridge over Hell (*ṣirāṭ*), the Scale (*mīzān*), the Reckoning (*ḥisāb*), the Basin of the Prophets (*ḥawḍ*) with their Intercession (*shafāʿa*), the Torments of the Grave (*ʿadhāb al-qabr*), Heaven (*janna*) and Hellfire (*nār*), Chastisement and Bliss. Ultimately, it comprehends what the encounter (*liqāʾ*) with God is, what it is to behold His Face and what nearness to Him means. The heart will fully apprehend all the terms he had heard of and to which he had ascribed vague and obscure meanings.[1]

The science of unveiling uncovers these matters until the Truth is fully disclosed with such clarity that certainty is experienced, as though visualized, without any need whatsoever for study or acquisition. As we explained earlier, it is possible to reach this state through the subtle reality, which was itself barred from this very vision because of being tarnished by the full spectrum of humanness and burdened with corporeal chains.

The science of the soul's interaction [with God], which is the science of the way to the Hereafter (*ʿilm ṭarīq al-ākhira*), is also the method applied to cleanse the heart (*al-ʿilm bi-kayfiyya taṭhīr al-qalb*) from its evils and impurities by controlling the passions, subduing human forces, severing all corporeal chains and emulating the prophets in all their states (may God's blessings be upon them). The more polished the heart is, the more turned towards the Truth [it becomes] and the more divine realities shine in it. This is the ascetic discipline and the struggles mentioned earlier.

The science of interaction is of two types. If salvation only is the disciple's goal and ultimate aspiration, then moral care and struggle of the heart suffice. The wayfarer needs to observe the limits imposed by God in both his outward and inward deeds. As we mentioned earlier, this is called 'the science of the inward', but it used to be called Sufism during the first Islamic era, before the aspirations of the Sufis led them towards the struggle for unveiling. *Al-Riʿāya*, the well-known book by al-Ḥārith b. Asad al-Muḥāsibī (may God be pleased with him), is designed for this particular path.

If the wayfarer aspires to the ultimate felicity, the loftiest levels and wishes to realize the means leading to them, namely walking on the straight path and the lifting of the veil in this life, he must know the following: the nomenclature used by the Sufis, their rules of proper conduct, the particulars followed in the struggles and their methods of teaching, the different levels of the struggles and the stations (*maqāmāt*), as well as the manner in which a struggle varies according to the station in which it takes place. The wayfarer must apply all this and commit himself to the emulation of the masters. All this ultimately became known as Sufism. The book designed for this path is the *Risāla* by the teacher Abū al-Qāsim al-Qushayrī, and among the later authors Suhrawardī's *ʿAwārif al-maʿārif*.

Since the struggle for unveiling depends on both struggles—walking on the straight path and God-wariness—the wayfarer who hopes to see the veils lifted must know the rules governing all struggles. Ghazālī wrote the *Iḥyā'* and his book encompasses both ways: moral care and the science of the inward described in the *Riʿāya*, as well as [the matters of how to] go straight and unveiling that are dealt with in the *Risāla*. As to the science of unveiling, the fruit and result of all struggles, it does not have a set path for the wayfarer to engage in because the Sufis (may God be pleased with them) warn against recording it in books or discussing it at all, except through symbols, allusions, examples or in very general way. The Sufis do not divulge these meanings to anyone because they know others cannot understand them. Besides, they watch the limits set by the Law, which cautions against questioning that which is not a direct concern to man and respect the rules of proper conduct towards God by keeping divine mysteries hidden. However, if an allusion related to these meanings happens to emanate from the mystic, it is called an ecstatic utterance (*shaṭḥ*). It can arise when a state of absence and intoxication overwhelms the wayfarer, and at that moment he expresses the inexpressible. It is reported that Abū Yazīd said, 'Glory be to me, how great is my majesty!' and 'I have traversed seas at the shores of which the prophets halted.'[2] As to Rābiʿa, she exclaimed, 'If I were to remove my veil, there would be no one left inside it [but Him].'[3] There are many more examples.

Know that it is forbidden to become absorbed in such statements for a number of different reasons.

Firstly, it is so because it is difficult, not to say impossible, to talk about perceptions or meanings emanating from the Dominion. In all languages, words were set to express that which is tangible, imaginary or conceivable and hence known by people. Words state the well-known and the familiar, not that which has been perceived by one single person in a generation or in a century. Furthermore, words should not be used figuratively because a metaphorical expression implies the existence of a common quality or ground for comparison, and there is none between the the Dominion and the Corporeal World (*ʿālam al-mulk*), and between the Unseen World (*ʿālam al-ghayb*) and the Visible World (*ʿālam al-shahāda*). Describing the realities of the Dominion (*aḥwāl ʿālam al-malakūt*), therefore, is difficult not to say impossible. Can one talk—let alone write books—about that which has not been understood? Indeed, when Sufis start expressing themselves through examples and in a general way their Path becomes obscure.

Secondly, because of their primordial nature, the prophets (may God be pleased with them) are the masters of unveiling and witnessing. The glimpse perceived by some saintly or sincere men is discerned through labour (*takalluf*) and acquisition. The prophet's knowledge of the Dominion is more complete than that of the gnostic or saint; indeed, there is no comparison between the two. God enlightens the prophet who is then able, with His assistance, to talk about the Dominion. In spite of this, the Prophet (may God bless him and grant him peace) did not divulge this knowledge. When asked to talk about the Spirit, he replied, '*Say: the Spirit is of the bidding of my Lord. You have been given of knowledge nothing except a little*' (Q.xvii.85). '*Say: the Spirit is of the bidding of my Lord*' was his reply to the Jewish scholars who knew that his non-answering proved the truthfulness of his prophecy and the sincerity of his message. The prophets did call upon all the people to seek salvation and informed them of its different levels. They alluded to some aspects of the Dominion because these had to be conveyed as doctrines of faith (*ʿaqā'id al-īmān*). Some can be understood literally in the Corporeal World, like [certain] Divine Attributes and the circumstances of the Resurrection, while others, like many of the Divine Attributes, are considered ambiguous. In contrast, some scholars even considered all these aspects ambiguous. What, then, is your opinion of those who are not prophets, who cannot pretend to a prophet's perception, who have not drunk from the basin of prophethood, and above all whose mission did not include the disclosure of the above?

Thirdly, according to the Law, sciences and knowledge divide into forbidden and permissible.[4] The rule inferred from the Law is the following: that which does not concern a man subject to the Law in his daily life or faith must not be investigated. The Prophet (may God bless him and grant him peace) said, 'One of the signs of a good Muslim is to disregard that which does not concern him.'[5] This tradition has been said to constitute a third of the religion.[6] That which does concern the man subject to the Law in his daily or religious life is permissible, indeed so essential that it becomes an obligation.

Since that which does not concern the individual subject to the Law in his faith and life is forbidden, this led to the study of the believer's essential duties because they become most important with regards to religion. Reflect upon the words of God Most High, '*They will question thee concerning the Spirit. Say: the Spirit is of the bidding of my Lord. You have been given of knowledge nothing except a little*' (Q.XVII.68). This denial connotes a prohibition (*ḥaẓr*). He also said, '*They will question thee concerning the new moons. Say: They are appointed times for the people, and the pilgrimage*' (Q.II.189). In other words, you only need to know that new moons herald the pilgrimage, a religious matter. There are also signals for people in their farming and commerce, matters of daily life. You do not need to know more than this. This statement is followed by another of greater importance still, in which God Most High disapproves of the custom of some pilgrims who, during the pilgrimage, would enter the houses from their back doors. Thus, His injunction not to interpret signs is succeeded by a divine rule; in this instance, there is a sign and a warning to the man subject to the Law who is asked to forgo such questioning.

Some later Sufis occupied themselves with the sciences of unveiling, engaged in discussing it and made it another science or technical domain. They taught their own personal method, arranged existents in a special way according to their own perception and claimed that it stemmed from intimate finding or witnessing. At times, some Sufis made different allegations. Consequently, the schools of thought proliferated, whereby different claims and dissensions arose. The various ways and itineraries contradicted each other and the diverging groups isolated themselves one from another. The name Sufism came to refer to the sciences of unveiling and the search for the secrets of the Dominion (*asrār al-malakūt*) through technical and acquired sciences. The Sufis started explaining ambiguous points in the Law, such as the Spirit, the Corporeal World, Revelation, the Throne, the Footstool, with explanations that were obscure, even impossible to grasp, and that sometimes contained reprehensible statements and heretical doctrines.

The Bāṭinī school, for instance, saw hidden meanings in many obviously clear Qur'ānic verses, thus veiling their transparent meaning with the cloud of their interpretation. To them, Adam and Eve symbolized the soul and nature (*ṭabīʿa*); the slaughter of the cow referred to [the fight against] the animal soul (*nafs*); the People of the Cave were those who drifted towards an existence of passions, and so forth.[7] Many misguided hearts revel in these kinds of statements because they covet the goals while still in the beginning stages and wish to enjoy the butter without going through the tiresome whisking process. They answer their opponents' questioning claiming their allegations stem from intimate finding; and this can neither be proved nor ascertained by anyone else besides themselves. '*Had God willed, they would not have done so*' (Q.VI.137). Indeed, they should have followed their predecessors who forbade delving into this. Moreover, what is the use of explanations if they are but vague and cryptic? It is then safer to resume the study of the Law and accept its meanings as set by traditional commentaries. Even though these are not altogether devoid of vagueness, referring to them is safer than relying upon some unintelligible postulates that are based neither on reasonable evidence nor on the Law.

In spite of their numerous divergent ways, these schools can be thought of as [representing] two main opinions (*ra'y*).[8]

THE FIRST OPINION believes in Self-disclosure and loci of manifestation (*maẓāhir*, sing. *maẓhar*), in Divine Names (*asmā'*) and Presences (*ḥaḍarāt*). This is a strange and philosophical approach. Among its most well-known advocates are Ibn al-Fāriḍ,[9] Ibn Barrajān,[10] Ibn Qasī,[11] Būnī,[12] Ḥātimī[13] and Ibn Sawdakīn.[14] The essence of this theory lies in the order it ascribes to the emanation (*ṣudūr*) of existents from the Necessary Truth (*al-wājib al-Ḥaqq*), the existence (*aniyya*) of which is Oneness (*waḥda*). From Oneness, Unity (*aḥadiyya*) and Unicity (*wāḥidiyya*) arise, which are both aspects of Oneness. If Oneness is considered in terms of the exclusion of multiplicity and the negation of apprehensions (*iʿtibārāt*), then it is Unity; whereas if it is considered in terms of multiplicity and infinite realities, then it is Unicity. Unicity is to Unity what the outward is to the inward and the visible (*shahāda*) is to the hidden (*ghayb*). Unicity is the locus of manifestation of Unity. Unicity is to Unity what the locus of manifestation is to the revealed Object (*mutajallī*). Then, that all-encompassing Oneness (*al-waḥda al-jāmiʿa*), which is the Essence itself and the source behind the existence of these two apprehensions—namely the inward with the exclusion of multiplicity and the outward with the inclusion of multiplicity—stands between the inward and the outward like the man who speaks to himself with himself.

The first of the degrees of manifestation (*ẓuhūr*) is His manifestation to Himself. The first consequence of this manifestation is the perfection relating to the Divine Names in order for Him to address Himself. The first of the Self-disclosures is that of the Most Sanctified Essence to Itself. This particular group of Sufis quotes the following tradition of the Prophet as the point of departure for their creed: 'I was a hidden treasure; I wanted to be known; so, I created mankind so that they would know Me.'[15] Only God knows the soundness of this tradition! However, if sound, it does not account for all the developments in their theory, neither does it support it with any clear proof.

To these Sufis, Self-disclosure contains perfection; it is the effusion (*ifāḍa*) of existentiation (*ījād*) and manifestation. Perfection here does not relate to Unity, which is the exclusion of multiplicity, but to Unicity, which is the locus of manifestation. It is divisible into perfection relating to Oneness (*kamāl waḥdānī*) and perfection relating to the Divine Names. If multiplicity is considered as a totality that happens in a single instant, or as a unique entity (*aynan wāḥida*) in the witnessing of God, then one is referring to the perfection that stems from Oneness (*al-kamāl al-waḥdānī*). On the other hand, if multiplicity is considered in terms of the particularization of realities and apprehensions descending successively into existence, and in terms of its role as the intermediate world (*barzakh*) containing all these separate individuals, then one is referring to the quality of perfection stemming from the Divine Names as it descends divided into the realities. It is the world of ideas (*ʿālam al-maʿānī*), the Nebulous Presence (*al-ḥaḍra al-ʿamāʾiyya*), that is the Muḥammadan Reality (*al-ḥaqīqa al-Muḥammadiyya*). Among these entities are the realities of the Pen, then the Preserved Tablet, then nature and then the body, leading up to Adam both in his essence and existence. According to these Sufis, the Nebulous Presence encompasses, in its plurality and divisibility, the realities of the seven Divine Names which are the Attributes. The most universal and comprehensive reality is the reality of life, then the realities of the prophets, messengers and perfect men among the Muḥammadan saints, who are the Poles (*aqṭāb*) and the seven Substitutes (*abdāl*). All these realities are a particularization of the Muḥammadan Reality. These realities are the origin and source of other realities, other disclosures and loci of manifestation for the Unique Essence (*al-dhāt al-aḥadiyya*). They are ordered according to several established hierarchies, ending with the sensorial and visible world (*ʿālam al-ḥiss waʾl-shahāda*) that is the world of rending (*ʿālam al-fatq*). They call them worlds (*ʿawālim*) or Presences; they are also called the domains of realities that are at times connected with the Truth and at times related to the created universe (*kawn*).

The first presence that followed the Presence of the Dark Clouds (*al-ḥaḍra al-ʿamāʾiyya*), according to these Sufis, was the Presence of Fine Dust (*al-ḥaḍra al-habāʾiyya*), which is called the Level of the Image (*martabat al-mithāl*). It is followed by the Throne, the Footstool, the celestial spheres (*aflāk*) in their particular order, the world of elements (*ʿālam al-ʿanāṣir*) and, finally, the world of composition (*ʿālam al-tarkīb*) from beginning to end. So long as these realities are related to the Truth and seen in respect to the essence of that intermediate world (*al-dhāt al-barzakhiyya*) that encompasses all particularization and successive hierarchies, they are in the world of mending (*ʿālam al-ratq*). But, when they are related to the created universe and reveal themselves in its loci of manifestations, then they are in the world of rending (*ʿālam al-fatq*). This is explained with many details, vague sentences and irregular terminology. In short, if this topic with all its issues were to be sorted out and clarified, the existential hierarchy of these Sufis would appear similar to that of the philosophers in their discursive thinking and theories but built neither on proof nor evidence.

THE SECOND OPINION believes in Oneness (*waḥda*), and their opinion is even stranger than the first group's, both in content and argumentation. Among its most famous advocates are Ibn Dahhāq,[16] Ibn Sabʿīn, Shushtarī and their followers. In brief, after they carefully examined and considered what had been said about the One (*al-Wāḥid*) and that which originates from the One, they stated that the Creator (*al-Bārī*) (may He be exalted and glorified) is the totality of what is visible and invisible: there is nothing besides this. The multiplicity of this Absolute Reality and the All-encompassing Existence (*al-aniyya al-jāmiʿa*)—which is the source of every existence—and of the Essence (*huwiyya*)—which is the source of every essence—is only the consequence of illusions (*awhām*), such as time, space, difference, occultation and manifestation, pain and pleasure, being and nothingness. This opinion affirms that all things, if delved into, are but illusions that refer back to the elements of information in the conscience and they do not exist outside it. If there were no such illusions, the whole world and all it contains would be the One and the One is the Truth. The servant has two sides: one is true, the other false. When falsehood—the side connected to illusions—vanishes, only the Truth remains.

These Sufis went astray as they meddled with the Law and its ambiguous aspects. To them, only he who understands the hidden secret of existence has attained the level of the gnostics who have reached realization (*taḥqīq*), which is the word they use to designate this type of science that [they claim] the prophets, learned men and saints taught those they considered worthy of it. According to them, there are several degrees [of realization]: the Sufi reaches detachment (*tajrīd*); the realized sage (*muḥaqqiq*) reaches gnosis of Oneness (*maʿrifat al-waḥda*); and the one who is close to God (*muqarrab*) is content with the Essence of His Essence (*ʿayn ʿaynihi*) rather than with its effect (*athar*). ʿAbd al-Ḥaqq says in one of his books that this is a new theory: 'We wish to call attention to something that was never heard of in past centuries, which did not arise ever in past times, and was never recorded in desert or city.' Then he added, and here he is not truthful, 'It stems from the word of God and His Prophet.'[17]

From the interest of this group in the science of unveiling there arose the belief in the Divine Names related to perfection, in which [it was claimed that] their loci of manifestation are the spirits of the celestial spheres and stars. Since the first creation (*al-ibdāʿ al-awwal*), the nature of the letters (*ḥurūf*) and their secrets pervade the Divine Names and the universes, moving within their phases and expressing their secrets. This gave rise to the science of the symbolism of letters. It is impossible to examine all the problems and aspects of this science. Būnī, Ibn ʿArabī and their school wrote extensively on the subject. In sum, they believe that the power of the spiritual souls can freely dispose of the world of nature (*taṣarruf al-nufūs al-rabbāniyya*) by means of the Most Beautiful Names of God (*al-asmā' al-ḥusnā*) and the Divine Words (*al-kalimāt al-ilāhiyya*) arising from the letters that encompass the secrets pervading the universe. Then, they disagreed concerning the secret of the power of the letters (*taṣarruf al-ḥurūf*), as they wondered where this power stems from.

Some say it depends on the temperament (*mizāj*) of the letter; and they divide letters into four groups, like the four elements. Each nature is linked to its group of letters, so that its influence, active and passive, is implemented through that particular group. Letters are classified, according to an artificial rule they call 'breaking down' (*taksīr*), into fiery, airy, watery and earthy, reflecting the same classification as the elements. The *alif* is fiery, the *bā'* is airy, the *jīm* is watery, the *dāl* is earthy and so on, through the alphabet and elements. Thus, seven letters are fiery: *alif, hā', ṭā', mīm, fā', sīn* and *dāl*; seven are airy: *bā', wāw, yā', nūn, ḍād, tā'* and *ẓā'*; seven are watery: *jīm, zay, kāf, ṣād, qāf, thā'* and *ghayn*; finally, seven are earthy: *dāl, ḥā', lām, ʿayn, rā', khā'* and *shīn*. Fiery letters repel cold diseases and multiply the power of heat whenever desired, in its physical or figurative sense; for instance, during wars, massacres and destruction, the power of the planet Mars can be increased. Watery letters repel hot diseases, such as fevers and other disorders, and multiply the power of cold whenever desired, either physically or figuratively, thus increasing the power of the moon or other such things.

These Sufis claim that the secret of the letters' power lies in their numerical value so that the letters of the alphabet assume a well-known numerical value, both intrinsic and conventional. Furhermore, because of the existing correspondence between the numbers, there is also a correspondence between the letters themselves—for instance, between the letters *bā', kāf* and *rā'*, because they all have a numerical value of two, in units, tens and hundreds, respectively. A similar relation exists between the letters *dāl, mīm* and *tā'* because they all have a value of four; and since four is a multiple of two, there is also a relation between two and four. The Sufis established 'magic squares' (*awfāq*) for letters and numbers in which each group of letters belongs to a corresponding magic square depending on the numerical value of the figure and number; and from this interrelation between the secret of the letters and the secret of the numbers stems the power above-mentioned:

Fire	a ا	h ه	ṭ ط	m م	f ف	s س	dh ذ
Air	b ب	w و	y ي	n ن	ḍ ض	t ت	ẓ ظ
Water	j ج	z ز	k ك	ṣ ص	q ق	th ث	gh غ
Earth	d د	ḥ ح	l ل	ʿ ع	r ر	kh خ	sh ش

It is very difficult to understand the secret of the interrelation between the letters and their temperamental nature, or between letters and numbers. Indeed, it is neither a scientific domain nor is it an analogical deduction. Rather, according to these Sufis, it rests upon mystical tasting and unveiling. Būnī said, 'Do not think that the secret of the letters can be understood through rational analogy (*al-qiyās al-ʿaqlī*); it can only be understood through witnessing and with divine help (*al-tawfīq al-ilāhī*).'[18] Nevertheless, it is undeniable that letters, and the Divine Names composed with these letters, have power over the natural and created worlds; this fact has been repeatedly established by many.

One might think that this type of power and the power exerted by the people who believe in talismans (*ṭalāṣim*) is one and the same; but this is not true. Indeed, according to the makers of talismans, the nature of the talisman and its influence stem from spiritual powers deriving from the substantial nature of Might (*jawhar al-qahr*). The powers exert their ruling and constraining control over the object of the talisman with the help of the secrets of the spheres, numerical interrelations and incenses. They draw out from the talisman in question an influence that is concentrated in it by means of a purposeful energy (*himma*); and as a consequence, superior natures become tied to the inferior ones. Their makers think the talisman is like ferment, made of earthy, airy, watery, fiery elements and their combinations. The talisman can transform and transmute the object it penetrates into its own essence and form, as does the philosophical stone which ferments and transmutes into itself the metals it infiltrates. In this way, they say that the subject matter of alchemy is 'a body in a body' because the philosophical stone is a corporeal substance and so is the metal it penetrates. On the contrary, the subject matter of the talisman is 'a spirit in a body' because it links superior natures to inferior ones, the inferior being corporeal and the superior spiritual.

Before one asserts the real difference between those who use the power of talismans and those who use the power of the Divine Names, one should realize that any influence on the natural world stems from the human soul and human energies because the human soul by its essence embraces and governs nature.[19] Nevertheless, the power exerted by those who use talismans is one based on calling down the spiritual force of the spheres and connecting it to forms or numerical relations, which causes some kind of fusion that, because of its nature, transforms and transmutes, in the way the fermenting agent acts with the substance it is mixed with. Yet, the power used by those who deal with the Divine Names is the result of spiritual struggle and unveiling, and it is achieved with divine assistance and His light. These people are able to compel nature to obedience rather than rebellion. They do not need the help of astral powers or any other, because the help they dispose of is a higher one. Those who operate with talismans need very little ascetic discipline, or just enough, to give the soul power to call down upon the spirits of the spheres. And what a worthless discipline and aim! The ascetic discipline practised by those who use the Divine Names is the great ascetic discipline (*al-riyāḍa al-kubrā*). They do not aim at interfering in the created world because that is a veil. Their own influence is but one of God's graces (*karāma*), accidentally bestowed through them.

If the one who is concerned with the Divine Names fails to understand them and the realities of the Dominion, which is the result of witnessing and unveiling, and if he limits himself merely to the relations between the Divine Names and the natures of the letters and words and exercises his power therein in that fashion, then he becomes a practitioner of magic—as it is well known. In that case, there is no difference between him and the maker of talismans. Indeed, the latter is more trustworthy for he relies upon scientific natural principles and structured laws. As to the one who works with the Divine Names' secrets and is not able to lift the veil from their reality and the effects of the interrelationships, and is not guided by any demonstrative rule in these technical matters, he occupies an inferior position. He might mingle the power of words and the Divine Names with the power of the spheres and so determine times for the remembrance of the Most Beautiful Names of God, drawing up magical squares for these Names—or for all Names—and determining times for their remembrance depending on the interrelationship between the star and the Name in question. This is what Būnī did in *Al-Anmāt*.

For them, the interrelationship [between the Divine Names and the stars] stems from the Presence of the Dark Clouds (*al-ḥaḍra al-ʿamā'iyya*), that is intermediary (*barzakhiyya*) for the perfection relating to the Divine Names.[20] It causes the differentiation of the Nominal perfection to descend in detail upon the realities in accordance with this very interrelationship, which is, as we said earlier, established through witnessing. If the one who believes in the Divine Names lacks the witnessing and has learned the interrelationship through transmission only, then his activity resembles that of the talisman maker, although the latter is more trustworthy, as we have already noted.

In the same way, a talisman maker can mingle his actions and the astral powers with the power of invocations that are composed of special words reflecting the interrelationship between words and stars. However, for the talisman makers, the interrelationship between words is not what it is for the people who believe in the Divine Names and have been granted the witnessing. Rather, it is based upon their own magical practices that allocate stars to all things in the created world, from substances to accidents, essences to minerals and letters to names, amongst other things. The talisman makers build strange and blameworthy theories according to this system, such as dividing the Qur'ānic verses and chapters, in the way Maslama al-Majrīṭī did in his *Ghāya*.[21]

From the *Anmāṭ*, it is clear that Būnī accepted their method. If you read through the *Anmāṭ* and the invocations that are divided according to the times of the seven stars, and then you examine the *Ghāya* with its standing invocations to the seven stars, you will see that either the *Anmāṭ* drew its inspiration from it, or this was made necessary by the interrelationship that exists between the root of creation (*aṣl al-ibdāʿ*) and the intermediary knowledge (*barzakh al-ʿilm*). And '*You have been given of knowledge nothing except a little*' (Q.xvii.85). One cannot deny the existence of everything the Law declares reprehensible. Indeed, even though magic is forbidden, it still exists. However, we are content with the knowledge God gave us.

With time, the works written by the Sufis who engaged in the science of unveiling multiplied, their involvements were protracted and their explanations abstruse. Many idle people became involved in perusing these works. They did so out of laziness and weakness, evils against which the Prophet (may God bless him and grant him peace) warned us.[22] They thought happiness lay in knowing the secrets of the Dominion and they believed these secrets were buried between the pages of their books. How wrong this is! That which led to this madness is nothing else besides the involvement in the sciences of unveiling, the very sciences great Sufis warned us not to rush into—it is God's secret and no gnostic should divulge it.

Al-Ḥusayn b. Manṣūr was put to death following a juridical opinion issued by legists and mystics.[23] The best excuse his defenders could provide was that he was in a state of intoxication and revealed the secret; therefore, his punishment became necessary. Otherwise, he is most often subject to anathematization (*takfīr*). The authors of the *Ghāya* did report one of his magical activities that no ordinary Muslim would ever practice, much less a gnostic. Indeed, it is a sign of idleness to engage in the science of unveiling, and to become absorbed in its subjects and in the texts written by those who follow this Path.

If the soul of the wayfarer aspires to gnosis and to the understanding of the Dominion (*al-ʿilm bi-aḥwāl al-malakūt*), then it is through struggle and proper conduct that he will be led to it. There is no possible way to attain knowledge and to the understanding of the conditions of the Dominion through mere nomenclature and sheets of paper, since—as we explained earlier—words cannot convey the meaning of these realities: they have never before been recorded and cannot possibly be interpreted through [attempted understandings of] interrelationship either.

If the soul is lazy and does not aspire to such knowledge, if it is reduced to the lowest conformism (*ḥaḍīḍ al-taqlīd*), then why should the wayfarer need to study a nomenclature which would only lead him to a type of science that is close to that of the philosophers?[24] Philosophy at least is a mentally conceived argumentation based upon the organization of analogies and sequences of proofs. Anyway, this contradicts the method of the partisans of Oneness for whom technical demonstration (*al-burhān al-ṣināʿī*) should be relinquished in favour of intimate finding. This leaves one sole alternative, namely acceptance of their words out of sheer trust in them; yet, the latter is, of course, [only possible] whenever they are able to expound their goals. Nevertheless, how can they be trusted, when many of the literal meanings of their words are in contradiction with the literal text of the Law? Those who are at variance with the Law cannot be trusted neither in word nor in deed. Abū Yazīd was told of a man well-known for his gnosis (*ʿirfān*) and wished to visit him.[25] When he arrived, he saw the man spit in the mosque, upon which Abū Yazīd immediately turned back saying, 'How can we trust someone with God's secrets when this person does not even believe in one of the rules of proper conduct prescribed by the Law?'[26]

If the Law forbids these people from plunging into the sciences of unveiling, and still they do not forsake these sciences, how can they be trusted in their knowledge of the divine secrets of God Most High, and how can one accept in good faith what they have to say? And this, when their words are not cryptic, but what if their words are laden with innovation and misbelief? May God protect us from this! What they call 'Sufism' is not Sufism, nor is it the lawful goal. And God knows best!

CHAPTER FIVE

On the Shaykh and When His Presence Is Required in the Spiritual Struggle

Know that our study has led to the conclusion that basically Sufism consists of spiritual struggle and wayfaring, the perfecting of which leads to unveiling and witnessing. Subsequently, the wayfarer is given the knowledge of God, His Attributes, His acts and the mysteries of His Kingdom (*asrār mulkihi*), as well as all the above-mentioned. We have demonstrated why the knowledge resulting from unveiling and witnessing should not be registered in books. We also explained why some later Sufis erred when they labelled these very stations as Sufism, turning them into a 'codifiable' science that can be acquired in books and records.

Actually, Sufism is a light that God sends forth into the heart that has been purified through spiritual struggle and orientated towards the Truth. At times, this light elucidates a divine mystery, a lordly wisdom, an obscure legal problem or an ambiguous aspect of the Book and the Sunna. However, the Sufi must neither dwell upon this gift nor be contented with it lest it become a veil that disrupts the Path. He must persevere on his way to God and never disclose the secret. God's secret is most deserving of being kept hidden.

We have explained how spiritual struggles differ according to their underlying motives. If the goal is salvation only, then the novice struggles towards God-wariness and moral care. If the goal is felicity and the loftiest levels of realization (*al-darajāt al-ʿulā*) in the Hereafter, then the wayfarer struggles towards walking on the straight path.[1] Finally, if the goal is knowledge through the lifting of the veil and witnessing of God in this world, the combat is unveiling. We have also mentioned that the name Sufism applies to all three struggles, in spite of the fact that it eventually referred to the last two. The great Sufis and their followers, whose lives are compiled in the *Risāla*, spoke of Sufism as these last two struggles, together with their properties, rules and nomenclature.

The teacher Abū al-Qāsim al-Qushayrī has explained how the difference between the struggles towards walking on the straight path and unveiling lies in their different underlying motives. He said, 'If the wayfarer believes in the Sufis' teachings and in gradual wayfaring (*sulūk wa-tadarruj*) towards the goal, he will share in the knowledge Sufis have been given, namely the unveiling of the Unseen World (*mukāshafat al-ghayb*). The disciple will not need to intrude upon and seek support from anyone foreign to their Path. But if the disciple is not of an independent nature and wishes to follow a more conventional way within a conforming pattern (*taqlīd*) until he reaches realization, then he should imitate his predecessors and travel their Path, for it is best for him to follow them rather than anyone else.'[2]

Know that the need for the teaching master (*al-shaykh al-muʿallim*) and for the advising educator (*al-murabbī al-nāṣiḥ*) varies according to the struggle. Sometimes his presence renders the struggle more complete and appropriate, or worthier and safer, and sometimes his presence is so imperative that the struggle cannot be without him. Let us explain and describe this in detail.

The Struggle for God-wariness

Firstly, the struggle for God-wariness, which is achieved through moral care, does not require the presence of a shaykh. It suffices to know God's decrees and His limits, and this knowledge can be drawn from a book, taught by a teacher (*muʿallim*) or transmitted by a master (*ustādh*). This is so because, as we said earlier, this particular struggle is incumbent upon every man subject to the Law. How could it be right, then, that a man should wait for a shaykh and thus neglect his duty and delay the fulfilment of God's commandment? Anyway, the shaykh will not add anything to the writings of the scholars who transmit the teachings of the Book and the Sunna, informing us of their references and sources.

Nevertheless, this particular struggle is bettered if the wayfarer follows a teaching master who will set an example to act upon. Indeed, the use of the senses in the teaching of any science is a condition for perfecting it. The science of God's decrees and limits is to know how to perform actions. The science of this performance is based either on transmission (*naql*) and a conveyed report (*khabar*), or on senses and observation (*muʿāyana*). The reliance on senses is more perfect.

This is why the *Ṣaḥīḥ* tells us that the Prophet (may God bless him and grant him peace) was actually shown how to pray: 'Gabriel came and prayed, so did the Prophet (may God bless him and grant him peace); then he prayed and so did the Prophet (may God bless him and grant him peace); then he prayed and so did the Prophet (may God bless him and grant him peace); then he prayed and so he prayed...'; thus [this happened] five times.[3] Gabriel taught the prayer entirely through example. This was necessary to make His teaching perfect, as it had to be.

When Arab delegations came to the Prophet (may God bless him and grant him peace), asking to be taught their religious duties, he would not only convey oral information, but he would send one of his eminent Companions to teach them by visually showing them how to perform their duties, and the men imitated them. Sometimes these men were given directions only, as in the tradition about the delegation from the tribe of Rabīʿa: 'He ordered you four things and forbade you four.'[4] Another time: 'Remember them and transmit them to those who will come after you.'[5] However, this was rare; usually the Companions would be sent to instruct the inquirers.

In the same vein, we see that it is often more effective to perform duties like prayer or ablution in front of Muslim children through example rather than statements and words. So much so that the pilgrimage rituals, for instance, are taught during the pilgrimage season on the days set for them, by those who had learned and taught them. Notice that the legist who writes the chapter on the laws regulating the pilgrimage—although he has thoroughly memorized the subject—will rely more on the knowledge of these instructors than on his own memory. He is taught by them and learns the rituals by watching them. Indeed, the soul trusts sensory perception more than words. Thus in this struggle [to attain God-wariness], to follow a shaykh is only a condition for its perfection (*sharṭ kamāl*), not a condition for its validity or an obligation (*sharṭ siḥḥat wa-wujūb*).

The Struggle Towards Walking on the Straight Path

Secondly, in the struggle towards walking on the straight path, wherein the wayfarer must be moulded by the good character traits of the Qur'ān (*al-takhalluq bi'l-Qur'ān*) and the character traits of the prophets (*khuluq al-anbiyā'*), the wayfarer may need a teaching master.[6] Indeed, not only is it difficult to know the character traits of the self (*khuluq al-nafs*) and the hidden colourations of the heart (*talawwunāt al-qalb*), but it is also arduous to cure them and set them free. As the struggle towards walking on the straight path is not an obligation binding upon everyone subject to the Law, it is strongly recommended that the wayfarer should look for a shaykh who knows its path and its difficulties. This, however, is not an obligation or compulsion because the source of this struggle is the Book, the Sunna and customary nomenclature. Even the many obscure aspects of the teaching and wayfaring in this combat do not escape free choice, and they remain part of the acquirable sciences (*al-maʿārif al-kasbiyya*). The wayfarer who clings to the Sunna is safe from the dangers of this Path and can set it right again if he errs. He can refer to his own judgement, whilst also benefitting from talks and discussions and from the writings of the scholars on the practices and theories [of this particular Path].

The Struggle for Unveiling and Witnessing

As to the third struggle for unveiling and witnessing, its aim is the lifting of the veil and spiritual perception of the spiritual world, and the Dominion of the heavenly and earthly realms. In it, the wayfarer must have an educating teacher (*al-muʿallim al-murrabī*), the one referred to as shaykh. It is not only an imperative but a necessity, without which this goal can seldom be attained, for several reasons.

Firstly, the foundation of this struggle is the Book and the Sunna. Yet, as we said earlier, its recent monastic trends are heretical innovations (*bidʿa*); and the Path set by the Law is considered the common way for everyone subject to this Law. It leads to salvation and felicity after death occurs. But this particular [last] struggle is a select way for the wayfarers with spiritual aspirations (*ahl al-himam*) who wish to attain, before death, the seed of ultimate felicity and the unveiling which normally occur at the time of death only. Therefore, this struggle has its own law, principles and rules of proper conduct. In it, the wayfarer can only imitate those who have turned this particular way into a tradition to follow. All do agree on the need for a shaykh in this struggle and warn against self-reliance and solitude in the wilderness of its Path. They enjoin the wayfarer to lay the reins of his life into the hands of a shaykh who has travelled this Path. Their shaykh has been led to the goal and has experienced—rather than just heard of—its perils, hidden ambushes, dangerous moments and adversities. The wayfarer is like the corpse in the hands of the mortician, or the blind man on the seashore who holds on to the hand of his guide.[7] Since our knowledge of this struggle and its laws comes from the shaykhs only, how could we forgo a condition set by them in their own Path?

Secondly, in this struggle, the wayfarer is liable to realize two qualities. The first quality lies within his power of acquisition and free choice, and is the purification and cleansing from blameworthy traits through the acquisition of praiseworthy virtues. The second quality does not lie within his power of acquisition and free choice, and has to do with the spiritual states that befall the wayfarer before, during and after the unveiling. The teacher Abū al-Qāsim said, 'A servant is characterized by his deeds, virtues (*akhlāq*) and spiritual states. Deeds are the actions he does by free choice. Virtues are his innate disposition—although they can change with work, time and repetition. Spiritual states prevail as from the beginning [of the way] and their purity is in accordance with the purity of his deeds.' (Those are his words.)

The spiritual states that do not depend on free choice are the fruits of acquired virtues (*al-ṣifāt al-muktasaba*), namely deeds (*aʿmāl*) and their results. They depend on each other and eventually lead to witnessing. They are hidden and uninterrupted. If imperfection has penetrated a spiritual state, the ensuing one is affected inasmuch as the prior state has been because every state rests upon what precedes it. Corruption in a spiritual state reaps its opposite: leading the wayfarer to his ruin—may God protect us! One can never remedy or reform such a state because it escapes free choice. If corruption takes place and triggers a series of like states damaged by the initial corruption, then the duration and importance of the evil increases thereon and its impact spreads. Neutralizing this corruption is no longer possible except by setting forth on another way which would deal anew with the virtues that are to be acquired. In this manner, the wayfarer opens himself to divine compassion for the eradication of the corruption that has crept into his heart in the initial states.

Sometimes it is difficult to resume the Path because the heart, the seat of all states, is unable to free itself from what might have settled in it. Corrupted spiritual states breed heresy (*zandaqa*), licentiousness (*ibāḥa*), rejection of the Law (*rafḍ al-sharīʿa*), ensuing slackness (*futūr*) and laziness (*kasal*). The wayfarer thereby loses his incentive and motivation. It becomes extremely difficult to cure this condition and it may in fact be too late to repair the damage. God Most High says [by way of quoting those who are damned], '*Would that we might be returned, and then not cry lies*' (Q.VI.27); but it is too late [for them] to then lament.

It is different if the wayfarer is closely watched over by a shaykh, as the disciple's deeds and wayfaring are amended. The shaykh himself has walked this Path and can differentiate between corrupt and sound spiritual states. He knows what fosters progress and what causes an interruption in the Path. He understands the relation between the states that are not submitted to will power and the deeds that are submitted to it.[8] He is aware of the correlation between the degree of purity of deeds and states, and has realized all this by test, hardship and training—not via books and stories. If all these conditions are fulfilled, then the wayfarer is following the right path, fears can be dispelled and perils avoided.

The wayfarer in his endeavour is similar to the dyer who tries out red, yellow or green dyes but the assimilation of the colour by the cloth is neither within his competence, nor does it depend on his choice. His responsibility is merely to immerse the cloth in special dyes, either mineral or vegetal, according to set proportions and dosages. The cloth must be ready for the absorption of the envisaged colour. For this, a skilled master is indispensable, one who knows the dosages of the different elements, their proportions, the amount of time necessary for the mixture, the call for cooking or fermentation, the immersion method and the timing of the whole process. The master teaches his apprentice by showing him, lest the latter apply a dye other than the one suggested. Since it is the first colour that settles into the cloth and renders it impervious to other dyes, the dying process is irreversible. So it is with the wayfarer who wishes to colour his heart with gnosis that leads to felicity. If the wrong colour has settled in his heart, the damage can no longer be rectified. For this reason, the educating shaykh (*al-shaykh al-murabbī*) will show the wayfarer how to apply the dye, its ingredients, dosages, proportions and the durations of the process. A shaykh is therefore indispensable because a dye cannot be applied at random and approximately. One is always careful not to damage a fine cloth; so how much more careful one should be not to ruin the heart when eternal suffering may be the result! May God protect us from this!

Thirdly, the essence of this Path is premeditated death (*al-mawt al-ṣināʿī*), which is, as we said earlier, the extinction of all human forces until the wayfarer is dead in body but alive in spirit. Hence the wayfarer tries to experience death before he actually dies in order to reach the spiritual vision that normally happens at the moment of natural death only (*al-mawt al-ṭabīʿī*). If ultimate spiritual perception has not been reached, the wayfarer strives to attain the spiritual states closest or most similar to it. He longs to enjoy this perception before he leaves his physical body; and for that reason, he submits it to ascetic discipline in order to experience death. These wayfarers refer to the above-cited words of the Prophet (may God bless him and grant him peace) in order to justify their ascetic discipline, 'Die before you die.'[9]

Any mentally conceived teaching will parallel some natural phenomenon and a man cannot grasp it by himself. To learn it, he must have a guide who teaches him the secrets of its workings because the ways of nature are hidden and—almost always—very difficult to see. If the teacher is competent, then the ascetic discipline is successful and useful; otherwise, it is not. This is true for all mentally conceived sciences.

Fourthly, and the following is the most obvious reason in our discussion of the issue, this particular wayfaring rests on meanings that are of two kinds.

The first meanings belong to the category of the conventional, namely sensorial and rational perceptions (*al-maḥsūsa wa'l-maʿqūla*). These meanings are set down in rules and expressed in books and words. They deal with the tangible part of the wayfaring; the severing of the ties binding the soul; the observance of spiritual retreat; the remembrance of God in particular ways; and after the struggles for God-wariness and walking on the straight path have been traversed, the adequate observance of obligatory prayers and supererogatory acts of devotion.

The second kind of meanings does not belong to the category of the conventional and is not familiar to the minds (*adhhān*) or set in concepts (*taṣawwurāt*). These meanings cannot be grasped by the senses, the intellect or through acquired sciences. They rely on mystical tasting and intimate finding (*umūr dhawqiyya wa-wijdāniyya*). A man will discover these meanings in his self, but will not be able to describe them to others except through metaphors or remote examples. It is not possible to capture them with scientific rules and nomenclature, or to classify them in artificial chapters and sections. They come forth in the shape of unexpected ailments (*ʿilal*), spiritual states, ephemeral inrushes, castings (*ilqā'āt*) and mystical findings (*mawājid*), as well as in all that befalls the itinerant from the beginning to the end of his wayfaring until his immersion in the sea of gnosis and divine unity (*baḥr al-maʿrifa wa'l-tawḥīd*).

This set of meanings deals with the core of the wayfaring, its secret and reality, without which nothing can be achieved. So long as the wayfarer does not understand these meanings, distinguish them from one another or differentiate between that which tends towards the goal and that which withholds him from it, his effort is useless and his search is neither partially nor fully realized. Books are of no avail at all in this and his mind will not grasp the explanations. The wayfarer must have a shaykh who, because of his mystical tasting, recognizes their existent entities (*aʿyān*) and differentiates between the harmful and beneficial. He can call the wayfarer's attention to these realities the way the dumb man does, by pointing his finger to sensorial objects without being able to describe them with words. Pointing out realities is more eloquent than using words. This is why you will not find these matters summarized in books or set out in manuals on the meanings of 'Sufism'. They are only hinted at in allusions or stories, the words of which do not uncover the essence of the goal. The teacher Abū al-Qāsim al-Qushayrī said, 'This group of people communicates with a specific terminology that discloses the meanings particular to their own Path to each other exclusively while hiding them from those who oppose their way. Thus, the meanings remain vague to outsiders and their secrets are jealously protected from outsiders. Indeed, these realities are neither gathered through personal effort, nor collected in a clever system. They are meanings deposited by God into the hearts of some men He purified in order to safeguard them in their innermost being.'[10] (This is the end of Qushayrī's statement—may God have mercy upon him!)

CHAPTER SIX

Arbitration between the Two Debaters: Ascertaining the Truth of Their Words and the Soundness of Their Arguments

Now that we have provided the reader with the necessary background to this debate and described the Sufi Path, its various routes and determined when a shaykh is needed or not, we can, as we promised earlier, arbitrate between the two disputants. The adjudication has been eased by our introductions and we shall proceed by citing the exact words of the two parties. Then, we shall intervene at each point of divergence by referring to the introduction.

First Argument

Those who believe in the need for a shaykh say to those who do not believe in this need—and advocate reliance on books and teachers in legal matters, rather than on guides in spiritual detachment—'Why do you rely on books and reject the guidance of spiritual masters (*shuyūkh al-ṭarīqa*) when the Sufis themselves followed shaykhs and ignored books?'

THE SHAYKH-DENIER[1] WILL ANSWER [the above in this manner]: The foundation of the wayfaring is the Qur'ān, the Sunna and that which has been derived therefrom. These are recorded and available to us; their transmitters are appointed to teach us and the spiritual masters are among them. Why should we, then, be unable to fare without them?

THE SHAYKH-PARTISAN'S REPLY IS the following: If mere transmission through written material were enough to attain this—or that—goal in any science or skill, then those who memorize the external description of sciences and skills without having acquired any experience in them should be the equals of those who have actually practised and mastered them. This is impossible. Therefore, you are in the wrong when you fancy one can succeed through mere [bookish] transmission.

I SAY: We have previously described the different types of spiritual struggles and concluded that the struggle for unveiling necessitates an educating master (*al-shaykh al-murabbī*) for the following reasons: its Path is peculiar and very dangerous. Its spiritual states and fruits are not liable to the wayfarer's efforts, power and free choice. It is a specific Path, different from the common way of the Law. As you well know, this is a recent struggle that had not yet surfaced during the time of our Predecessors. We never came across instructions [from the Predecessors] concerning a method for its wayfaring, spiritual retreat, remembrance, or a description of its fruits, such as the disclosure of the lights or the lifting of the veil. Besides, were it not for the valid interpretations of its itinerants, many of the sayings and rules in this struggle seem to contradict the Law on its external plane. The saints of God and His elite found this Path when they isolated themselves and severed the ties binding their hearts to the world. They did explain its wayfaring and clarified its ascending steps (*maʿārij*) so that the aspirant could reach felicity and goodness. They wished to find sources for their Path in the Qur'ān and the Sunna, and this in spite of the meddling of the legists and supporters of the Law; but, then, we mentioned this earlier. As to God-wariness, it is the main way of the Law, the course to salvation. Unveiling is the main way of 'Sufism', the ascending steps towards spiritual vision (*miʿrāj al-maṭlaʿ*), the seed for ultimate felicity (*al-saʿāda al-ʿudhmā*) and the highest degrees (*al-darajāt al-ʿūlā*). Walking on the straight path is the main way of the Qur'ān and prophethood. Law is clearly the source and explanation of both struggles [God-wariness and walking on the straight path], and its transmitters are many.

When the shaykh-denier says: 'The foundation of the wayfaring is the Qur'ān, the Sunna and that which has been derived therefrom. These are recorded and available to us; their transmitters are appointed to teach us and the spiritual masters are among them. Why should we, then, be unable to fare without them?' I say: if they are referring to the two struggles, the way of which is the Qur'ān and the Law, namely God-wariness and walking on the straight path, then this is true and we are not in want of a shaykh, as we said earlier. On the other hand, if this statement refers to the struggle for unveiling, which is the main way of Sufism, then this is impossible. When the shaykh-denier claims that some aspects of this last struggle have been recorded, it is only true for some notions that were put in writing in a general and indirect fashion because most of them do not partake of the habitual and conventional. So it is for all the spiritual states and ephemeral inrushes the Sufis claim. When words can no longer describe a reality because it is indescribable, the presence of one who has 'witnessed' (*ʿiyān*) becomes necessary. The witness can attest to the genuineness of the conveyed report and brush illusory presumptions aside. Only the itinerant who has experienced this wayfaring will recognize witnessed perceptions (*al-mudrakāt al-ʿiyāniyya*). He is aware of the delusions that threaten the wayfarer who believes in solitary progress and mere [unguided] imitation of conveyed reports, as we said earlier.

When the shaykh-denier says 'the spiritual masters are among them', my answer is the following: shaykhs can educate, discipline and lead to spiritual states and observation; yet, the above-mentioned are not submitted to free choice and are not part of sensory or known sciences. The teachers who issue legal edicts and transmit the Law relayed the tradition by showing us and teaching us how to perform an action that, on the contrary, is submitted to human power. Many among them have both functions [as spiritual master and legal authority]. However, if we assume that when the shaykh-denier says '[the spiritual masters of this Path] are among them' they mean that all shaykhs must be recognized, honoured and followed, then this is true. Many stories support our belief, that of ʿUmar and Uways,[2] Shībān the shepherd[3] and Shāfiʿī,[4] Muḥāsibī and Ibn Ḥanbal,[5] as well as others.

The shaykh-partisan also argues that when the itinerant relies on transmitted knowledge (*naql*) and does not seek the guidance of a teacher, then this implies a certain conclusion, namely: 'If mere transmission through written material were enough to attain this—

or that—goal in any science or skill, then those who memorize the external description of sciences and skills without having acquired any experience in them should be the equals of those who have actually practised and mastered them.'

However, I say that this is a weak argument because the shaykh-denier could refute it in the following manner: it is true that there is a difference in level between the one who has experienced knowledge and the one who has not, but this does not prove that a shaykh is needed. It only says that he who has spent energy learning with a shaykh might reach a certain level of knowledge, while he who has learned without a shaykh might, through books, reach a level less exalted. In reality, we believe the wayfarer needs a Shaykh, and books alone do not lead him to his goal not because of a possible difference between the levels achieved, as was mentioned, but because the perceptions (*madārik*) in this Path are not amongst the known, acquirable sciences and skills; rather, they are findings of an intimate inspirational nature (*wijdāniyya ilhāmiyya*). Most of the time, they escape free choice. They are the outcome of performed deeds and manifest themselves in specific ways. Thus, these perceptions cannot be ascertained through acquired sciences but need a shaykh who knows because he witnesses, testifies and teaches the nature of the various deeds and their ensuing spiritual states.

Second Argument

THE SHAYKH-DENIER PROCEEDS TO SAYING: The Path of Sufism rests on good work (*ʿamal*) and detachment (*tajarrud*) in view of service (*khidma*) that needs to be depicted in a book, by a shaykh or a transmitter which fulfils the need.

THE SHAYKH-PARTISAN ANSWERS: This is not so! The Path is divided in two sections. The first section is of lesser importance. It is a guideline for good works, given by way of a simple description or the help of a book. For the time being, we shall tolerate and accept this view without discussing it. The second section is grander. It is the Path of Sufism. It calls for a sound diagnosis of the sicknesses that can befall the wayfarer in his self, heart or spiritual state, as well as the science of the cure of the above.[6] It requires recognizing the nature of the ephemeral inrushes that befall the heart and knowing whether these stem from the self, the Devil, the angels or God. It involves understanding the mystical experiences along with their preliminary and ensuing stages, determining their authenticity or their fallacy and displaying a great deal of experience as to the particular instances when wayfarers can err. Indeed all of the ambushes and dangerous areas must be known, lest the wayfarer—when he sets out on this Path—lose his faith and become an unbeliever, slide away from the Sunna towards heretical innovation, or give up his freedom and turn into a slave of the world. The itinerant could call a halt to all further spiritual states, pursue charismatic gifts, unveiling or sound dreams (*ru'yā ṣāliḥa*). From the onset of the Path and throughout his faring, the seeker must be equipped to face these issues as well as other minor aspects that cannot be encompassed in definitions or described in books.

I SAY: This argument is sounder than the preceding one. Knowing the above uncodifiable issues does not mean acquiring them, but rather finding them. The shaykh is the only one able to do this, as he identifies these matters and points them out to the disciple singly and visually.

As to the comment about the issues [in the wayfaring] 'that cannot be encompassed...in books', I say: in any case, it is neither the would-be compilation in books of these matters nor their apprehension through scientific definition that would lead to gnosis. On the contrary, had these matters been encompassed in books, they would have become part of the acquired sciences rather than remaining in their own category. Only the discerning teaching shaykh and the inquiring disciple who pursue these matters as they are in their realness can return them to their own category.

Third Argument

THE SHAYKH-DENIER SAYS: All this is recorded in books and you only need to read the book [*Iḥyā' ʿulūm al-dīn*] of Abū Ḥāmid [al-Ghazālī] (may God be pleased with him). In it, he speaks about all these things extensively and really more than sufficiently. He is recognized as a spiritual master by the Sufis themselves and by other knowledgeable and fair men. So why should not his words, advice, or the books written by other great spiritual teachers be followed?

THE SHAYKH-PARTISAN ANSWERS: You have called upon us to talk about three levels.

FIRSTLY, it is said that the shaykh on the Path to God (may He be glorified) compares to a guide on a tangible road at the end of which is a treasure. The road is full of precipices and dangerous lands inhabited by brigands and highwaymen from whom very few travellers escape. If the shaykh were to describe the road to you, its dangers and perils, the traps set by the enemy with the manner to avoid them—and if you decide to rely only on this description in order to travel this journey for the very first time in your life—you will find that the guide's instructions are totally pointless. There are several ways and ramifications in the road, which all look alike, and at every turn you dread that the highwaymen and enemies will attack you unexpectedly. A description is only an approximation of the truth and cannot lead to it, particularly when its object is hidden and remote from all imaginings and conjectures. This is what will happen unless a guide accompanies you, urges you to follow the main road, helps you in the perilous places or prepares you to face dangers. When the foe appears, the shaykh will have readied you with the amount of strength and device you need to face it. Then, victorious, you reach the treasure, seize it and leave the enemy territory protected and safe. Otherwise, you would have been imprisoned or killed. Such is the way towards the self-realization of the gnosis of God (*al-taḥaqquq bi-maʿrifat Allāh*).

There are two expanses the wayfarer must traverse in order to reach it: the world that is inhabited by the enemy Satan, and the Hereafter that is ruled by the desire to reach it. The enemy has strewn both expanses with so many schemes that no book could possibly comprehend or describe them adequately, because of the remoteness of their purposes, covert targets and subtle planning. These schemes are not related to the familiar; and therefore a mere description, without an insight borrowed from the Divine through the light of His wisdom, is not sufficient. How could a man cross this Path without a guide? In most cases, it is not possible.

SECONDLY, the books indicated above are loaded with stories about great spiritual masters (*arbāb*); and some were enslaved by their spiritual states while others mastered them. However, most of the stories concern the first type, who cannot be emulated so long as they are in this [enslaved] condition. The wayfarer who tries to follow them might deviate from the commendable path and disrupt it. Indeed, this befalls most of the wayfarers who have emulated the state-enslaved mystics; they divide into several groups:

i. Some harm their bodies, wear it out, or almost so.[7]

ii. Some lose their minds or almost so.

iii. Some do violence to the religion by overstepping the boundaries of the divine orders and finally become overcome by it.

iv. Some wayfarers on their way to God despair of the Divine Soul, or almost so.

v. Some follow a good path in their action or learning; however, it is disrupted by some obstacle, such as dissemblance, vanity, love of the world or glory. They do not know if the obstacle is real or insinuated by the Devil. They give up all action and learning, thinking they are giving them up for God's sake, when in fact they are merely presenting the Devil with what he had intended to obtain.

vi. Others doubt this Path and its adherents and call it a lie, and there are many other cases.

Following Sufi books does not help solve the above-mentioned problems; but, on the contrary, ignites them. These are matters that only great spiritual masters know thoroughly; and indeed, never in the past or present have such ills befallen a wayfarer who placed himself under the protection of a realized Sunni shaykh (*shaykh sunnī muḥaqqiq*). The shaykhs who have mastered their spiritual states are the ones to be emulated because they control their selves and states, and because they themselves have emulated [the predecessors]. As to those who could not control their spiritual states, they contradict—at least outwardly—the Sacred Law, for which they may—or may not—be excused or justified. The difference between the two groups is difficult to construe with the above-mentioned books. Yet, it is this very difference that determines when emulation is valid and when it is not. Therefrom, if we do not ascertain this difference, how shall we, with total trust, emulate [a shaykh]?

This is why we say: the wayfarer who is guided by books can either reject the guidance of the shaykh who deserves to be followed and emulate the one who should not be emulated, or else he may attempt to follow both shaykhs at once. The spiritual states of the two shaykhs followed concomitantly differ and they may disagree on many points; and as a result, the wayfarer's behaviour becomes contradictory. Furthermore, a given man can be simultaneously enslaved by some spiritual states and in control of others, and therefore the imitation is valid in the second instance and not in the first. Only a shaykh can ascertain the difference. Besides, those who evince spiritual states are of many types:

I. Some do not truly experience a mystical state.
II. Some truly experience authentic spiritual states.
III. Some experience a spiritual state that is triggered by a sickness of the self. [They experience] loss of consciousness, trances, tears, screaming or such usual patterns for spiritual states that are but sheer simulation (*mubṭal*). In the same manner, the person in question can perform some charismatic acts, but in reality he has fallen into the Devil's grip.
IV. Some are trustworthy in all these things.
V. Some are untrustworthy.
VI. Some did in fact experience a certain spiritual state but let up in the practice that had brought it about.[8] As a consequence, the state abated and they were driven to despair. This is the door to disorder and [surrender to one's] caprices (*hawā*).

Moreover, while some spiritual states and mystical experiences are integrally authentic, others are integrally fraudulent; some belong to both categories at once; others are authentic from one angle and fraudulent from another; and some are questionable. In all cases, it is the shaykh who must examine these spiritual states, as he is the only one who can explain them. It is upon the examination of and differentiation between all the various states that the legal and dogmatic matters (*fiqhiyya wa-iʿtiqādiyya*), as well as the matters related to the wayfaring (*sulūkiyya*), are based. Therefore, he who wishes to become a Sufi without a shaykh who has been taught by a shaykh, connecting him through an initiatic chain (*sanad sulūkī*) to the First Teacher (*al-muʿallim al-awwal*) and True Guide (*al-murshid al-ḥaqq*) (may God bless him and grant him peace), will have a difficult voyage to a distant harbour.

THIRDLY, even though there is essentially one path to Him, the ways to God Most High are as many as the breaths of all His creatures. Each wayfarer deserves an education (*tarbiya*) that corresponds to his nature and not to others'. Spiritual states and mystical experiences, ephemeral inrushes, divine gifts, sciences, inspirations (*ilqā'āt*) and accidental manifestations (*ʿawāriḍ*) on the way vary with each individual, their experiences, the beginning and end of their journey, their strength and weakness. The method of spiritual travelling varies with each wayfarer. Two men might be on equal footing as far as action, learning and the sequential order in their ascetic discipline, but if they are faced with two different obstacles they will need specific remedies. One unique remedy for both individuals would be useless and many different remedies for both would prove just as useless. Besides, two men might come across the same obstacle and yet the same remedy may help one of them and be useless for the other. Mystical states, experiences and inspirations will befall both wayfarers in a similar way or in a different way. In accordance with what God shows him, it is the shaykh who separates between the similar and links together the different.

This is what befalls the wayfarer who strives to assume good character traits and travels on the path to self-realization. Now the self-realization of divine unity is the most powerful. Instead of trying to apprehend it by means of a book, it is better and safer to attain it guided by a shaykh who has traversed the sea of unity and halted at its shore, inviting wayfarers to follow him there. This journey is most important; and safety is indispensable because the obstacles that can befall the wayfarer are most formidable and calamitous, most numerous and bitter. Nonetheless, destruction is closer to him than his shoelace. Most of the Bāṭinīs, Ḥulūlīs,[9] Zanādiqa,[10] Ibāḥīs,[11]

Tanāsukhīs,[12] Jabarīs[13] and all such sects originally strayed from the right path. Either they travelled it without a knowing realized shaykh or they escaped his surveillance. The wayfarer needs the shaykh like the body needs sustenance.

I SAY: This is a long debate, difficult to grasp for the one who tries to understand its content. To start with, let us summarize it since our comments are based on the above.

To recapitulate: Those who deny the need for a shaykh as a condition in this Path claim, as mentioned above, that the course to follow needs to be clarified through a description—which in turn becomes an image in the mind of the wayfarer, whose subsequent actions can conform to this image. Regardless of whether this is achieved through a shaykh, a shaykh's transmitted teaching or a Sufi book, the wayfarer must act according to this image within him and must be contented with it.

Those who believe in the need for a shaykh answer that, in this Path, we need to understand the course to follow. But that we also need to know the particulars that befall the wayfarer by way of ailments, spiritual states, ephemeral inrushes, mystical experiences, their varieties and differences and the differences between their diverse and infinite repercussions. If mere description is sufficient to understand the nature of the Path, it is not for the [particulars listed] above; rather, a shaykh endowed with insight is indispensable because he understands the Path as an entity and in its particulars.

The shaykh-denier claims that books—such as the *Iḥyā'* or others—deal with all the above-mentioned matters sufficiently and even more than sufficiently.

The shaykh-partisan replies that there are three notions that render the shaykh's teaching necessary.

Firstly, by and large, the mystical wayfaring resembles the tangible road wherein many fears, dangers, perils, enemies and risks are to be expected. A mere description of the road is generally insufficient and the traveller needs to be accompanied by a guide endowed with insight in all these matters. Only then can the traveller hope for a safe journey. This is also the case for the mystical wayfaring.

Secondly, books tell about ailments, ephemeral inrushes, spiritual states and mystical experiences, but in truth they only tell tales of wayfarers [in the main]. Yet, wayfarers are different from each other since they can either be in control of their spiritual state or they can be controlled by it. A spiritual state can be sound or corrupt, authentic or fraudulent, in harmony or in contradiction with the Path in which case it becomes the source of undesirable results. A book cannot ascertain all this. Only a teacher endowed with insight can expose these differences and point them out to the wayfarer.

Thirdly, there is more than one road in the mystical wayfaring and the ways to God are as many as the breaths of all His creatures. Each wayfarer follows a course and a tutoring that correspond to his nature. Just as the roads in the wayfaring vary, the ailments, spiritual states and ephemeral inrushes also differ. Furthermore, each way has its corresponding experiences. The wayfarer cannot discern these differences unless he is in direct contact with a teacher endowed with insight into all these matters, and this is especially relevant when the itinerant reaches the station of professing divine unity.

This is, in substance, what the interlocutor mentioned. As you can see, the discourses of both debaters totally lack proofs. The one who rejects the need for a shaykh merely offers allegations, and the one who opposes a path without a shaykh does not provide any proof. The shaykh-partisan discusses the three issues that he calls 'stations' (*maqāmat*). In the first, he draws a concrete comparison [between the mystical wayfaring and a tangible road] and postulates the dangers within, with the intention of disavowing book guidance and dismissing it as uncommon. In the second level, he spells out the itinerants' spiritual states, mentions the difference between states and between wayfarers, and then concludes that none of this can be realized with books only. Finally, in the third level, he enumerates the number of paths and their various types, and then simply concludes again that the wayfarer cannot do with books only.

We believe the need for a teaching master is substantiated by the following proof, as we mentioned earlier. All the perceptions in this Path and all that befalls the one who travels it—namely ailments, spiritual states and ephemeral inrushes—are related to intimate finding and mystical tasting. They do not pertain to the conventional, acquirable sciences (*al-ʿulūm al-kasbiyya al-mutaʿārifa*) and cannot be apprehended with conventional linguistic usages or fixed in artificial rules. Furthermore, most of the spiritual states, ailments and mystical experiences are not only unconventional, but they are not subject to free choice either. So they must be dealt with according to their place of origin. The information that has been recorded in books is related to the acquired, conventional sciences, but the spiritual states pertaining to this Path are only described by way of metaphors; and their reality is unknown. A shaykh is therefore indispensable for conveying to us a knowledge that we do not possess at all. This is the true answer to the debate; and it also provides clear evidence. Nonetheless, this answer only applies to the struggle for unveiling. In the struggles towards walking on the straight path and God-wariness, it is safe and sound to rely on the written, the recorded and valid legal opinions. And God knows best!

Fourth Argument

THE SHAYKH-DENIER THEN SAID: If the Sufis' writings implement the purpose for which they were written, then we are in the right and all you said is useless. But if their writings are useless and even, in your opinion, misleading, then they were written in vain. This is an opinion that belittles the great Sufis who are actually and unanimously recognized guides. Therefore, your discourse—which dispossesses them of their function—is unanimously declared vain.[14]

THE SHAYKH-PARTISAN ANSWERED: The statements of the Sufis in their books are true. I refer here to Sufis like Abū Ḥāmid, Muḥāsibī, Ibn ʿAtā', all those who followed the same recognized way, the people of the Sunna and the leaders to the right path. We exclude those who departed from their way and turned it into a philosophy (*falsafiyyan*).

All that was said above is correct. The statements of Abū Ḥāmid and the other authors stem from their self-realization and adoption of virtuous traits (*iṭṭisāf*). But their statements never implied that descriptive books suffice in the Path. They do not exempt from [following] the guidance of the above-mentioned Sufis or their followers who tried to fall heir to their predecessors. This is the point of the debate. The Sufis' writings are useful in that they exhort and instigate the aspirant to seek lawful conduct and sound spiritual states, and to embark upon [the Path] according to the rules. Any book will suffice to teach any given field but [Sufi] books are useless unless imparted to the disciples by the masters, personally. Truly, the most necessary condition in the Path is the presence of a shaykh who does not merely explain written material matters as related in books, but who points at the contents of books in your own self.

The Path rests solely on that which is acquired through finding. The content of books on Sufism is fully grasped by the one who has found these realities and turned them into qualities of his own. Only those who have attained mystical experiences can understand the Sufis' occasional testimony. As to the others, they assume true is false and false is true because all this is so remote from familiar notions. Sometimes, the wayfarer will understand the Sufis' experiences correctly, but errs when it comes to applying them in the wayfaring because he is ignorant of its occurrences. In all this, the wayfarer needs a shaykh.

Moreover, Sufi authors disclosed little and withheld much more. Their statements are but general rules the outer meaning of which needs to be explained in innumerable cases. Their expressions are extreme and must be interpreted. Their summaries must be expounded and their generalizations specified. As we said earlier, this is necessary because of the differences between the circumstances of the paths and the spiritual states of the wayfarers.

I SAY: We have spoken about spiritual struggles and their degrees. The first struggle involves experiencing God-wariness through moral care, which is a duty incumbent on all men. In the second struggle, walking on the straight path, the wayfarer needs to assume the character traits of the Qur'ān and the prophets. This particular struggle is an obligation upon the prophets and is lawful to those who aspire to the higher levels in the community. The discourse on both struggles is part of common knowledge and their learning part of the acquirable sciences. The writings of the recognized Sufi guides are filled with rules concerning these two struggles, namely God-wariness and walking on the straight path. Among these writings are the *Iḥyāʾ*, the *Riʿāya*, the *Qūt*, the works of Ibn ʿAṭāʾ and others.[15]

The goal of the third spiritual struggle, namely unveiling and spiritual perception, is the lifting of the veil in a specific way and manner. As we previously mentioned, there are disagreements regarding the lawfulness of this particular combat. Since its realities are not part of the acquirable customary sciences, most of its rules are transmitted by competent masters who have grasped them by personally finding them (*al-wājidīn lahā*). As no words in the conventional language can express these realities, very few are set down in the Sufis' books, besides a few describing the nature of the wayfaring methods and some rules. The latter are not found through mystical tasting (*al-mawājid al-dhawqiyya*) and thenceforth can be transcribed. As to the rules and concepts that are found through mystical tasting, they are not touched upon or deposited in books. It is the duty of the shaykh to transmit them since, at most, the Sufi writers will relate some vague stories and make general hints about a spiritual state, an ephemeral inrush or a mystical experience (*wajd*). Yet, all this lacks clarity and needs the interpretation of a shaykh. And do not ever imagine that the nomenclature adopted by the Sufis can help non-Sufis conceive of their real meaning! They set it down in order to communicate with one another, and not to address those who have not tasted what they have tasted; we have cited the teacher Abū al-Qāsim in this respect.

When the shaykh-denier says: 'If the Sufis' writings implement the purpose for which they were written, then we are in the right and all you said is useless. But if their writings are useless and even, in your opinion, misleading, then they were written in vain.' We say the following: what is the meaning of the word purpose (*maqṣūd*) here? If purpose refers to the spiritual effort towards God-wariness and walking on the straight path, then the writings of the Sufis help insofar as their principles and rules of proper conduct are concerned. If purpose refers to the effort towards unveiling and spiritual perception, there is nothing wrong with the fact that these writings do not fully answer the need of this purpose—although they partly do so, namely by describing the methods of this last struggle's wayfaring. However, the Sufis' writings will not deal with ailments, ephemeral inrushes, mystical findings, spiritual states and all that occurs in this particular wayfaring. Doubtlessly, these occurrences are the pillar of this journey and the main road in its wayfaring, and can only be clarified and transmitted by a shaykh.[16] Truly, it is impossible to express them and neither explanatory words nor man-made rules prove adequate because these perceptions are not part of the acquirable sciences, as we have already stated.

As to the claim of the shaykh-partisan, namely: 'The Sufis' writings are useful in that they exhort and instigate the aspirant to seek lawful conduct and sound spiritual states.' We wonder: how can the debater limit the usefulness of the books to these achievements only? How is this possible when such books are filled with laws about the struggles towards walking on the straight path and moral care that ensure salvation and lead the wayfarer to the level of the sincere believers (*marātib al-ṣiddīqīn*)? And is there anything greater than the spiritual struggle of the prophets and assuming the good character traits of the Qur'ān? It is only the wayfaring towards unveiling that escapes these writings because mystical tasting can hardly, if ever, be put into words. There is no harm in the fact that these writings cannot contain this last wayfaring, and certainly their other benefits outweigh this omission. We also expounded earlier on the disagreements concerning the legality of the Path to unveiling, but be that as it may, the shaykh will make sure the itinerant harvests the books' benefits.

The shaykh-partisan was ending his speech when he added—if only he had said it earlier!—'Truly, the most necessary condition in the Path is the presence of a shaykh who does not merely explain written material matters as related in books, but who points at the contents of books in your own self. The Path rests solely on that which is acquired through finding.' And the rest of his discourse is related above. Indeed, here his words are pertinent and they provide a summary of the substance of our topic.

Fifth Argument

THE SHAYKH-DENIER ARGUES: A shaykh does not possess knowledge of all this. If he draws his knowledge from the aforementioned books, then there is nothing wrong with this. But if he does not refer to such books, he is claiming a new law, and enough it is to hear this evil claim!

THE SHAYKH-PARTISAN ANSWERS: No, indeed! The [shaykh's] knowledge relies on the Book and the Sunna. His knowledge is the spirit behind the books and the foundation of all that derives from the sources of the Law. This is why the realized Sufi enlightens the legist in his knowledge of the Law; the [Qur'ānic] commentator in his commentary; the specialist in legal theory in his knowledge of the sources of the Law; the physician in his medical science; the leader in his government; the artisan in his art; and all men in their trade and life. The shaykh pinpoints their mistakes and errors and indicates how to correct them. This is a knowledge he alone possesses, to the exclusion of books and of those who have not experienced what he has realized.[17] The knowledge God bestowed upon the shaykh relates to all sciences and the directing of all beings, the way jurisprudence relates to the Law itself. In fact, it is an even clearer and more accurate science.

I SAY: The shaykh possesses two kinds of knowledge. Firstly, he can explain the conditions of this wayfaring and its method. He describes the course to follow beforehand, namely the spiritual efforts towards God-wariness and walking on the straight path, as well as the principles concerning all this. This type of knowledge has been presented in the Sufis' books along with their numerous aspects and detailed rules, and it suffices to follow them.

Secondly, there is the knowledge of the spirit behind this wayfaring, its secret truth, and it relates to the unforeseen events mentioned earlier. It relies on mystical tasting and cannot be expressed in words or conveyed through books and codified material. When the wayfarer experiences some event through mystical tasting, it is the shaykh who will point out the genuinely real therein and lead him to their understanding thereon.

The shaykh-denier argues that, 'If he does not refer to books, he is claiming a new law, and this is an ignominious accusation!' We have explained earlier that the wayfaring [towards unveiling] is a special path (*ṭarīq khāssa*) different from the common way of the Law (*al-sharᶜ al-ᶜāmm*). The sincere believers found it and followed it, hoping to attain the loftiest levels of realization. When they tasted its realities and grasped its perceptions through finding, they understood how this wayfaring relates to the five legal principles of behaviour (*al-aḥkām al-khamsa*).[18] Subsequently, they instructed therein those who plunged into its waves and traversed its seas, tasting of what they had tasted. Truly, these realities are comprehended in the five legal principles of behaviour the way the particular is in the general. However, it is difficult to phrase the relation between the five principles of behaviour and this Path—which, anyhow, the majority does not feel a need for. Therefore, the relation was concealed from all but the enlightened few who were given the knowledge of its realities and gnosis of God's decree in all this.

As to the argument of the shaykh-partisan: 'No, indeed! The [shaykh's] knowledge relies on the Book and the Sunna. His knowledge is the spirit behind the books and the foundation of all that derives from the sources of the Law.' I assert this is a rhetorical argument that cannot convince an opponent who negates the relation between the five legal principles of behaviour and the unforeseen events, claiming it is non-existent in the Book. As aforementioned, the truth is that it is not recorded in books because its masters—the saints of God—do know the interrelation between the unforeseen events and the legal principles, having understood their realities by finding them.

As to the shaykh-partisan's words concerning 'the realized Sufi who enlightens the scientists and artisans in their sciences and arts', we say: this is a true statement and we discussed the subject earlier. To him whose knowledge is inspired by God, all the realities and hidden secrets of existence are disclosed as they are, because he contemplates them with the eye of his heart. The God-inspired person guides men to truth and protects them from error because his knowledge results from his perceptions. Are not the acquired and applied sciences but a mere shadow of his knowledge? The human perceptions of the realized Sufi are enhanced by the light God cast into his heart and the divine knowledge that replenished his whole self.

Sixth Argument

THEN, THE SHAYKH-DENIER CONTENDED THAT: If the science the shaykh alone possesses can be expressed in words, then it is possible to acquire and transmit it. The recorded is transmittable, as seen in the cases of Abū Ḥāmid (may God be pleased with him) and others as well. If the shaykh's science is not recorded, it is virtually part of that which could be recorded, since it is actually acquired by him, apprehended and imagined in his mind. In both cases, this science can be acquired, read and taught and hence recorded. Therefore, it is right to draw from books what is relevant therein. If this is not so, then what is this "science"?

THE SHAYKH-PARTISAN ANSWERS: It is a science that cannot be acquired, enclosed, contained in rules, or gathered in one code of laws. This is why when we ask the shaykh who has reached realization (*al-shaykh al-muḥaqqiq*) what he knows about the science of Sufism, he answers he knows nothing. He is in a state of poverty from all points of view. Rather, he is like an empty tablet (*lawḥ*) ready for what will be imprinted on it. God confers upon the shaykh a discerning light wherewith he discriminates between true and false in all things. The shaykh cannot describe this light, nor pass it on to a wayfarer or to any other man. He can only describe it via parables (*mithāl*) that are but a manifestation of this light, the reality of which is hidden as it was before. He who possesses this light will understand, while he who does not possess it will not. And this is the reason many book-followers were misled—'*But they split up their religion into sects, each party rejoicing in what is with them*' (Q.xxx.32). Each group adapted the Book and the Sunna to what they knew of Sufi realities.[19] They correlated the Sufis' mystical states to some religious law, other than the one transmitted to the community by the Prophet (may God bless him and grant him peace), thinking that the Sufis were addressed differently to everyone else. This is proof enough for the negative state of the book-followers.

I SAY: It has been determined that the perceptions in this Path are not acquirable or recordable, but are related to intimate finding and mystical tasting (*wijdāniyya dhawqiyya*). It is impossible to talk about them except to the one who shares in this finding and tasting; but we have already said that.

As to the shaykh-denier's argument: 'If the science the shaykh alone possesses can be expressed in words, then it is possible to acquire and transmit it. The recorded is transmittable...If the shaykh's science is not recorded, it is virtually part of that which could be recorded...'. I answer saying that this kind of knowledge cannot be put in words. The sciences that can be explained have a technical, acquirable nomenclature; yet, this is not the case for the sciences that stem from intimate finding.

The shaykh-denier added the following: 'It can be acquired, [read] and taught.' If the deniers are referring here to the science related to God-wariness or walking on the straight path, then this is true. If they are referring to the knowledge particular to the struggle for unveiling, then this is forbidden (*mamnūʿ*) because, as we said, the perceptions of this knowledge are beyond sciences and nomenclatures. The shaykh-partisan had alluded to this when he said 'a discerning light wherewith he discriminates between true and false in all things', to the end of his discourse.

Furthermore, the shaykh-partisan asserts that book-followers strayed by claiming that the Sufis were addressed differently to everyone else. To this we answer: if the reason for this deviation is indeed book-following and the reliance on transmission, then the solution to this discussion lies in the aforesaid: the perceptions in this wayfaring are related to intimate finding and mystical tasting. He who relies on writings—but without discrimination—does not understand how this particular wayfaring is correlated to the five legal principles of behaviour and will claim the principles underlying Sufism are at variance. And God knows best! We have demonstrated earlier how wrong it is to claim that the Law is liable to different interpretations in accordance with its application to different people and according to two levels: an outward and an inward.

Seventh Argument

THE SHAYKH-DENIER SAID: Wayfaring without a shaykh is impossible either because of the essence of the Path itself—which is not likely—or because of external reasons such as customs or the Law. Customs do not forbid it since many fared forth without a shaykh and were taught the Path by a book, or a transmitter who had learned its method from a book.[20] God guided them and did not entrust them to anyone else. The biographies testify to this. As to the Law, wherefrom comes the argument stating that the way (*sulūk*) must be fared forth with a shaykh or without one? On the contrary, there are instances when the opposite is stated, as in God Most High's words, '*O ye who believe! If ye keep your duty to God, He will give you discrimination between right and wrong*' (Q.VIII.29). This asserts that whoever is wary of God is given the discriminating light (*al-nūr al-furqānī*) that you claim is a quality reserved to the shaykh. In fact, this light is the result of God-wariness, which entails conforming to His orders and avoiding the forbidden. This can safely be drawn from books since it merely consists in acting upon the matters of substantive law and the experiences of the Sufis who lived according to it. So why would a shaykh be needed? It says in the noble Qur'ān, '*But those who struggle in Our cause, surely We shall guide them in Our Ways*' (Q.XXIX.69). This reiterates the meaning of the aforementioned verse as well as many other verses too.

THE SHAYKH-PARTISAN ANSWERED: To travel the way without a master is not impossible because of the essence of the Path itself, but for reasons pertaining to custom and the Law. According to custom, current tradition and recorded precedents, we see that those whose lives have been related in books relied on shaykhs and did not fare without them. Most of those who slid off the straight path did so because they embarked upon it without a shaykh, or because they opposed him in some matter. We have seen this with our own eyes and we have read it in books. By 'reliance on a shaykh', I do not mean that a wayfarer should follow one master only. Although this is preferable, it is not a universal condition. As to the case of the wayfarer who follows the Path without a shaykh at all, it is possible theoretically but almost impossible in actual fact. A certain man might indeed follow a master and yet you might not know he does, or else you might not know his shaykh; your ignorance of something does not imply its non-existence. The shaykh is one of the means through which God assists His servant.

But let us assume that a man can proceed along the Path without a shaykh; this is a rare case that fits in the category of exception and cannot be turned into a general law, just as the grammatical exception is memorized but not turned into a rule. The same held true for the sale of the palm trees' fruits, the making of loans and the contracts for irrigation;[21] all these are specific rules without being a measure for everything. Our problem here is best illustrated with the story of Khuzayma's testimony[22] and that of Abū Burda's sacrifice of the new-born goat.[23] Furthermore, one might come across a wayfarer who does not follow a shaykh, but such a wayfarer is seldom of benefit to others in the Path; instead he is a community (*umma*) to himself.

The need for a shaykh is made even more evident in the Law: '*Question the people of the Remembrance, if it should be that you should not know*' (Q.xvi.43); and also in His words, '*O believers! Obey God, and obey the Messenger and those in authority among you*' (Q.iv.59). In addition, it is also said that 'learned men are the heirs of the prophets'.[24] To be in no need of the heirs of the Prophet compares to being in no need of the Prophet. The Prophet is sent to explain the Book, as is his heir. Every man who transmits a religious legal science is the heir of the Prophet therein; there are innumerable proofs for this and your arguments do not refute anything. Even at the stage of God-wariness, the wayfarer needs the guidance of a shaykh who knows the method to follow for each individual and in every circumstance, and who shows caution with regards the obstacles that could divert the disciple from his way. Just as God-wariness is gradually achieved, so is its result, namely discrimination, which is attained by degrees, little by little, with the perfection of its later stages being in proportion to the perfection of the earlier ones.

As the God-wary believer (*muttaqī*) advances through the progressive stages of development, his discriminating faculty increases. At the respective levels of submission, faith and excellence, he is given the discrimination that corresponds to their particular phases. Each level of discrimination has its sources, principles, ephemeral inrushes, mystical findings, and accidental manifestations with their befitting results, namely walking on the straight path or not, performing sound or corrupt action. Therefore, we reiterate, a shaykh is needed in the spiritual struggle that guides the wayfarer to the straight path, just as God-wariness is needed to lead him towards discrimination. The itinerant will traverse vast expanses of perilous lands familiar only to its native inhabitants. When the shaykh sees that the wayfarer has gained insight in all these matters, that the voyage led him back to his starting point and original centre, and when he sees the wayfarer clad in divine light, endowed with discerning light, he will entrust him to God in whom is guidance from the beginning until the end. Thereafter, when more opportunities towards further training cross the path of the itinerant, he will seek them out with full awareness but without relinquishing the guidance of his shaykh, whether the latter is alive or dead.[25] Indeed, it is on this Path that the itinerant has been endowed with and clad in this light; and if he departs from it, the light in him will become extinct. The tradition binding shaykh and disciple is absolute and epitomizes the uninterrupted initiatic chain (*al-silsila al-muttaṣila*) that connects to the Prophet (may God bless him and grant him peace). He who holds on will reach, and he who severs is stranded.

I SAY: The shaykh-denier refuted the impossibility of the Path without a shaykh either because of the essence of the Path itself or for of external reasons, such as customs or the Law. The shaykh-partisan concurs with the reason linked to the essence but contests the legal and customary impossibility.

Know that one cannot restrict impossibility to the abovementioned three factors. It is impossible to journey without a guide because of the nature of the wayfaring, which is based on intimate findings and mystical tasting. The oral explanations of a shaykh competent in these matters are therefore needed. Yet, anything impossible by nature can become possible the day its nature is altered; thence, the discernment of intimate findings (*al-madārik al-wijdāniyya*) is made possible by God, who leads towards and infuses into some individuals the gnosis of these realities (*aʿyān*), by way of a charismatic gift, akin to the prophetic miracle (*muʿjiza*).[26] This reverses the normally possible or impossible by altering their nature. However, the soundness of the particular cases in wayfaring is confirmed to the wayfarer and his brethren only after spiritual vision—its fruit—is reaped. When the wayfarer is absolutely certain that he has reaped the fruit, he understands that God has taken over his affairs and guidance.

If God, in His providence and guidance, disrupts customs—that call for the presence of a shaykh in the wayfaring—and lifts its interdiction, this exceptional circumstance should not be taken as an example to imitate. The wayfarer must not disregard this injunction and undertake this course without a shaykh, assuming God Most High has taken over his guidance in a Path wherein perceptions are filled with ambiguity for the one who is unassisted in this experience. This is a foolish action and idle talk! If he does so, the wayfarer will be acting like the man who walks alone into the fire saying, 'I shall walk into the fire and God will protect me', claiming God made the fire '*coolness and safety*' for Abraham (Q.XXI.69). So it is with the one who drinks deadly poison alleging the charismatic act whereby Khālid b. al-Walīd drank poison and was not harmed.[27] The possible does not become impossible and the impossible possible just because the custom has been disrupted once (by way of a prophetic miracle or a charismatic act. If the wayfarer fancies he is guided [by God], this could be but a test for him, and he must be alert at all times until he reaches the desired object and is certain that God has truly favoured him. Yet, this is rare and consequently the wayfarer must not rely on this possibility.

Thus, both sides agree that wayfaring without a shaykh is not impossible because of the essence of the path (*al-imtināʿ al-dhātī*). The shaykh-partisan rejects the customary impossibility (*al-imtināʿ al-ʿādī*). He does not reject the essential impossibility [or impossibility by nature], as long as the nature justifying the impossibility is valid; and since this essential impossibility is rarely invalidated by an isolated case, the argument rejecting the necessity of the shaykh in this Path is unfounded.[28] On the contrary, his presence is a condition, as we proved earlier. As to the legal impossibility (*al-imtināʿ*

al-sharʿī), I do not know why the shaykh-denier refutes it. They claim God-wariness will necessarily grant the wayfarer the light of discrimination, and its struggle will lead him to guidance. This is absolutely correct. But then, why not consider shaykh-following a requirement in their claim? Is it not a requirement for many of the absolute statements in the Qur'ān and the Sunna? This is all the more true if by struggle and God-wariness the shaykh-denier is actually referring to the Path of unveiling and spiritual perception, wherein—as proven earlier—the presence of a teacher endowed with knowledge about its perceptions is most necessary.

As to the struggles towards walking on the straight path and God-wariness, we explained that their perceptions are familiar and can be understood with the Law transmitters' discourses. Since their perceptions are not grasped through intimate finding, these can be secured from books and compiled material, without help from a shaykh—although, again, his presence does perfect these struggles. We have already said this. This was also stated in the two Qur'ānic verses quoted above and we do not need to reiterate.[29]

Concerning the argument of the shaykh-partisan that 'learned men are the heirs of the prophets', to be in no need of the heirs of the Prophet compares to being in no need of the Prophet. The Prophet is sent to explain the Book, as is his heir. Every man who transmits a religious legal science is the heir of the Prophet therein.' Know that the Prophet has three statuses:

A general one, namely the guidance of the people (*hidāya li'l-khalq*) towards salvation; and this applies to all men subject to the Law.

A second special status related to his own personal spiritual struggle, an individual obligation upon him, which inheres in walking on the straight path and assuming the traits of the Qur'ān.

The third and even more restricted status involves the Prophet's path towards spiritual perception, through meditation (*taḥannuth*) in the cave of Hīrā'.[30] There, away from people, he was exposed to ephemeral inrushes and mystical findings whereby God guided him and taught him. This is the way to unveiling, and [the way of the Sufis] is but a drop of water in the sea, a shadow of the goal [compared with the way of the Prophet]. The difference between the two is like the difference between the lamp and the sun; or rather the lamp is closer to the sun [than is their Path to His]. The comparison is only an allegory and an approximation. The first goal for the believers subject to the Law is salvation by following the prophets and imitating them. Therein is the true meaning of the 'inheritance of the learned men'. This inheritance is the capital and wealth of faith. It is impossible to proceed without the heir who inherited from the Prophet.

As to walking on the straight path and assuming the prophets' good character traits, it is an individual obligation upon them. But when the believers subject to the Law undertake this course, they may reach a more perfect level and ascend to loftier levels [than the level attained with the first struggle, God-wariness]. He who searches for these levels learns from books and learned men, and must abide by their teachings. Consequently, it is impossible to dispense with the heir in this. In both cases, [the search for salvation and the effort towards walking on the straight path], the word heir signifies the one who understands the legal principles that are part of known realities familiar to us.[31]

As to the 'even more restricted way' in this Path, its legality troubles the heirs—the learned men. Basically, one may just ignore this specific Path; and even more so—according to those who do not believe in the guidance of a shaykh—one must ignore it because during the early Islamic times the Companions and the Predecessors were not aware of it and did not follow it. They either sought salvation or walking on the straight path, striving to assume the good character traits of the Prophet (may God bless him and grant him peace). How could they not dispense with a path wherein the presence of the teacher or some other tutor is a prerequisite?

The shaykh-partisan believes that God-wariness and struggle are achieved differently according to the stations at which they take place, and the reaped results vary with the struggles. We believe that this is true. In the struggles towards God-wariness and walking on the straight path, wariness manifests itself in perceptions that can be understood. Whether these manifestations are sources, principles, ephemeral inrushes, mystical findings, accidental manifestations or befitting results, they all belong to the realm of the familiar. As to the perceptions belonging to the wayfaring towards unveiling, its meanings (*maʿānī*), sources, principles, accidental manifestations or befitting results, they are not accessible because they are not part of the conventional, as we said earlier; hence, the need for a shaykh to spell out all these elements. As to the rest of the discourse of the two debaters, it is clear.

Eighth Argument

THE SHAYKH-DENIER THEN SAYS: All you said is feasible, but only if a shaykh is available and accessible. Yet, these days there are no shaykhs around! Besides, even if such a shaykh exists we might not know of him. What then is the solution for the wayfarer who wishes to follow a Path besides reliance on books?

THE SHAYKH-PARTISAN ANSWERED: If the shaykh for this special Path is not available, that does not mean he does not exist. [In fact, he will exist] until '*We shall inherit the earth and all that are upon it*' (Q.XIX.40). On the other hand, the shaykh for the path common to all is available. His follower is either a wayfarer to God (*sālik*) or one attracted to Him (*majdhūb*).

If the seeker is a wayfarer, he only needs to observe commandments and avoid prohibitions, as indicated by the shaykh versed in the Law. He must not be negligent or excessive, careless or unduly rigorous. If he is an artisan, he will not abandon his trade—provided it is licit, of course—and if he is a scholar or a student, [he will maintain] his studies. This wayfarer will not impose upon himself too many supererogatory or pious acts of devotion (*nawāfil wa-mandūbāt*) if these affect his livelihood or his peace of mind. In doing so, he will not isolate himself or be different from other people, except in the illicit matters which he avoids while they do not, or in the obligatory matters which he performs while they do not.

Perhaps, the wayfarer does need a shaykh for all the above-mentioned, but an expert legist (*al-faqīh al-muftī*) is sufficient because these matters are easy to solve. The wayfarer will act as the student of Law and its sources, traditions of the Prophet, or any other science related to the legal sciences. At the same time, he will look for a teacher, inquire and inwardly pray with ardour for God to lead him towards a master who answers his needs and whom he loves. If he hears about such a realized teacher who fulfils the quality of the shaykh as attested by all, he will go to him if he can; and if he cannot, he will write him and tell him about his spiritual state. If the wayfarer does not find a shaykh, he should persevere in his search and prayers, and that which God has foreordained for him will no doubt be granted.

As to the one attracted by God, he is enraptured, bereft of his self, absorbed in his Lord and withdrawn from the world. He belongs to Him only. As he does not—and cannot—take charge of himself, he must not consult books in the event of encountering an obstacle on his way. If the obstacle is related to the domain of the legist, he consults with him. If the obstacle is related to some other domain, he must trust in the service of the One who has attracted him to Him and who will guide him the way He chooses to. But he must not rely on books or on the one who relies on books and does not have knowledge or realization of what he is transmitting. And only God leads to the truth.

I SAY: The denier's position that such a shaykh is unavailable [is supposed to] prove that he is not a condition to the Path. Unquestionably, this would be proof enough had the Law or reason declared this specific Path to be an obligation; and only then would this wayfaring without a master substantiate that he is not a condition therein. Yet, how could that be when we have discussed earlier the difficulty facing the legists in determining its legality? But we do not ratify this. Rather, we say: if the wayfarer finds a shaykh, let him follow this Path; and if he does not find one, let him renounce this Path—lest he be faced with dangers and exposed to perils—until God brings forth a shaykh for him.

The shaykh-partisan claims there will always be a shaykh available until 'We shall inherit the earth and all that are upon it.' This is a strange postulation on the part of certain Sufis who speculate about the sciences of unveiling, the Pole (*quṭb*), the Pillars (*awtād*) and the Substitutes (*abdāl*). We already exposed their theories, declaring them to be false and perverse. The truth is that the shaykh—who is a wayfarer and a guide (*al-shaykh al-sālik*)—is like all particular beings:

he exists at times and does not at other times. If a shaykh is found, the wayfaring will go straight (*istiqām al-sulūk*). If a shaykh cannot be found, then this Path must be forsaken because it is not an inherent condition [for the believer]. Thus, [it will be] until God (may He be exalted) sends forth a shaykh. Then, God will guide the wayfarer by way of a charismatic act, and He will inspire, favour and lead him to one of His saints. It is [only right for] the shaykh to convey the teaching and education [particular to this Path], generation after generation, until the chain of transmission is discontinued after many ages and successive periods. At that time, one must wait until God, in His mercy, again sends forth a shaykh. And God knows best!

The shaykh-partisan added: 'On the other hand, the shaykh for the path common to all is available.' These words seem to infer that the need for a shaykh is a condition not only in the struggle towards unveiling, but also in the struggles towards walking on the straight path and God-wariness. However, we have previously clarified the difference between these struggles: unlike the first two, the last struggle does require the presence of a shaykh. 'The path common to all' must designate the way of the Law, whose shaykh is the mostly available expert legist (*muftī*). If the latter happens to be unavailable, then juridical principles can [possibly] be drawn from those books which are consulted—provided their sources are valid and their chains of transmitters sound. This may continue in such a way until some teachers acquire again a deeply-rooted proficiency and can resume their teaching [of the Law]. Unlike the path of unveiling, there is no harm, danger or peril in faring this way without a shaykh [if performed with the aforementioned proviso].

Furthermore, the shaykh-partisan divided seekers into two groups: the wayfarer and the one attracted by Him. He also claimed that if the seeker does not have a shaykh, he must limit himself to obeying the Law, following the directives of the legist, earning his livelihood, professing his trade, and ardently praying that God guides him to a shaykh. If I only knew! What would the seeker lose if he does not follow this specific way? By God, this Path is so dangerous and perilous to everyone except he whom God has protected and guided to the goal! Besides, is there another path anyone could aspire for, besides walking on the straight path wherein the wayfarer assumes the character traits of the prophets, the sincere believers and the Qur'ān?

The shaykh-partisan added: 'If he hears about such a realized teacher who fulfils the quality of the shaykh as attested by all, he will go to him if he can; and if he cannot, he will write him and tell him about his spiritual state.' I say the following: how can communicating in writing [with a shaykh] be ever valid or useful, when this same debater has been declaring since the beginning of the discussion that book learning is useless, written transmission unreliable and book followers are in great danger? What is the difference between a written work and a letter sent by a shaykh from a distant land? Both rely on recorded transmission and writing. The only difference is that, in the letter to the shaykh, there is distance in place, whereas in written books, there is distance in time.

The shaykh-partisan then goes on to define the duty of the one attracted by God. I say: know that he has no duty (*waẓīfa*) whatsoever! For the Sufis, the ones attracted by God—like Bahlūl and other madmen of the people of wayfaring (*majānīn ahl al-sulūk*)—were ravished to themselves by the spiritual vision (*ʿinda al-maṭlaʿ*). Hence, they completely lost the requisite level of intellect that would bind them to the Law, so they have no duty to it anymore. Indeed, they have reached the goal (*wuṣūl*), and duties are mere means to the goal. The one attracted by God has arrived, seen the light, been ravished out of himself and is out of his mind. He does not know the Book, faith or transmission; rather, he is constantly immersed in the sea of gnosis and divine unity, oblivious to senses and sense objects.

CONCLUSION AND ASCERTAINMENT

There is yet one unresolved question on my mind. The one attracted to God has lost his mind and is not accountable for legal observance. He occupies the lowest level in humankind and is considered peripheral to the mass of believers inasmuch as he is exempted from religious duties and especially from worship. How can he then reach the level of God's saints and be considered one of them, as has been attested and never denied in both past and present times?

Consequently, God in His grace and guidance inspired me and my question was answered. The intellect, by virtue of which a man is liable for the religious duties imposed by the Law, applies to worldly life and conducts man in his daily domestic life. If a man has lost this intellect owing to a lack in his self and in his subtle soul (*laṭīfa rūḥāniyya*)—as is the case with fools and idiots—then he sinks below the human level and has nothing to do with faith, not to mention sainthood (*walāya*).[1] On the other hand, if a man has lost his intellect because he has been drowned in the sea of divine lights and is little inclined towards the sensorial world and its burden, then he is not debased and does not sink below the level of humankind. On the contrary, his faith increases and he is worthy of sainthood because he has contemplated the lights of gnosis (*anwār al-maʿrifa*). As to keeping his lofty rank, in spite of his exemption from the religious duties and his relinquishing the means to a goal—which anyway he has already reached—the one who is attracted by God enjoys and is granted a specific legal statute (*ḥukm sharʿī*), agreed upon by the Sufis who are entrusted with the knowledge therein.

We said earlier that the Sufis' legal principles stem from their intimate finding and mystical tasting. If these legal principles escape us, it is not because they are obscure or intricate, but because the mystical perceptions—from which they stem—are concealed. If the Sufis happen to intuitively perceive one of these spiritual states—through an inrush, a casting onto the heart or the like—they know how these spiritual states relate to God's rule. Occasionally, a judgement passed by Sufis on a fellow Sufi might strike us as strange, but it is only so because of the strangeness of the perception that relies on tasting (*madārik dhawqiyya*). This should not be apprehended as farfetched, as the Sufis know best their own perceptions. God bestows upon them special divine graces (*takhṣīṣ*), wherein lies their felicity.

Here ends my discourse and the debate between the two protagonists.

May God guide us to Him, grant us felicity through gnosis of Him, lead us to the straight path and infuse sincerity in our deeds so that they be performed for His sake only. May He be pleased with us and may He protect us from His wrath. Truly, He is all-powerful.

Here ends our work. Praise be to God for His bountiful help. May His prayers and blessings be upon our master Muḥammad, His Prophet and His servant, and on his family and Companions! This was completed on Monday 29 Jumādā I, 890 [AH].[23] May God bestow upon us His grace and generosity!

NOTES

Translator's Introduction

1. A Sufi Debate and the Origins of the *Shifā'*

1 Ibn ʿAjība, *Īqāẓ al-himam fī sharḥ al-Ḥikam wa'l-futūḥāt al-ilāhiyya fī sharḥ al-Mabāḥith al-aṣliyya* (Cairo: Matbaʿat Aḥmad Ḥanafī, n.d.), p. 147.

2 The clash between two epistemologies, the methods of the Law and the Path of the Sufis or 'the illuminative knowledge acquired by mystics vis-à-vis juridically circumscribed teachings of the *fuqahā'*...seems to be a continuation of the *Karāmāt al-awliyā"* polemic that began in the 4th/10th century, as Yousef Casewit states in 'The Forgotten Mystic: Ibn Barrajān (d. 536/1141) and the Andalusian Muʿtabirūn' (PhD thesis: Yale University, 2014), pp. 54–55.

3 For Aḥmad Zarrūq, see C. Brocklemann, *Geschishte der Arabishen Litteratur*, 2 vols. (Leiden: E. J Brill, 1943), henceforth cited as *GAL*, vol. II, p. 253, and suppl. II, pp. 360 and 362; Ibn al-Qāḍī, *Durrat al-ḥijāl fī ghurrat asmā' al-rijāl,* 2 vols. (Cairo: Dār al-Turāth, 1971), vol. I, p. 90, and *Jadhwat al-iqtibās* (n.l.: n.p.,1892), p. 64; Aḥmad Bābā, *Nayl al-ibtihāj bi taṭrīz al-dībāj* in Ibn Farḥūn, *al-Dībāj al-mudhahhab fī maʿrifat aʿyān al-madhhab* (Cairo: Maktabat Dār al-Turāth, 1932–3), pp. 84–6; Ben Cheneb, 'Etude sur les personages mentionnés dans l'Idjazah du Cheikh Abd al-Qadir al-Fasy', in *Actes du XIVe Congrès International des Orientalistes* (Algiers: n.p., 1978), p. 51. In *Qawāʿid al-taṣawwuf* (Cairo: n.p., 1976), p. 40, Zarrūq mentions the debate that took place between 'the later-day initiates of Andalusia who disagreed among themselves as to whether reading books sufficed, to do without shaykhs. So they wrote various parts of the Islamic world and received answers, each one answering according to his own enlightenment', as translated by Z. Istrabadi, *The Principles of Sufism* (ProQuest/UMI: 2002), p. 101. In *ʿIddat al-murīd* (lith. edition: n.p., 1943)—as found in Ibn Tāwīt al-Ṭanjī, *Shifā' al-sā'il li-tahdhīb al-masā'il* (Istanbul: Osman Yalçın Matbaası, 1957, hereinafter refered to as 'Ṭanjī, *Shifā*'')—Zarrūq tells us Ibn Khaldūn was among those who answered this question. Finally, in *al-Naṣīḥa al-kāfiya* (lith. edition: n.p., n.d.), p. 61 m, Zarrūq mentions Ibn Khaldūn in connection with one of the subjects dealt with in the *Shifā'*. For the last two references, see Ṭanjī, *Shifā'*, p. 'ḍ'.

4 For Aḥmad al-Wansharīsī, see *GAL*, vol. II, pp. 248 and 356, and suppl. II, p. 348. The reference is given as Aḥmad al-Wansharīsī, *al-Miʿyār al-mughrib wa'l-jāmiʿ al-muʿrib,* vol. XII, p. 291, as found in Ṭanjī, *Shifā'*, p. 'ḍ'.

5 For Abū Muḥammad ʿAbd al-Qādir al-Fāsī, see *GAL*, suppl. ii, p. 708. The reference is found in ʿAbd al-Raḥmān al-Fāsī, 'Qiṣṣat makhṭūṭ Ibn Khaldūn', *Risālat al-Maghrib*, vol. x: 1948, pp. 570–1.

6 For Abū ʿAbd Allāh Muḥammad b. Aḥmad al-Masnāwī, see *GAL*, suppl. ii, p. 685. The reference is found in Fāsī, 'Qiṣṣat', p. 571.

7 Ibn ʿAjība, *Īqāẓ al-himam*, p. 147.

8 For Abū Isḥāq Ibrāhīm b. Mūsā al-Shāṭibī, see *GAL*, suppl. ii, p. 374; Ibn al-Qāḍī, *Durrat*, vol. i, p. 182, and *Jadhwa*, p. 60; *Nayl*, pp. 46 *ff.*; Ben Cheneb, *Ijāza*, p. 277.

9 For Abū al-ʿAbbās Aḥmad b. al-Qāsim b. ʿAbd al-Raḥmān al-Qabbāb, see *GAL*, suppl. i, p. 346; *Dībāj*: p. 187; Ben Cheneb, *Ijāza*, p. 328; *Nayl:* pp. 72–3.

10 For Muḥammad b. Ibrāhīm b. ʿAbbād al-Rundī, see *GAL*, suppl. ii, p. 358; *Encyclopeadia of Islam*, henceforth cited as *EI*[2], s.v. 'Ibn ʿAbbād'; *İslam Ansiklopedisi*, henceforth cited as *IA*, s.v. 'Ibn Abbād er-Rundī'; see also Aḥmad b. Muḥammad al-Maqqarī, *Nafḥ al-ṭīb min ghuṣn al-Andalus al-raṭīb wa-dhikr wazīriha Lisān al-Dīn b. al-Khaṭīb,* 10 vols. (Beirut: Dār al-Kutub al-ʿArabī, 1949), vol. vii, p. 261; Ibn al-Khaṭīb, *al-Iḥāṭa fī tārīkh Garnāṭa*, 3 vols., edited by M. A. Inan (Cairo: al-Tibāʿa al-Miṣriyya, 1974), vol. iii, pp. 252–6; Ibn al-Qāḍī, *Jadhwa*, pp. 200–1; *Nayl*, pp. 279 *ff.*; Ben Cheneb, *Ijāza*, p. 343. See also Paul Nwyia, *Ibn ʿAbbād de Ronda* (Beirut: Imprimerie Catholique, 1961); Ibn ʿAbbād al-Rundī, *Lettres de Direction Spirituelle, al-Rasā'il al-Ṣughrā*, edited by Paul Nwyia (Beirut: Dār al-Mashriq, 1974), pp. 130–140. For the latter, we shall be quoting the English translation by John Renard in *Ibn ʿAbbād of Ronda: Letters on the Sufi Path* (New Jersey: Paulist Press 1986), pp. 184–94.

11 Wansharīsī, *Miʿyār*, vol. xii, pp. 201 *ff.*; texts as found in Ṭanjī, *Shifā'*, pp. 110–34.

ii. A Historical Overview

12 Ashʿarism is a school of orthodox theology that bears the name of its founder Abū al-Ḥasan al-Ashʿarī (d. 324/935); *Shorter Encyclopeadia of Islam*, edited by H. A. Gibb and J. J. Kramers (Leiden: E. J. Brill, 1974), henceforth cited as *SEI*, s.v. 'al-Ashʿarī'.

13 The Mālikī *madhhab* is the school of *fiqh*, or Islamic law, that dominated North Africa and bears the name of the Imam Mālik b. Anas; see *SEI*: s.v. 'Mālik b. Anas'. For a thorough analysis of these pillar elements and their interrelations in Andalusian and North African medieval history, refer to Vincent J. Cornell, *Realm of the Saint, Power and Authority in Moroccan Sufism* (Texas: University of Texas Press: 1998) and Yousef Casewit, 'The Forgotten Mystic'.

14 ʿAlī b. Yūsuf b. Tashufīn the Almoravid reigned from 500/1106 to 538/1143. See ʿAbd al-Raḥmān b. Khaldūn, *al-Taʿrīf bi-Ibn Khaldūn wa-riḥlatihi sharqan wa-gharban*, edited by Muḥammad b. Tāwīt al-Ṭanjī (Cairo: Matbaʿat Lajnat al-Ta'līf wa'l-Tarjama wa'l-Nashr, 1951), p. 56; Ahmad b. Khālid, al-Nāṣirī, *Kitāb al-istiqṣā lī-akhbār duwal al-Maghrib al-aqsā*, vol. ii, in *Archives Marocaines*, vol. xxxi: 1925, pp. 197–209.

15 For Abū Ḥāmid al-Ghazālī, *Ḥujjat al-Islam* or 'Restorer of the Faith', see *GAL*, vol. I, p. 419 and suppl. I, p. 744-756; *EI²*: s.v. 'al-Ghazzālī'; Ibn al-Qāḍī, *Jadhwa*, pp. 65–6; A. Dermeersemann, 'Le Maghrib a t'il une Marque Ghazalienne?', *Revue de l'Institut des Belles-Lettres*, vol. LXXII: 1958, pp. 109–12, and 'Ce que Ibn Khaldūn pense d'al-Ghazālī', *Revue de l'Institut des Belles-Lettres*, vol. LXXII: 1958, pp. 109–12 and 161–93; Alfred Bel, *La Religion Musulmane en Berbérie* (Paris: Librairie Orientaliste Paul Geuthner, 1938), pp. 229–30. Concerning the upheaval that surrounded Ghazālī's books in general and the *Iḥyā' ᶜulūm al-dīn* in particular, see the detailed description of Nāṣirī, *Istiqṣā*, vol. II, pp. 216–20. Note that the extent of Ghazālī's influence on Andalusian Sufism is challenged by Casewit in 'The Forgotten Mystic', p. 23, and Cornell in *Realm of the Saint*, pp. 15–29.

16 Casewit, 'The Forgotten Mystic', p. 15.

17 Qāḍī Abū Bakr b. al-ᶜArabī had studied with Ghazālī while in the East and had introduced the *Iḥyā'* to the Maghrib about eight years before the book burning. He had two disciples, Abū Yaᶜzzā al-Ḥazmīrī and ᶜAlī b. Ḥirzihim, who in turn would be the masters of one of the towering figures in Western Sufism, Abū Madyan. About Abū Bakr b. al-ᶜArabī, see *GAL*, suppl. I, p. 663; *EI²*: s.v. 'Ibn al-ᶜArabī'; *IA*: s.v. 'Ibnü'l-Arabi, Ebu Bekir'; *Nafḥ*: vol. VII, pp. 303–6: Nāṣirī, *Istiqṣā*, vol. III, in *Archives Marocaines*, vol. XXXII: 1927, pp. 59–60; Ibn al-Qāḍī, *Jadhwa*, pp. 147 *ff.*; Ben Cheneb, *Ijāza*, p. 278; Ibn Qunfudh, *Uns al-faqīr wa-ᶜizz al-ḥaqīr* (Rabat: Editions Techiniques Nord Africaines, 1965), pp. 42, 71, 93; Casewit, 'The Forgotten Mystic', pp. 29–30. See also Emile Dermenghem, *Le Culte des Saints dans l'Islam Maghrébin* (Paris: Gallimard, 1954), p. 73.

18 Abū al-Ḥasan ᶜAlī b. Ḥirzihim, commonly called Sīdī Ḥrāzim, the above-mentioned legist and Sufi who is said to have met Ghazālī when travelling in the East. Ibn Ḥirzihim was instrumental in teaching and spreading Ghazālī's works in the Maghrib; Ibn Qunfudh, *Uns*, pp. 12–3; Nāṣirī, *Istiqṣā*, vol. II, pp. 216–9 and vol. III, p. 179, pp. 184–5; *Nayl:* p. 198; Ibn al-Zayyāt, *al-Tashawwuf ilā rijāl al-taṣawwuf* (Rabat: Matbūᶜāt Ifrīqya al-Shimāliyya al-Fanniyya, 1958), pp. 71 *ff.* and pp. 147–150. See also Cornell, *Realm of the Saint*, pp. 23–26.

19 Abū al-Ḥākam ᶜAbd al-Salām al-Ishbīlī b. Barrajān, commonly called Bū al-Rijāl, was a Sevillian mystic who was executed in Marrakesh by order of the Sultan ᶜAlī b. Yūsuf; see *GAL*, vol. I, p. 434, and suppl. I, p. 775; *IA*: s.v. 'Ibn Berrecān'; Nāṣirī, *Istiqṣā*, vol. II, p. 218. See also Cornell, *Realm of the Saint*, pp. 20–21 and 25–6; and Casewit's 'The Forgotten Mystic'.

20 Aḥmad b. Muḥammad b. Mūsā b. ᶜAṭā' Allāh al-Ṣanhājī al-Mārī al-Andalūsī, known as Ibn al-ᶜArīf or Ibn al-ᶜIrrīf, a native of Tangiers, or according to some sources, Almeria. Ibn al-ᶜArīf died in Marrakesh in strange circumstances for some chroniclers say that he was poisoned by order of the Sultan ᶜAlī b. Yūsuf. In *Maḥāsin al-majālis*, his classification of the mystical stages is that of Ghazālī; see Ibn al-ᶜArīf, *Maḥāsin al-majālis*, edited and translated by Asin Palacios (Paris: Librairie Orientaliste Paul Geuthner, 1933), pp. 6–7; Paul Nwyia, 'Notes

sur Quelques Fragments Inédits de la Correspondance d'Ibn al-ʿArīf avec Ibn Barrajān', *Archives Berbères et Bulletin de L'institut des Hautes Etudes Marocaines Hespéris*, vol. XLIII: 1956, pp. 217–22. Yet, as Casewit notes, even though 'Ibn al-ʿArīf was exposed to Ghazālī's teachings early in his career...his writings are not preponderantly Ghazālian' (Casewit, 'The Forgotten Mystic', p. 65). Concerning Ibn al-ʿArīf, see *GAL*, vol I, p. 434, and suppl. I, p. 776; *IA*: s.v. 'Ibnü'l-Arif'; *Nafḥ:* vol. I, p. 344; Nāṣirī, *Istiqṣā*, vol. II, p. 218; *Nayl*, pp. 59–63; *Tashawwuf*, pp. 96 *ff.* See also Cornell, *Realm of the Saint*, pp. 19–23.

21 Casewit, 'The Forgotten Mystic', p. 36.

22 Abū al-Qāsim b. Qasī claimed to have been a disciple of Ibn al-ʿArīf, and organized a *ribāṭ* (a religious centre sometimes used for military purposes) in southern Portugal. His followers rebelled against the Almohad government and won several victories over their armies until Ibn Qasī was killed ten years after the beginning of the uprising. See *IA*: s.v. 'Ibn Kasī Ebü'l-Kasim'; Bel, 'Le Soufisme en Occident Musulman', p. 148; Cornell, *Realm of the Saint*, pp. 21–23.

23 Casewit, 'The Forgotten Mystic', p. 58.

24 As Casewit points out, 'The burning of Ghazālī's works was a crucial moment for Andalusī Sufism because it further marked out the Andalusī mystical movement's distinctive self-awareness. But an understanding of Andalusī Sufism cannot begin with Ghazālī. Ibn al-ʿArīf, Ibn Qasī, and Ibn Barrajān in the early 6th/12th century were not Ghazālī's *alter egos* but highly original thinkers who drew primarily from their local tradition in al-Andalus.' Casewit, 'The Forgotten Mystic', p. 63.

25 Al-Mahdī Abū ʿAbd Allāh Muḥammad b. Tūmart was born in a little village of the Atlas Mountains that he left in order to perfect his education in the East. Back in Morocco, he tried in vain to convince the legists that they should return to the study of the sources, that is the Qur'ān and the Sunna, rather than limit themselves to the study of the treatises of Islamic law which was, most of the time, but a means to accede to higher official positions. In 514/1520, Ibn Tūmart named himself *al-Mahdī*, or The Rightly-Guided, and preconized the doctrine of divine unity (*tawḥīd*) as a code impregnated with mystical ideas and more particularly with those of Ashʿarī and Ghazālī whom—he claims—he met while in the East. From *tawḥīd* came the name of the dynasty, al-Muwahhidūn, or Almohads ('Unitarians'). See *EI²*: s.v. 'Ibn Tumart'; *IA*: s.v. 'Ibn Tūmert'; Henri Terrasse, *Histoire du Maroc*, 5 vols. (Casablanca: Editions Atlantide, 1930), vol. IV, pp. 261–81; Rachid Bourouiba, *Ibn Tūmart* (Algiers: Societé Nationale d'Edition et de Diffusion, 1974); Vincent Cornell, 'Understanding Is the Mother of Ability: Responsibility and Action in the Doctrine of Ibn Tūmart', *Studia Islamica*, vol. LXVI: 1988, pp. 71–103. On The Almohads, see *EI²*: s.v. 'Almohades'; Nāṣirī, *Istiqṣā*, vol. III; Terrasse, *Histoire*, vol. IV; Jamil Abun-Nasr, *A History of the Maghrib in the Islamic Period* (Cambridge: Cambridge University Press, 1987), pp. 87–102; ʿAbd Allah Laroui, *L'Histoire du Maghrib*, 2 vols. (Paris: Libraire

François Maspero, 1975), vol. I, pp. 159–84; Philip Hitti, *History of the Arabs* (New York: Summit Books, 1981), pp. 546–9. 'The popularity and politicization of Ghazālī's Sufism in the mid 6th/12th century is evidenced by the fact that Ibn Tūmart would seek rally to support for his cause by appealing to Ghazālī and by masquerading as his direct disciple.' (Casewit, 'The Forgotten Mystic', p. 61)

26 Note that Casewit mentions the gap that could occur in the juridical methodolody of some state legists and the Maliki *madhhab* as such and regrets the cliché descriptions of the *madhhab* as 'pharisaical, inflexible, dry, intolerant, and monolithic' (Casewit, 'The Forgotten Mystic', pp. 3–4). See also Ibn al-ʿArīf, *Maḥāsin al-majālis*, p. 5.

27 ʿAbd al-Mu'min b. ʿAlī, also known as ʿAbd al-Mu'min al-Kūmī, was one of Ibn Tūmart's followers. After the latter's death, he appointed himself successor and reigned from 524/1130 to 558/1163; see Ibn Khaldūn, *The Muqaddimah: An Introduction to History*, 3 vols., translated by Franz Rosenthal (Princeton: Princeton University Press, 1980), vol. II, p. 472; Nāṣirī, *Istiqṣā*, vol. III, pp. 31–97; Bourouiba, *Ibn Tūmart*, pp. 37–42; Abun-Nasr, *A History*, pp. 90–95.

28 Abū Madyan Shuʿayb b. al- Ḥusayn al-Anṣārī, commonly called Sīdī Bū Madyan, is the patron saint of Tlemcen where he is buried. His mausoleum, al-ʿUbbād, is one of the most frequented places of pilgrimage. Abū Madyan was a master of both *sharīʿa* and *ḥaqīqa*, or legal and mystical matters, and is venerated as one of the greatest masters in Maghribi Sufism. See *GAL*, vol. I, p. 438, and suppl. I, p. 784; *EI*[2]: s.v. 'Abū Madyan'; *IA*: s.v. 'Ebū Medyen'; Nāṣirī, *Istiqṣā*, vol. III, pp. 184–7; Ben Cheneb, *Ijāza*, p. 350; *Nayl*, pp. 127–9; *Nafḥ*, vol. IX, p. 342; ʿAbd al-Wahhāb al-Shaʿrānī, *al-Ṭabaqāt al-kubrā*, 2 vols. (Cairo: n.p., n.d.), vol. I, pp. 122–4; as well as the many important passages devoted to Abū Madyan throughout Ibn Qunfudh, *Uns*. See also Cornell, *Realm of the Saint*, pp. 131–8 and 283–4.

29 Abū ʿAbd Allāh al-Daqqāq al-Fāsī was one of the teachers of Abū Madyan; see *IA*: s.v. 'Dekkāk Ebū Ali'; *Tashawwuf*, pp. 135 *ff.*; Ibn Qunfudh, *Uns*, p. 27; ʿAbd al-Ḥaqq al-Badīsī, '*Al-Maqṣad*, Vie des Saints du Rif', translated by G. S. Colin, in *Archives Marocaines*: 1926, p. 92; Alfred Bel, 'Sidi Bou Medyan et son maître el-Deqqaq à Fez', *Mélanges,* edited by René Basset (Paris: Leroux, 1923), pp. 31–68; Cornell, *Realm of the Saint*, pp. 29–30; Casewit, 'The Forgotten Mystic', p. 69. The 'Malāmatī' is the Sufi who follows 'the path of blame' deliberately in order to be discredited publicly and reach a state of perfect sincerity; *EI*[2]: s.v. 'Malāmatiyya'.

30 Abū Yaʿzzā Yalannūr (ʿAlannūr) al-Azmīrī, or Mūlāy Bū ʿAzza, the ascetic shepherd and Berber saint of the Atlas Mountains who is said to have been Abū Bakr b. al-ʿArabī's disciple in Fez and who had a deep influence on Abū Madyan. See Nāṣirī, *Istiqṣā*, vol. II, pp. 219–20 and vol. III, pp. 184–7; *Tashawwuf*, pp. 195–205; Dermenghem, pp. 59–68; Victor Loubignac, 'Un Saint Berbère, Moulay Bou ʿAzza, histoire et légende', *Hespéris*, vol. XXXI: 1944, pp. 15–34; Shaʿrānī, *Ṭabaqāt*, vol. I, p. 109; Cornell, *Realm of the Saint*, pp. 67–79 and pp. 279–80.

31 Mūlāy ʿAbd al-Salām b. Mashīsh al-Idrīsī was an ascetic saint who lived in Jabal al-ʿAlam where his tomb is still an object of pilgrimage and veneration; *GAL*, vol. I, p. 440, and suppl. I, p. 787; *EI*[2]: s.v. 'ʿAbd al-Salām'; *IA*: s.v. 'Abdüsselām b. Meşiş el-Haseni'; Nāṣirī, *Istiqṣā*, vol. III, pp. 245–5; A. M. Mohamed Mackeen, 'The rise of al-Shādhilī', *JAOS*: 1971, vol. XCI, pp. 479–82; M. Xicluna, 'Quelques Légendes relatives a Moulay ʿAbd al-Salām Ben Mashīsh', *Archives Marocaines*, vol. III: 1905, pp. 119–33. Concerning the actual Sufi investiture (*khirqa*), Bel states that Abū Bakr b. al-ʿArabī received the investiture at the hands of Ghazālī, and then passed it on to Abū Yaʿzzā and Ibn Ḥirzihim, who in turn initiated Abū Madyan, Ibn Mashīsh and Shādhilī. Alfred Bel, 'Le Sufisme en Occident Musulman', *Annales de l'Institut des Etudes Orientales* (Algiers: Editions Maisonneuve 1934–5), p. 146, note 2.

32 Abū al-Ḥasan al-Shādhilī, the *Quṭb al-zamān* or 'Pole of the Time', founder of the Shādhilī order, was born in Morocco, moved to Tunis and finally settled in Alexandria; see *GAL*, vol. I, p. 449, and suppl. I, p. 804; *IA*: s.v. 'Ṣâzelī'. About the Shādhiliyya order, see *EI*[2]: s.v. 'Shādhiliyya'; *IA*: s.v. 'Şazeliyye'. Ben Cheneb, *Ijāza*, p. 338; *Nayl*, p. 206; Shaʿrānī, *Ṭabaqāt*, vol. I, pp. 4–10; Mackeen, 'The Rise of the Shādhilī order', *JAOS*, vol. XCI: 1971, pp. 482–6; Cornell, *Realm of the Saint*, pp. 146–49.

33 Marinid refers to the Banū Marīn tribe founders of the dynasty that succeeded the Almohads. The Marinids established their capital in Fez and were in power from 592/1196 to 956/1549. See *EI*[2]: s.v. 'Merinids'; Nāṣirī, *Istiqṣā*, vol. IV, in *Archives Marocaines*, vol. XXXIII: 1934; Terrasse, *Histoire*, vol. V; Robert Brunshwig, *La Berbérie Orientale sous les Hafsides des Origines à la fin du XV Siècle*, 2 vols. (Paris: Adrien Maisonneuve, 1940–47), sections 3–4 ; Laroui, *L'Histoire du Maghrib*, pp. 186–206; Abun-Nasr, *A History*, pp. 103–118.

34 'Those who appear as the great ancestors of Maghribi Sufism had lived and died under the Almohads, but their spiritual descendants were multiplying.' Terrasse, *Histoire*, pp. 5 and 80. On Sufism during the Marinid Period, see Cornell, *Realm of the Saint*, pp. 125–154.

35 Abū ʿAbd Allāh Shūdhī al-Ḥalwī (d. beginning of the 7th/13th century) was a *qāḍī* in Seville at the onset of the Almohad dynasty. He was named al-Ḥalwī because he abandoned his functions, books and family in order to sell sweets to the children in the streets of Tlemcen. He was the teacher of Ibn Dahhāq al-Awsī, who is mentioned by Ibn Khaldūn in the *Shifā'*, p. 62 (see also p. 116, note 35 and p. 138, note 16). On him, see also Yaḥyā b. Khaldūn (brother of our historian), *Histoire des Beni ʿAbd al-Wād, Rois de Tlemcen*, 2 vols., translated by Alfred Bel (Algiers: Imprimerie Orientale Fontana Frères and Cie, 1911), vol. II, pp. 83–7; Ibn Maryam, *al-Bustān fī dhikr al-awliyā' wa'l-ʿulamā bi-Tilimsān*, in the summarized translation by A. Delpech in *Revue Africaine*: 1883–4, p. 391; see also Brosselard, 'Les Inscriptions Arabes de Tlemcen', *Revue Africaine*: 1860, pp. 161–74 and pp. 321–31; Dermenghem, pp. 87–95.

36 For Abū al-Ḥasan ʿAli b. ʿUthmān, see Ibn Khaldūn, *Taʿrīf*, pp. 51–2; Terrasse, *Histoire*, vol. v, pp. 51–62; Nāṣirī, *Istiqṣā*, vol. iv, pp. 189–285; and Régis Blachère, 'Quelques Details sur la Vie Privée du Sultan Merinide Abu'l-Ḥasan', *Memorial d'Henri Basset*, 2 vols. (Paris: Librairie Orientaliste Paul Geuthner, 1928), vol. i, pp. 83–8.

37 For Abū ʿInān Fāris b. ʿAlī, see Ibn Khaldūn, *Taʿrīf*, pp. 62–66; Nāṣirī, *Istiqṣā*, vol. iv, pp. 293–334.

38 Qāḍī Abū ʿAbd Allāh Muḥammad b. Aḥmad al-Fishtālī was appointed judge by Abū ʿInān and sent to Granada as an ambassador. He was one of the masters of Qabbāb who, as mentioned above, was involved in the polemic around which Ibn Khaldūn's *Shifāʾ* is written; see Ibn al-Khaṭīb, *Iḥāta*, vol. ii, pp. 187–91; *GAL*, suppl. ii, pp. 346*ff.*; Ibn al-Qāḍī, *Durrat*, vol. ii, p. 270; *Jadhwa*, pp. 146 ff; *Nayl*, p. 265; Nwyia, *Ibn ʿAbbād*, p. 51.

39 Abū al-ʿAbbās Aḥmad b. ʿUmar b. ʿĀshir al-Anwas was born in Jimena (Spain), lived in Algeciras before he left to perform the pilgrimage to Mecca, and finally settled in Salé, where he was recognized by all as one of the greatest saints and teachers. Among his disciples was Ibn ʿAbbād al-Rundi. See *IA*: s.v. 'Ibn Aşir'; *Nafḥ*, vol. ix, p. 195; Ibn al-Qāḍī, *Durrat*, vol. i, pp. 148–9; *Jadhwa*, pp. 78 ff; *Nayl*, pp. 70–1; Ibn Qunfudh, *Uns*, pp. 7–10 and 79; Ben Cheneb, *Ijāza*, p. 188; Nāṣirī, *Istiqṣā*, vol. iv, pp. 323–4; Cornell, *Realm of the Saint*, pp. 142–44.

40 Let us mention in passing that Sufism in North Africa is often split into two separate trends, namely an intellectual urban elitist spiritualism on one side, and a folkloric rural popular maraboutism on the other. Such dichotomies seem artificial, as Cornell cogently demonstrates in *Realm of the Saint*, pp. xxv–xxviii, 3–32 and 32–63.

41 Ibn Marzūq, *al-Musnad al-ṣaḥīḥ al-ḥasan fī maʾāthir wa-maḥāsin mawlānā Abī al-Ḥasan*, translated into Spanish by Maria Viguera (Madrid: Instituto Hispano Arabe de Cultura, 1977), pp. 337–40.

42 Abū al-ʿAbbās Aḥmad b. ʿAlī b. al-Khaṭīb b. Qunfudh al-Qusṭanṭīnī (d. 810/1407) was a Sufi from the school of Abū Maydan. Interestingly, among his teachers were Ibn al-Khaṭīb (Ibn Khaldūn's friend), Qabbāb and Ibn ʿAbbād who answered the question underlying Ibn Khaldūn's *Shifāʾ*, and Abū Zayd ʿAbd al-Raḥmān al-Lujāʾī, fourth disciple of Ibn al-Bannā who was himself the teacher of Ābilī (Ibn Khaldūn's teacher). See *IA*: s.v. 'Ibn Kunfuz'.

43 The most important *ṭāʾifa*s were the following: the Shuʿaybiyyūn in Azzamur, followers of Abū Shuʿayb, patron Saint of Azzamur (d. 560/1165) and one of the masters of Abū Yaʿzzā; the Ṣanhājiyyūn, followers of the Banū Amghar, whose *zāwiya* was located near Tit; the Mājiriyyūn, followers of Abū Muḥammad Ṣāliḥ (d. 631/1233); the Aghmatiyyūn (or Ḥazmīriyya), disciples of the venerated saint Abū Zayd ʿAbd al-Raḥmān al-Ḥamzīrī (d. 706/1307); and the Hāhiyyūn in the High Atlas Mountains, followers of Abū Zakariyyā Yaḥyā al-Hāhī. For some more detailed information concerning these *ṭāʾifa*s, see Ibn Qunfudh, *Uns*, pp. 63–6;

Badīsī, *Maqṣad*, in Colin's translation, pp. 207–8; Spencer Trimingham, *The Sufi Orders in Islam* (Oxford: Oxford University Press, 1971), pp. 50–1; Nwyia, *Ibn ʿAbbād*, p. xxv; Edouard Michaux-Bellaire, 'Les Confréries Religieuses au Maroc', *Archives Marocaines*, vol. XXVII: 1927, pp. 17–55; Mackeen, 'The Early History of Sufism in the Maghrib prior to al-Shadhili', *JAOS*, vol. XCI: 1971, pp. 398–408 and 'The Rise of al-Shadhili', pp. 477–86; Terrasse, *Histoire*, vol. v, pp. 80–4; Cornell, *Realm of the Saint*, pp. 44–45, 61–62 and 139–145.

44 For the Shādhilī order, see Mackeen, 'The Rise of al-Shādhilī', p. 486; Eric Geoffroy, *Le Soufisme en Egypte et en Syrie* (Damas: Institut Français d'Etudes Arabes de Damas, IFEAD, 1995), pp. 207–8; Cornell, *Realm of the Saint*, pp. 144–154.

45 Tāj al-dīn Ibn ʿAtā'Allāh al-Iskandarī was the third Shaykh of the Shādhilī order. He lived in Egypt and his *Ḥikam* had an immense influence on the Moroccan mystics; on him see Victor Danner in Ibn ʿAṭā'illāh, *Ṣūfī Aphorisms* (*Kitāb al-Ḥikam*), translated by Victor Danner (Leiden: E. J. Brill, 1984); Paul Nwyia, *Ibn ʿAbbād*, p. LVIII and *Ibn ʿAtā'Allāh et la Naissance de la Confrérie Shadhilite* (Beirut: Dār al-Mashriq, 1972); *GAL*, vol. II, p. 117, and suppl. II, p. 145; *EI*[2]: s.v. 'Ibn ʿAtā'Allāh'; *IA*: s.v. 'Ibn Atāullah el-Iskenderi'; Ibn al-Qāḍī, *Durrat*, vol. I, p. 12; *Dībāj*, vol. I, p. 242; Ben Cheneb, *Ijāza*, p. 341; Shaʿrānī, *Ṭabaqāt*, vol. II, p. 17.

46 Ibn ʿAbbād's thirteenth letter is headed as follows: 'A letter explaining a saying of my master Abū al-Ḥasan al-Shādhilī'; see *Letters on the Sūfī Path*, p. 176. Cornell examines the question of Ibn ʿAbbād's connection with the Shādhiliyya in *Realm of the Saint*, pp. 153–4.

47 'The majority of the doctors of the Law at the time, if not themselves affiliated, was at least favourable to Sufism, and it could be said without exaggeration that a wave of mysticism washed over the intellectual milieus of the Maghrib. A. Bel correctly points to the fact that scholars believed their training was insufficient if they had not followed the teachings of a Sufi Shaykh. This is why we see the rising, in the Maghrib, this new type of *fuqahā'*, described in the works of Ghazālī as people who joined to legal science (*ʿilm al-ẓāhir*) a theoretical knowledge, or even an internal experience, of mysticism (*ʿilm al-bāṭin*)'; Nwyia, *Ibn ʿAbbād*, p. XLII.

48 The Ayyubid dynasty that ruled Egypt from 564/1169 to 648/1250 was founded by Ṣalāḥ al-Dīn al-Ayyūbī, the first leader who was able to unite the Arabs against the Crusaders; see C. E. Bosworth, *The Islamic Dynasties* (Edimburgh: Edimburgh University Press, 1981), pp. 61–2; *EI*[2]: s.v. 'Aiyubids'; Aḥmad Taqī al-Dīn al-Maqrīzī, *al-Mawāʿiz wa'l-iʿtibār fī dhikr al-khiṭaṭ wa'l-āthār* (Baghdad: n.p., n.d.), vol. II, pp. 232–6.

49 The Mamluks were originally the professional slave guards of the Ayyubid sultans and were mainly Kurds, Circassians and Turks; their dynasty divides into two important lines: the Bahrī Mamluks, who ruled from 648/1250 to 784/1382 and the Burjī Mamluks, who ruled from 784/1382 to 922/1517. The Mamluks were able to protect Egypt from the Mongol invasions that had devastated the other Arab kingdoms; see Bosworth, *The Islamic Dynasties*, pp. 63–67; *EI*[2]: s.v.

'Mamluks'; Hitti, *History*, pp. 665–705; Maqrīzī, *Khiṭaṭ*, vol. II, pp. 241–4.

50 For Abū al-Fayḍ Thawbān b. Ibrāhīm Dhū'l-Nūn al-Miṣrī, the celebrated Sufi of Nubian descent who lived in Cairo, see *GAL*, vol. I, p. 198, vol. II, p. 82, and suppl. I, p. 353; *SEI*: s.v. 'Dhū'l-Nūn'; *IA*: s.v. 'Zünnūn el-Mısrī'; Shaʿrānī, *Ṭabaqāt*, vol. I, p. 54; ʿAlī Hujwirī, *Kashf al-Maḥjūb*, translated by R. A. Nicholson (Lahore: Luzac and co., 1976).

51 Abū Fityān Aḥmad al-Badawī, the venerated Egyptian saint of Maghribi background, settled down in Egypt and was the founder of the *ṭarīqa* Badawiyya or Aḥmadiyya. See *GAL*, vol. I, p. 450, and suppl. I, p. 808; *SEI*: s.v. 'Aḥmad al-Badawi'; *IA*: s.v. 'Bedeviyye'; Shaʿrānī, *Ṭabaqāt*, vol. I, pp. 145–9.

52 Ibrāhīm al-Dasūqī (or Dusūqī or Disūqī), native of Dusūq, a village in lower Egypt, was the founder of the Dasūqī order of dervishes. See *SEI*: s.v. 'Dasūkī'; *IA*: s.v. 'Desūkī, Ibrāhīm b. Abdülaziz'; Shaʿrānī, *Ṭabaqāt*, vol. I, pp. 131–45.

53 Abū al-ʿAbbās al-Mursī was the successor of Shādhilī as the head of the Shādhiliyya order; see *Nafḥ*, vol. II, p. 389; Shaʿrānī, *Ṭabaqāt*, vol. II, pp. 10–16.

54 Jamāl al-Dīn Yūsuf b. Taghribirdī, *al-Nujūm al-zāhira fī mulūk Miṣr wa'l-Qāhira*, 16 vols. (Cairo: al-Hayʿa al-Miṣriyya al-ʿĀmma li'l-Kitāb, 1972), vol. XVI, p. 146.

55 *Khanaqa* is a Persian word, originally a compound: *khān* (from *khandan*), meaning 'remembrance of God' (*dhikr*), and *qah*, meaning 'place'.

56 'Since the old days of their masters, the Ayyubid rulers, the members of this Turkish dynasty in Egypt and Syria, have been erecting colleges (*madāris*) for the teaching of the sciences and monastic houses (*khawāniq*) for the purpose of enabling the Sufis (*fuqarā'*) to follow the rules for acquiring orthodox Sufi ways of behaviour (*adab al-ṣūfiyya al-sunniyya*) through remembrance of God and supererogatory prayers. They took over that custom from the preceding caliphal dynasties. They set up buildings (those institutions that are mortmain gifts) and endowed them with lands that yielded income sufficient to provide stipends for students and Sufi ascetics. Their example was imitated by men of wealth and high rank under their control. As a result, colleges and monastic houses are numerous in Cairo. They now furnish livings for poor jurists and Sufis. This is one of the good and permanent deeds of this Turkish dynasty.' Ibn Khaldūn, *Taʿrīf*, p. 279.

57 Abū Muḥammad b. ʿAbd Allāh b. Baṭṭūṭa, the famed traveller of the Middle Ages, was born in Tangiers. He journeyed all over the Muslim world and related his travels and adventures in the *Riḥla*. On Ibn Baṭṭūṭa, see *EI²*: s.v. 'Ibn Batuttah'. Quote in Ibn Baṭṭūṭa, *Riḥla* (Beirut: Dār Ṣādir li'l-Ṭibāʿa, 1960), pp. 37–9.

58 Shihāb al-Dīn Aḥmad al-Qalqashandī was an Egyptian historian whose *Subḥ al-aʿshā* is a manual devoted to all the holders of official governmental position. See *GAL*, vol. II, p. 134, and suppl. II, p. 164. Quote as found in Trimingham, *The Sufi Orders*, p. 19.

III. Sufism in the Life of Ibn Khaldūn

59 Eric Chaumont, 'Notes et Remarques autour d'un texte de la Muqaddima', *SI*, vol. CVIV: 1986, p. 152.

60 For extended detailed references on the different interpretations of Ibn Khaldūn's works, consult Ahmed Abdesselem, *Ibn Khaldūn et ses Lecteurs* (Paris: Presses Universitaires de France: 1983).

61 Ibid., p. 52.

62 Sir Hamilton Gibb, 'The Islamic Background of Ibn Khaldūn's Political Theory', *Bulletin of the School of Oriental Studies*, vol. VII: 1933–5, p. 28.

63 The theoretical ambitions of Wardi are already stated in the very title of his book, *The Social Logic of Ibn Khaldūn*, as critically assessed by Abdesselem in *Ibn Khaldūn et ses Lecteurs*, p. 96.

64 Baali and Wardi, *Ibn Khaldūn and Islamic Thought-Styles: A Social Perspective* (Boston: G.K. Hall & co, 1981), p. 49.

65 Yves Lacoste, *Ibn Khaldoun, Naissance de l'Histoire, Passé du Tiers Monde* (Paris: Maspero, 1985).

66 Gibb—while recognising the interest in the precision of Ibn Khaldūn's description, analysis and interpretation of the political, social and economic realities of the Arab Muslim world—says, 'Ibn Khaldūn was not only a Muslim, but as almost every page of the *Muqaddimah* bears witness, a Muslim jurist and theologian, of the strict Maliki school. For him religion was far and away the most important thing in life—we have seen that he expressly calls his study a thing of subsidiary value—and the shariʿa the only true guide; this means not just that Ibn Khaldūn was careful to safeguard himself in his arguments from the suspicion of unorthodoxy, but that he did not and could not introduce into his system anything that was logically incompatible with the Islamic standpoint...The ethical and Islamic basis of Ibn Khaldūn's thought is implicit throughout his exposition, quite apart from his constant appeal to texts from Quran and Tradition. His doctrine of causality and natural law is simply that of the *sunnat Allāh* so often appealed to in the Quran.' See Gibb, 'The Islamic Background of Ibn Khaldūn's Political Theory', p. 28. Far from pretending to give an exhaustive list, since the bibliography on Ibn Khaldūn is plethoric, I will mention only some example of sources that try to analyse the historian's thought in context: Hayden V. White, 'Ibn Khaldūn in World Philosophy of History: Review Article', *Comparative Studies in Society and History* (Cambridge: Cambridge University Press, 1959), vol. II, p. 1; Briton Cooper Busch, 'Divine Intervention in the "Muqaddimah" of Ibn Khaldūn', *History of Religions* (Chicago: Chicago University Press, 1968), vol. VII, p. 4; ʿAbd al-Madjīd Māziyān, *al Naẓariyya al-iqtiṣādiyya ʿinda Ibn Khaldūn wa-usūsuha min al-fikr al-Islāmī wa'l-wāqiʿ al-mujtamaʿī* (Algeria: Manshurāt al-Ikhtilāf, 2002); Aziz al-Azmeh, *Ibn Khaldūn in Modern Scholarship: A Study in Orientalism* (London: Thirld World Center for Research and Publication, 1981)

and *Ibn Khaldūn: An Essay in Reinterpretation* (London: Frank Cass, 1982); Johann Meuleman, 'La Causalité dans la "Muqaddimah" d'Ibn Khaldūn', *SI*, vol. LXXIV: 1991, pp. 105–142. See also Michel Chodkiewicz in the following book reviews: 'Ibn Khaldūn in Modern Scholarship', *SI*, vol. LXI: 1985, pp. 199–201; 'Ibn Khaldun and Islamic Ideology; Ibn Khaldūn, an Essay in Reinterpretation', *SI*, vol. LXII: 1985, pp. 173–5; his review of René Pérez, 'Ibn Khaldūn, La Voie et la Loi', *SI*, vol. LXXVII: 1993, p. 194, and Chaumont, 'Notes et Remarques', p. 37.

67 For Abū ʿAbd Allāh Muḥammad b. al-Ḥusayn al-Qurayshī al-Zubaydī, see Ibn Khaldūn, *Taʿrīf*, pp. 14–15; *Nafḥ*, vol. VII, p. 163; Ibn Baṭṭūṭa, *Riḥla*, p. 15. Concerning the religious orders in the city of Tunis, see Robert Brunschwig, *La Berbérie Orientale sous les Hafsides des Origines à la Fin du XV Siècle* (Paris: Adrien Maisonneuve, 1940–47), pp. 335–49.

68 Ibn Khaldūn, *Taʿrīf*, pp. 15–6. For further details on Ibn Khaldūn's early education and teachers, see Ibn Khaldūn, *Taʿrīf*, pp. 14–49.

69 See Muhsin Mahdī, *Ibn Khaldūn's Philosophy of History* (Chicago: The University of Chicago Press, 1964), p. 27.

70 For Abū ʿAbd Allāh Muḥammad b. Ibrāhīm al-Ābilī, see Ibn Khaldūn, *Taʿrīf*, pp. 33 *ff.*; Ibn al-Qāḍī, *Durrat*, vol. II, p. 265; *Jadhwa*, pp. 144 and 191 *ff.*; *Nayl*, pp. 245 *ff.*; Ibn Ḥajar al-ʿAsqalānī, *al-Durar al-kāmina fī aʿyān al-māʾa al-thāmina*, 6 vols. (Cairo: Dār al-Kutub al-Ḥadīth, 1966), vol. III, p. 375; Ibn Maryam, *Bustān*, pp. 246–53; Yaḥyā b. Khaldūn, *Histoire des Beni ʿAbd al-Wād*, vol. II, pp. 71–2; Nassif Nassar, 'Le Maître d'Ibn Khaldoun: Al-Ābilī', *SI*, vol. XX: 1965, pp. 103–14.

71 Ibn Khaldūn, *Lubāb al-muḥassal*, as cited in Nassar, 'Le Maître d'Ibn Khaldoun', p. 107.

72 Ibn Khaldūn, *Taʿrīf*, p. 37.

73 Abū ʿAlī al-Ḥusayn b. Sīnā was an eminent Persian physician, metaphysician and mystic whose philosophy combined Aristotelian and Neo-Platonic influences with Muslim theology. On him, see *GAL*, vol. I, p. 452, and suppl. I, p. 812; *EI²*: s.v. 'Ibn Sina'; *IA*: 'Ibn Sīnā'. Reference in Ibn Khaldūn, *Taʿrīf*, pp. 62–3.

74 Abū al-ʿAbbās Aḥmad b. al-Bannā was a renowned mathematician, theologian and mystic who had a deep influence on the eighth/fourteenth century Sufis, himself the disciple of shaykh Abū Zayd ʿAbd al-Raḥmān al-Ḥazmīrī, founder of the Ḥazmīriyya Sufi order; see *GAL*, suppl. II, p. 359; *EI²*: s.v. 'Ibn al-Bannā'; *IA*: s.v. 'Ibnü'l-Bennā el-Merrākūşī'; Ibn al-Qāḍī, *Jadhwa*, pp. 73 *ff.*; *Nayl*, pp. 65–8; Nwyia, *Ibn ʿAbbād*, pp. XLIII–XLIV; and Henri Renaud, 'Ibn al-Bannā de Marrakesh, Sufi et Mathématicien', *Hespéris*, vol. XXV: 1938, pp. 13–42.

75 Concerning Ābilī's Sufism, see Nwyia, *Ibn ʿAbbād*, XLIII–XLIV; Mahdi, *Ibn Khaldūn*, p. 35.

76 Abū Abd Allāh al-Maqqarī, theologian and Sufi of the eighth/fourteenth century, was an ancestor of the author of *Nafḥ al-ṭīb* and a teacher of Ibn al-Khaṭīb, Ibn ʿAbbād and Ibn Khaldūn. See *GAL*, vol. II, p. 296, and suppl. II, p. 407; Ibn al-Khaṭīb, *Iḥāta*, vol. II, pp. 191–226; Bel, *La Religion*, pp. 329–30. See also

Ignacio Saadé, *El Pensamiento Religioso de Ibn Jaldun* (Madrid: Imprenta de Aldecoa, 1974), p. 4. If one confronts the dates of Ibn ʿAbbād's life in Fez with those of his contemporary Ibn Khaldūn's visits to Fez, besides the fact that they had a common master, it is more than probable that the two men should have met.

77 Nwyia, *Ibn ʿAbbād*, p. XLII.

78 Al-Ḥārith b. Asad al-Muḥāsibī, (d. 243/857) was an Iraqi Sufi author of *Kitāb al-riʿāya li-ḥuqūq Allāh*. On him, see *GAL*, suppl. I, p. 351; *EI*²: s.v. 'al-Muhāsibī'; *IA*: s.v. 'Muhāsibī'. The story of Ibn ʿAshīr and Abū ʿInān is a well known episode related by many biographers, such as Maqqarī, *Nafḥ*, vol. IX, p. 195; Nāṣirī, *Istiqṣā*, vol. IV, pp. 323–4; Shaʿrānī, *Ṭabaqāt*, vol. I, p. 58.

79 Muḥammad b. Aḥmad al-Sharīf al-Tilimsānī, a student of Ābilī's and a brilliant legist 'through whom a Sunnite orthodoxy was to be restored and the Almohad heresy erased'; Bel, *La Religion*, p. 303; see also Nwyia, *Ibn ʿAbbād*, p. XXII. Note that Ibn ʿAbbād was not only a student of Ābilī but also of al-Sharīf al-Tilimsānī and al-Maqqarī. As to Maqqarī, he was one of the teachers of Ibn al-Khaṭīb and Ibn Khaldūn.

80 As cited in Bel, *La Religion*, pp. 322–9; see also Nwyia, *Ibn Abbād*, pp. XXVI–XXVII.

81 'The great pedagogical experience of al-Ābilī showed him some of the flaws in some methods that were particularly harmful to the transmission of knowledge. His disciples present to us four very interesting ideas: the proliferation of books is harmful to the presentation of sciences; the recourse to books only does not suffice for the acquisition of science, and one must travel, meet teachers and study under their direction; abstracts can only constitute a veil to real knowledge and therefore students must abandon these abstracts and look for knowledge at its source. Ibn Khaldūn obviously benefited from these pieces of advice in his studies, teaching, and writing. In the sixth part of the *Muqaddima*, he develops ideas that are exactly similar, and stresses the necessity of looking for a master of progress methodically in the studies, and on going beyond the difficulties that come along when numerous manuals and obscure abstracts are used.' Nassif Nassar, 'Le Maître d'Ibn Khaldoun', *SI*, vol. XVII: 1965, p.113.

82 Ibid., p. 112.

83 '...[Al-Maqqarī] whom all his contemporaries including the vizier of Granada Ibn al-Khaṭīb, or the historian Ibn Khaldūn..., present to us as one of the "luminaries" of Malikite *fiqh*, Qur'anic exegesis, ḥadīth and dogmatics. Yet, his knowledge of mysticism was far from being inferior to his knowledge of other sciences, and we saw he was explicitly affiliated to Sufism through an *isnād* going back to Junayd. Ibn al-Khaṭīb, who was his disciple, says he liked to talk about *taṣawwuf* and write books on this subject.' Bel, *La Religion*, p. 329; see also Nwyia, *Ibn ʿAbbād*, p. XIV.

84 ʿAbd Allāh al-Anṣārī al-Harawī (of Herat) was a contemporary of Ghazālī. Many commentaries and translations of his *Manāzil al-sā'irīn* are available. I consulted *Abdallāh al-Anṣārī al-Harawī, Les Etapes des Itinérants vers Dieu*, translated by

Laugier de Beaurecueil (Cairo: Institut Français d'Archéologie Orientale, IFAO, 1962), pp. 15–21. On Harawī, see *GAL*, suppl. II, p. 753; *EI*²: s.v. 'Herevi'; *IA:* s.v. 'Herevī, Hāce Abdullah'; Ben Cheneb, *Ijāza*, p. 41; Shaʿrānī, *Ṭabaqāt*, vol. I, p. 52. Quote as translated in Ibn Khaldūn, *Muqaddima*, vol. III, p. 98.

85 Ibid., vol. III, p. 99.

86 On *tawḥīd*, see also *Muqaddima*, vol. III, pp. 39 *ff.*

87 Nāṣirī, *Istiqṣā*, vol. IV, pp. 343–69, and especially pp. 369–79.

88 Ibn Khaldūn, *Taʿrīf*, p. 135.

89 Ibid., p. 149.

90 Ibid., p. 120.

91 Ibrāhīm b. al-Adham al-Balkhī was a prince of Balkh who left his kingdom and became a wandering ascetic. See *SEI*: s.v. 'Ibrāhīm b. Adham'; *IA*: s.v. 'Ibrāhīm b. Edhem'; Abū ʿAbd al-Raḥmān al-Sulamī, *Ṭabaqāt al-ṣūfiyya* (Cairo: Dār al-Kitāb al-ʿArabī, 1953), pp. 27–38.

92 Ibn Khaldūn, *Taʿrīf*, p. 125; Mahdi's translation in *Ibn Khaldūn*, p. 46.

93 Ibn Khaldūn, *Taʿrīf*, pp. 102–3, 134–5 and 226–7.

94 Even Lacoste, one of the most adamant Marxist interpreters, acknowledges Ibn Khaldūn's inward spiritual search: 'Ibn Khaldūn's decision to abandon political life cannot only be explained by a personal situation that has become delicate. Ibn Khaldūn seems to have deeper reasons. He seems to have been thinking about this withdrawal for a long time. He has already retired twice to the convent of al-ʿUbbād, but was forced to give up its quietude in the face of the imperative solicitations of the king of Tlemcen. For many years, the moments Ibn Khaldūn devotes to studying and meditating are more and more frequent; he becomes more and more impatient towards the interruptions political life imposed on his research. Therefore, it is more a fully thought-out decision rather than a compulsion that provides the explanation for his retreat.' Lacoste, *Ibn Khaldoun*, p. 77.

95 Ibn Khaldūn, *Taʿrīf*, pp. 311–3.

96 Saʿīd al-Suʿadā' was the name of a house confiscated from Qanbar, an enfranchised eunuch in one of the Fatimid palaces. Qanbar was put to death in 544/1173. Maqrīzī, *Khiṭaṭ*, vol. II, pp. 415–6.

97 Ibn Khaldūn, *Taʿrīf*, p. 279; see also *Muqaddima*, vol. II, p. 435.

98 Ibn Khaldūn, *Taʿrīf*, p. 121.

99 Trimingham, *The Sufi Orders*, p. 18.

100 Ibn al-Furāt, *al-Sulūk*, as cited in Ibn Khaldūn, *Taʿrīf*, p. 313.

101 Al-Ẓāhir Sayf al-Dīn Barqūq reigned from 783/1382 to 791/1389 and again from 792/1390 to 801/1399; see Ibn Khaldūn, *Taʿrīf*, p. 249; Maqrīzī, *Khiṭaṭ*, vol. II, p. 241, and *Kitāb al-sulūk li-maʿrifat duwal al-mulūk* (Cairo: Matbaʿat Dār al-Kutub, 1970), vol. III.

102 Ibn al-Furāt, *Tārīkh*, as cited in Ibn Khaldūn, *Taʿrīf*, p. 313, note 1.

103 Ibn Khaldūn, *Taʿrīf*, p. 314.

104 Shams al-Dīn al-Sakhāwī, *al-Ḍaw' al-lāmiʿ li-ahl al-qarn al-tāsiʿ*, 12 vols. (Beirut:

Dār Maktabat al-Ḥayāt, 1966), vol. IV, p. 146; Ibn al-ᶜImād, *Shadharāt al-dhahab fī akhbār man dhahab*, 8 vols. (Beirut: al-Maktab al-Tijārī li'l-Tibāᶜa wa'l-Nashr wa'l-Tawzīᶜ, n.d.), vol. VII, p. 77; *Nayl*, p. 170.

IV. The *Shifā'*, a Manuscript on Sufism

105 According to Muhsin Mahdi, this discretion concerning his early writings and training is deliberate, but 'must not prevent us from seeking to explore this subject; for he gives us enough hints to make us suspect that this reticence is intentional and that the problem is of major significance'. Mahdi, *Ibn Khaldūn*, p. 29.

106 Ibn Khaldūn, *Taᶜrīf*, pp. 62–3. Mahdī explains: 'In his peculiar style, Ibn Khaldūn tells us the reason why he could not mention what he was studying with al-Ābilī directly: even the powerful and highly respected judge of Tunis had to go to his home and be alone with his teacher when reading such works.' Mahdi, *Ibn Khaldūn*, p. 35, note 2.

107 'The times in which the author lived were not such that a man of the world, a man who loved life for its glamour and adventure, could propound his theories if these savored of heresy. Did not Ghazālī, an equally comprehensive thinker but a more courageous thinker, had to observe a certain caution in this regard?...Ghazālī had the courage to withdraw from an honorable position, but Ibn Khaldūn had no such intention. He was not of the stuff martyrs are made of!' Miya Syrier, 'Ibn Khaldūn and Islamic Mysticism', *Islamic Culture*, vol. XXI: 1947, p. 267.

108 Ṭanjī's postulated date for authorship of the *Shifā'* is 774–776/1373–1375.

109 Ṭanjī, *Shifā'*, p. 'k'. For Abderrahmane Lakhsassi, Ibn Khaldūn 'did not breathe a word about this text [the *Shifā'*] (which is a real contribution to Islamic mysticism) in his autobiography. Both those who are surprised about his silence about these works as well as those who deny his authorship for the same reason often forget that an autobiography is necessarily subjective, and is not a biography. Whether the latter tries to be objective, the former looks mainly to the self as the author would like others to perceive him. Ibn Khaldūn probably wanted to be known only for his work on history, and, for him, nothing more is worth mentioning in his autobiography, which, as a matter of fact, is deliberately linked, in the form of an appendix, to the *Kitāb al-ᶜIbar*.' Abderrahmane Lakhsassi, 'Ibn Khaldūn', in *History of Islamic Philosophy*, edited by Seyyed Hossein Nasr and Oliver Leaman (London and New York: Routledge, 2001), p. 353.

110 For Abū al-Alī al-Ḥasan b. Masᶜūd al-Yūsī, see *GAL*, vol. II, p. 455, and suppl. II, p. 675. According to Muṭīᶜ al-Ḥāfiẓ, Yūsī died in 1102/1691; see Ibn Khaldūn, *Shifā' al-sā'il li-tahdhib al-masā'il*, edited by Muḥammad Muṭīᶜ al-Ḥāfiẓ (Damascus: Dār al-Fikr al-Muᶜāṣir, 1997), p. 207. Yūsī wrote a letter on the question of the need for a Shaykh. Ibid., pp. 209-14.

111 Ṭanjī, *Shifā'*, p. 'y, h'.

112 Ibid.

113 Abū al-Ḥasan al-Shushtarī al-Numayrī al-Fāsī (d. 668/1269) was a student of

Ibn Sabʿīn; see *GAL*, vol. I, p. 274, and suppl. I, p. 483; *EI²*: s.v. 'al-Shushtarī'; Maqqarī, *Nafḥ*, vol. II, p. 483; *Nayl*, pp. 202–3.

114 Zarrūq, *Qawāʿid*, pp. 39–40; reference to *ʿIddat al-murīd* and to *al-Naṣīḥa al-kāfiya* as found in Ṭanjī, *Shifā'*, p. 'y, h'.

115 Zarrūq, *Naṣīḥa*, p. 61.

116 Reference in Ṭanjī, *Shifā*, p. 'y, w'. The commentator of Zarrūq's *Naṣīḥa* is Abū ʿAbd Allāh b. Abd al-Raḥmān b. Zikrī al-Fāsī (d. 1114/1704); on him, see Nāṣirī, *Istiqṣā*, vol. IV, p. 380.

117 As found in Fāsī, 'Qissat makhṭūṭ', pp. 570–1.

118 As found in Fāsī, 'Qissat makhṭūṭ', p. 571. See *Shifā'*, p. 68.

119 As found in Fāsī, 'Qissat makhṭūṭ', p. 571. See *Shifā'*, p. 62.

120 For Abū Abbās Aḥmad b. Yūsuf al-Fāsī, see *GAL*, suppl. II, p. 701.

121 In his poem entitled *al-Rā'iyya fī al-sulūk*, Muḥammad b. Aḥmad al-Sharīshī describes the relation between shaykh and disciple. On him, see *GAL*, suppl. I, p. 802.

122 As found in Ṭanjī, *Shifā'*, p. 'y, z' *ff*.

123 Ibn ʿAjība, *Īqāẓ al-himam*, p. 147.

124 Ṭanjī, *Shifā'*, p. 'y, z' *ff*.

125 ʿAbd al-Raḥmān Badawī, *Mu'allafāt Ibn Khaldūn* (Cairo: Mu'allafāt Ibn Khaldūn, 1962), p. 24, and Ṭanjī, *Shifā'*, p. 'ḍ'. Let me mention in passing here that, according to Khalifé, Ibn Khaldūn must have written his treatise between the years 787/1385 and 800/1398, because he shows more tolerance and sympathy towards Sufism in the *Muqaddima* than in the *Shifā'*, which according to Khalīfé is a sign of old age. Many commentators based themselves on Khalifé's edition and adopted the dates suggested by him. However, this date is cancelled by the above argument, namely the date 779/1377 marking the death of Qabbāb, who could not have taken part in the debate posthumously. ʿAbd al-Raḥmān Badawī also compares the *Shifā'* to the sixth chapter of the *Muqaddima*, 'On Sufism', and marks—like Khalifé—a definite change in Ibn Khaldūn's stance towards Sufism. Badawī believes the author shows a more positive and mature understanding of Sufism in the *Muqaddima*, which was completed in 779/1377, and so concludes that the *Shifā'* must have been written before that time. Badawī's conclusion is definitely accurate as far as the date is concerned. Yet, it seems to me that, although possible, it is not too likely that this change could have taken place so swiftly, over the couple of years that separate the second visit to Fez in 774–776/1372–1374 (the most logical postulate for the writing of the *Shifā'*) and the completion of the *Muqaddima*. Furthermore, the accretions to the *Muqaddima* concerned precisely this very sixth chapter, the chapter 'On Sufism', and were added towards the end of the historian's life, when Ibn Khaldūn was living in Cairo, indeed an older man and perhaps a more indulgent author. Besides, if it is true that Ibn Khaldūn shows more tolerance in the *Muqaddima*, he does indeed show more partiality and less 'historic objectivity' in the *Shifā'* wherein he gives away his sympathy

towards Sufism, or at least some of its endeavours. The *Muqaddima* is a historical work, whereas the *Shifā'*, although it betokens Ibn Khaldūn's historical mind, is nevertheless a treatise on mysticism that betrays the man's acceptance as well as his reservation with regards to the science of Sufism. See Ibn Khaldūn, *Shifā' us-sā'il litehzīb-il-masā'il, Apaisement a Qui Cherche Comment Clarifier les Problèmes*, edited by Ignace Khalifé (Beirut: al-Matbaᶜa al-Katūlikiyya, 1959), p. 9, note 2, and Badawī, *Mu'allafāt*, pp. 21–4. See also Fadlou Shehadi, 'Theism, Mysticism and Scientific History in Ibn Khaldūn', *Islamic Theology and Philosophy*, edited by Michael A. Marmura (Albany: State University of New York Press, 1984), p. 326, and the article on Ibn Khaldūn in *EI²*: s.v. 'Ibn Khaldūn'.

126 Ṭanjī, *Shifā'*, p. 'ḍ, b'.

127 Ibid., p. 'ḍ, n'.

128 Ṭanjī, who was able to study Ms.C, tells us it is 61 pages long. It is filled with mistakes, and many words and sentences are missing; its main interest lies in the fact that the order of the pages is not disturbed; Ṭanjī, p. 'ḍ, n'.

129 Ibid., p. 'ḍ, n'.

130 Badawi, *Mu'allafāt*, p. 15. There is at least one other edition which was not consulted in this study: *Shifā' al-sā'il li-tahdhib al-masā'il* by Muḥammad Muṭīᶜ al-Ḥāfiẓ (Dār al-Fikr al-Muᶜāṣir, 1997).

131 See Mahdi, 'The Book and the Master as Poles of Cultural Change in Islam', in *Islamic and Cultural Change in the Middle Ages*, edited by Speros Bryonis (Wiesbaden: University of California Los Angeles, 1975), p. 3.

132 *Muqaddima*, vol. III, p. 342.

133 *Muqaddima,* vol. III, p. 281.

v. Ibn Khaldūn's Understanding of Sufism

134 *Shifā'*, p. 11.

135 For ᶜAli b. Aḥmad Abū al-Ḥasan al-Būshanjī, (d. 348/959), see *IA*: s.v 'Būşenci'.

136 Lacoste, *Ibn Khaldoun*, p. 241.

137 'There would be a problem for Ibn Khaldūn if his commitment to the scientific study of the history of culture were part of a commitment to approach all problems of knowledge in the same way. Another way of putting this: If what is sometimes called his positivism in history were part of a general positivist theory of knowledge, then it would be difficult to understand how he can also subscribe to a Sufi theory of knowledge. The two would clearly be incompatible. But there is no evidence for this general positivism. On the contrary, the evidence is for a hierarchical theory of knowledge in which different ways of knowing are fitted in, the scientific-rational, the mystical and the prophetic.' Shehadi, 'Theism, Mysticism and Scientific History', p. 270.

138 As Shehadi comments, 'The concern for Ibn Khaldūn's case is imported from the experience with Western positivism and other endorsements of the scientific way. In the Western tradition, positivism has been offered as a

complete but restrictive theory of knowledge. And where positivism is not theoretically explicit, the rise of empirical science in the West has provided such a winning model of inquiry that scientific searchers became at least psychologically disinclined to have any commerce with, or even take seriously, claims based on other than scientific evidence. But this could hardly have been the cultural climate for Ibn Khaldūn. In Ibn Khaldūn's thought, the logical compatibility between scientific inquiry in one area and intuitive inquiry in another is reinforced by the cultural expectation that a place be found for the evidential-rational as well as for the supra-rational intuitive and revelatory.' Ibid. See also Chodkiewicz, 'Ibn Khaldūn and Islamic Ideology; Ibn Khaldūn an Essay in Reinterpretation', pp. 61–62.

139 He says '...those who claim that the essences, properties and distant causes of all beings, sensible as well as those that are beyond the senses, can be perceived by theoretical investigation (*al-anẓār al-fikriyya*) and rational syllogisms (*al-aqyisa al-ʿaqliyya*). They claim that the dogmas of faith are to be established by rational investigation and not through hearing (transmission), since they are among the things to be perceived by reason...They claim that happiness lies in the comprehension of all beings, sensible and those that are beyond the senses, through his investigation and those logical demonstrations...together with the expurgation of the soul and its embellishment with virtues. This they claim is possible for man in accordance with his reason, speculation and disposition toward praiseworthy acts, and abstention from the reproachable, even if no Law is revealed to distinguish between virtuous and vicious acts. They claim that when the soul acquires this happiness, it acquires joy and pleasure, and that ignorance of that happiness is eternal misery. This, according to them, is the meaning of felicity and torment in the world to come.' As translated by Rosenthal in *The Muqaddimah*, vol. III, pp. 246–7. (I quoted Mahdi's translation, *Ibn Khaldūn*, pp. 110–1.)

140 Ibid., vol. II, p. 436 (Mahdi's translation, p. 74).

141 'The intellect, indeed, is a correct scale. Its indications are completely certain and in no way wrong. However, the intellect should not be used to weigh such matters as the oneness of God, the other world, the truth of prophecy, the real character of the divine attributes, or anything else that lies beyond the level of the intellect. That would mean to desire the impossible... [The fact that this is impossible] does not prove that the indications of the scale are not true [when it is used for its proper purpose].' Ibid., vol. III, p. 38.

142 'Even in the circles in which a truce had been signed between the two parties, as was the case during the Marinid era, the Sufis were convinced that he who dedicated himself to *ʿilm al-ẓāhir* would become irremediably impermeable to *ʿilm al-bāṭin*, and incapable of opening his heart to the lights of *taṣawwuf*.' Nwyia, *Ibn ʿAbbād*, p. 248. Besides, the legists were criticized for being extremely corrupt and greedy, often immersed in canonical disputes and uninterested in providing

people with normative legal guidance. They were held responsible for provoking this breach between the Law and the Path.

143 Shehadi, 'Theism, Mysticism and Scientific Theory', 266. In an unpublished conference, 'Religion and Philosophy in Ibn Khaldūn's critique of Sufism' at the International Conference on Islamic Intellectual History (Harvard University, May 1988), James W. Morris reads criticism and irony into Ibn Khaldūn's analysis of Sufism. Personally, I did fail to see sarcasm behind each of Ibn Khaldūn's words. I saw but a selective apprehension of Sufism, a disapproval of the 'later-trend Sufis' and of their ultimate endeavour labelled 'struggle for unveiling' (rather than Sufism as a whole). For political reasons perhaps or because of the author's juridical background as mentioned above? One could, of course, argue that this last struggle for unveiling represents the core and goal of mystical realization. However, this seems to have been the limit set by Ibn Khaldūn in his approval of and insight into Sufism.

144 *Muqaddima*, vol. III, p. 101.

145 'The legist's viewpoint is not limited to this world as such because it is a worldly point of view but for other reasons related to his position.' *Shifā'*, p. 13.

146 *Shifā'*, ibid. Chaumont, 'Notes et Remarques', p. 156.

147 *Shifā'*, p. 15.

148 Ibn ʿAjība, *Īqādh al-himam,* p. 5. The statement of Mālik is widely quoted, but numerous authorities have done so without providing a chain of transmission for it from Mālik; see Gibrīl Fouād Ḥaddād, *The Four Imams and their Schools* (n.l.: Muslim Academic Trust, n.d.), pp. 179–180.

149 Nwyia, *Ibn ʿAbbād*, p. 229.

150 Wansharīsī, *Miʿyār*, as found in Ṭanjī, *Shifā'*, p. 127.

151 Ṭanjī, *Shifā'*, p. 128.

152 Ibid., p. 132. ʿAbd al-Karīm al-Jīlī tells us that his master, Shaykh Sharaf al-Dīn Ismaʿīl al-Jabartī (d. 805/1403), had forbidden his disciples to read Ibn ʿArabī's works because a disciple will comprehend the content of a book only if he has reached the level of knowledge of the writer. Otherwise, the disciple will misunderstand the author's words, waste his time and even try to put into practice what he reads at the peril of his life. 'I have tried to make you understand how lofty and valuable this knowledge [of God] is, so that you aspire to acquire it through reading, practising and learning its books with masters, wherever they are. The accomplished master will be more beneficial to you than all the books you could read throughout your lifetime. Indeed, you will grasp from the books that which you can comprehend, whereas the accomplished gnostic, if he wishes you to understand a matter as it is in its reality, will impart to you his own knowledge of it, and what a gap there is between his understanding and yours! Reading books with the realised sages (*muḥaqqiqqīn*) is better than the deeds of the wayfarers (*aʿmāl al-sālikīn*). Being in the presence of the people of Allah (*mujālasat ahl Allāh*) after whom you model your conduct (*ta'addub*) is

better than all the books in the world.' Abd al-Karīm al-Jīlī, *Marātib al-wujūd wa-ḥaqīqat kull mawjūd*, in *al-Kahf wa'l-raqīm*, edited by ʿĀṣim Ibrahīm al-Kayyālī (Lebanon: n.p., 2008), pp. 37–40.

153 Ibn ʿAbbād, *Letters on the Sufi Path*, pp. 184–94.

154 Ibid., p. 185.

155 Ibid., p. 186.

156 In an interesting article, Laury Silvers-Alario demonstrates that in early Sufism no distinction was made between the *shaykh al-taʿlīm* and the *shaykh al-tarbiya* (translated by her as 'lecturer' vs. 'director' or 'teaching shaykh' vs. 'shaykh of spiritual direction'). Laury Silvers-Alario, 'The Teaching Relationship in Early Sufism: A Reassessment of Fritz Meier's Definition of the *shaykh al-tarbiya* and the *shaykh al-taʿlim*', *The Muslim World*, vol. XCIII: 2003, p. 93.

157 *Shifā'*, p. 71.

158 ʿUmar b. Muḥammad Shihāb al-Din al-Suhrawardī was the official 'Shaykh of the Shaykhs' (*shaykh al-shuyūkh*) in Baghdad and left us the *ʿAwārif al-maʿārif*, one of the most popular books on Sufism. See *GAL*, vol. I, p. 440, and suppl. I, p. 778; *EI*[2]: s.v. 'Suhrawardi'.

159 See also *Iḥyā'*, vol. III, pp. 61 and 64; Zarrūq, *Qawāʿid al-taṣawwuf*, p. 40; Ibn al-Khaṭīb, *Rawḍat al-taʿrīf bi'l-ḥubb al-sharīf* (Cairo: Dār al-Fikr al-ʿArabī, 1968), pp. 448–53.

160 *Shifā'*, p. 76.

161 Najm al-Din Razi, *The Path of God's Bondsmen, from Origin to Return*, translated by Hamid Algar (New Jersey: Islamic Publications International, 1982), pp. 235–42. See also Emir Abd el-Kader *Écrits Spirituels*, translated by Michel Chodkiewicz (Paris: Editions du Seuil, 1982), pp. 60–1.

162 See *SEI*: s.v. 'Uwaysiyya'; *IA*: s.v. 'Üveys el-Karanī' and 'Üveysilik'; *Shifā'*, p. 109.

163 'Love' is a notion that is quasi absent in the *Shifā'*. Note also that Ibn Khaldūn refers to the 'love of God' (as in *Shifā'*, p. 43), rather than the feeling of love towards the *wasīla* or the means to God, namely the Prophet or one of his heirs, i.e. the spiritual master. Ibn Khaldūn only mentions once in passing that the wayfarer should love his master; see *Shifā'*, p. 92. See also Pérez, p. 275, note. 99.

164 Jalāl al-Dīn al-Rūmi, *Mathnawī of Jalālu'ddin Rūmī*, 3 vols. edited and translated by Reynold A. Nicholson (London: Luzac and co., 1977), vol. I, p. 10.

165 Chodkiewicz, 'Ibn Khaldūn, La Voie et la Loi', p. 196.

166 Personal communication of Victor Danner, May 1989.

Prologue

1 Abū Ḥāmid al-Ghazālī, *Iḥyā' ʿulūm al-dīn*, 5 vols. (Beirut: n.p., n.d.) and al-Ḥārith b. Asad Muḥāsibī, *al-Riʿāya li-ḥuqūq Allāh* (Cairo: Dār al-Kutub al-Ḥadith, 1970).

2 Note that *maṭlaʿ* is sometimes read as *muṭṭalaʿ*.

3 I chose to translate *abdāl* as 'saints' rather than 'Substitutes' in this context.

Chapter One

1 Bukhārī, *al-Ṣaḥīḥ* (Leiden: E. J. Brill, 1962–8), 'ʿIlm', p. 39. Note that Ibn Khaldūn did not quote the beginning of the *ḥadīth*, 'The lawful is clear and the unlawful is clear' (*al-ḥalāl bayyin wa'l-ḥarām bayyin*). See also Abū Zakariyyā Yaḥyā al-Nawawī, *Riyāḍ al-ṣāliḥīn* (Beirut: Dār Iḥyā' al-Turāth al-ʿArabī, 1399/1979), p. 204.

2 Ghazālī, *Iḥyā'*, vol. IV, p. 308; Murtaḍā al-Zabīdī, *Kitāb itḥāf al-sāda al-muttaqīn bi-sharḥ asrār Iḥyā' ʿulūm al-dīn li'l-Ghazālī*, 10 vols. (Cairo: Matbaʿat al-Muyammaniyya, 1984), vol. IX, p. 572.

3 Ghazālī, *Iḥyā'*, vol. III, p. 46. Ṭanjī references this tradition to Tirmidhī and Aḥmad; Ṭanjī, *Shifā'*, p. 6.

4 Ghazālī, *Iḥyā'*, vol. III, p. 46; Abū Nuʿaym al-Iṣfahānī, *Ḥilyat al-awliyā' wa-ṭabaqāt al-aṣfiyā'*, 10 vols. (Cairo: Matbaʿat al-Saʿāda, 1971), vol. IX, p. 38. Ṭanjī references this tradition to Bukhārī; Ṭanjī, *Shifā'*, p. 7.

5 Ghazālī, *Iḥyā'*, vol. III, p. 46. Ṭanjī references a similar tradition to Aḥmad; Ṭanjī, *Shifā'*, p. 7.

6 '*Ṣuwarikum*' or 'your external aspect' in Ms.A, p. 3; '*ajsāmikum*' or 'your bodies' in Abū Nuʿaym, *Ḥilya*, vol. VII, p. 46, and Nawawī, *Riyāḍ*, p. 9; '*aʿmālikum*' or 'your deeds' in Ms.B, 8; '*amwālikum*' or 'your riches' in Ibn Māja, *al-Sunan* (Cairo: al-Matbaʿa al-ʿIlmiyya, 1313 AH), vol. II, p. 278.

7 Reference to the Qur'ānic verse, '*Is he whose breast God has expanded unto Islam, so he walks in a light from his Lord (like one who disbelieves)?*' (Q.XXXIX.22).

8 ʿUmar b. al-Khaṭṭāb (d. 35/656); on him, see Abū Nuʿaym, *Ḥilya*, vol. I, pp. 38–55; Ahmad al-Khazrajī, *Khulāṣat tadhhib al-kamāl fī asmā' al-rijāl*, 3 vols. (Cairo: al-Matbaʿa al-Khayriyya, 1904), vol. II, p. 268; Ibn al-Jawzī, *Tārīkh ʿUmar b. al-Khaṭṭāb* (Damascus: Dār Iḥyā' ʿUlūm al-Dīn, n.d.).

9 Ḥudhayfa b. al-Yamān (d. 36/656); on him, see Abū Nuʿaym, *Ḥilya*, vol. I, pp. 270–83; Khazrajī, *Khulāṣa*, vol. I, p. 201; Ibn Ḥajar al-ʿAsqalāni, *al-Iṣāba fī tamyīz al-ṣaḥāba*, 4 vols. (Cairo: al-Maktaba al-Tijāriyya al-Kubrā, 1939), vol. I, p. 306.

10 Ghazālī, *Iḥyā'*, vol. I, p. 78; Zabīdī: vol. I, p. 430.

11 Ibn Māja, *Sunan*, vol. II, p. 289.

12 Bukhārī, *Ṣaḥīḥ*, '*waḥy*', p. 1; Nawawī, *Riyāḍ*, p. 7.

13 Muḥammad al-Tirmidhī, *al-Jāmiʿal-mukhtaṣar min al-sunan*, 4 vols. (Cairo: n.p., 1875), '*fitan*', p. 72; Ibn Ḥanbal, *al-Musnad* (Cairo: Muḥammad al-Zuhrī al-Gharnāwī, 1896), pp. 290-1.

14 The Muʿtazila was a school of speculative theology that was most active between the years 105–131/723–48; *SEI*: s.v. 'al-Muʿtazila'; *Muqaddima*, vol. III, pp. 35–75.

15 The Rāfiḍīs 'was a general abusive name for people considered as Shiʿites'; J. H. Kramers in *SEI*: s.v. 'Rāfidites'; *SEI*: s.v. 'Shīʿa'; *Muqaddima*, vol. II, pp. 156–200.

16 The Khārijīs were partisans of ʿAlī b. Abī Ṭālib, who dissented when the latter accepted the arbitrage that gave Muʿāwiya the caliphate. They relied mainly on the use of violence and insurrections; see *SEI*: s.v. 'Khāridjites'.

17 Sunnis or Followers of the Sunna has 'become the characteristic term for the theory and practice of the catholic Muhammadan community...and those who refrain from deviating from dogma and practice. The expression is particularly used in this sense in opposition to Shīʿa'. A. J. Wensinck, *SEI*: s.v. 'Sunna'.
18 Abū al-Qāsim al-Qushayrī, *al-Risāla* (Cairo: n.p., 1900), pp. 4–5.
19 Note a probable mistake in Ms.A, p. 4, and Ms.B, p. 9, which read 'afʿāl al-jawāriḥ' rather than 'afʿāl al-qulūb'. See Ṭanjī, *Shifā'*, p. 11, note 1.
20 See Ghazālī's discussion on commendable versus reprehensible knowledge. Ghazālī, *Iḥyā'*, vol. i, pp. 13–6; Zabīdī, vol. i, pp. 148–54.
21 For Abū al-ʿAbbās b. ʿAtā' (d. 311/923), see Sulamī, *Ṭabaqāt*, pp. 225 *ff.*
22 Ghazālī, *Iḥyā'*, vol. i, pp. 79–80; Zabīdī, vol. i, pp. 148–54.
23 'Al-tawajjuh bi'l-qalb', in Ms.A, p. 5, and Ms.B, p. 10; and 'al-tawḥīd bi'l-qalb', in Ṭanjī, *Shifā'*, p. 12.
24 Ghazālī, *Iḥyā'*, vol. i, p. 161; Zabīdī, vol. iii, p. 116. Ṭanjī references this tradition to Abū Dāwūd; Ṭanjī, *Shifā'*, p. 12.
25 Tirmidhī, *Sunan*, 'qiyāma', p. 60; Ibn Ḥanbal, *Musnad*, vol. ii, p. 152; Abū Nuʿaym, *Ḥilya*, vol. vi, p. 352, and vol. viii, p. 264; Nawawī, *Riyāḍ*, p. 205.
26 Zabīdī, vol. i, p. 159; Nawawī, *Riyāḍ*, p. 206; Ibn Māja, *Sunan*, vol. ii, p. 287.
27 Ghazālī, *Iḥyā'*, vol. i, p. 160.
28 Ibn Māja, *Sunan*, 'fitan' p. 1; Ibn Ḥanbal, *Musnad*, vol. iv, p. 207; Zabīdī, vol. i, p. 155; Nawawī, *Riyāḍ*, p. 142.
29 Bukhāri, *Ṣaḥiḥ*, 'shahādat', p. 27; Abū al-Ḥusayn Muslim, *al-Ṣaḥīḥ* (Cairo: n.p., 1374/1955), 'ʿaqīda', p. 4.
30 'Wa-ḥikman ʿalayhim min ḥaythu ẓāhiri aʿmālihim', Ms.A, p. 6. This sentence is missing in Ṭanjī, *Shifā'*, p. 14.
31 This group derives its name from *bāṭin* or 'inward'. 'The term means those who seek the inward or spiritual meaning of the Qur'an'; see *SEI*: s.v. 'Bātiniya'; and *IA*: s.v. 'Bātiniyye'.
32 On the importance of religious education, see *Muqaddima*, vol. ii, pp. 257–61.
33 Ibn Ḥanbal, *Musnad*, vol. ii, pp. 480 and 935; Ibn ʿArabī, *al-Futuḥāt al-Makkiyya*, 4 vols. (Beirut: Dār Ṣādir, n.d.), vol. i, p. 284.
34 Bukhārī, *Ṣaḥiḥ*, 'ṣawm', p. 6; 'buyūʿ', p. 49; Muslim, *Ṣaḥīḥ,* 'fitan', p. 8; Tirmidhī, *Sunan,* 'fitan', p. 10.
35 When translating the Qur'ān, the translation of A. J. Arberry has been adhered to in the vast majority of occasions, with only occasional deviation from it.
36 For Abū al-Qāsim b. Muḥammad al-Junayd (d. 297/909), see Qushayrī, p. 31; Sulamī, *Ṭabaqāt*, pp. 155–6; EI^2: s.v. 'al-Junayd'. Quote in Qushayrī, p. 217.
37 Qushayrī, p. 217.
38 Ibid.
39 Tirmidhī, *Sunan*, 'daʿawāt', p. 79.
40 Bukhārī, *Ṣaḥīḥ*, 'riqāq', p. 3; Abū Nuʿaym, *Ḥilya*, vol. iii, p. 301; Nawawī, *Riyāḍ*, p. 168.

41 Ibn al-Jawzī, *Talbīs Iblīs* (Cairo: Matbaʿat al-Manār, 1928), p. 187.
42 'Ahl al-Ṣuffa' was a name given to a group of Emigrants (*muhājirūn*) who settled in Medina with the Prophet; see *SEI*: s.v. 'Ahl al-Ṣuffa'.
43 Abd al-Raḥmān b. Ṣakhr is known as Abū Hurayra or 'the father of the little cat' (d. 57–8/676–8). See *SEI*: s.v. 'Abū Hureyra'; Abū Nuʿaym, *Ḥilya*, vol. I, pp. 376–385; Khazrajī, *Khulāṣa*, p. 397; Ibn al-Jawzī, *Ṣifāt al-ṣafwa*, 4 vols. (India: Matbaʿat Dā'irat al-Maʿārif, 1968), vol. I, p. 38.
44 For Abū Dharr al-Ghifārī (d. 32/652), see Abū Nuʿaym, *Ḥilya*, vol. I, pp. 156–170; *Ṣifāt al-ṣafwa*, vol. I, p. 38.
45 For Bilāl b. Ribāḥ al-Ḥabashī (d. 30/640), see *SEI*: s.v. 'Bilāl'; Abū Nuʿaym, *Ḥilya*, vol. I, pp. 147–51; Ibn Saʿd, *al-Ṭabaqāt al-kubrā*, 8 vols. (Beirut: Dār Ṣādir, 1958), vol. II, pp. 358–387; Khazrajī, *Khulāṣa*, p. 148.
46 For Ṣuhayb b. Sinān b. Mālik al-Rūmī (d. 38/658), see Abū Nuʿaym, *Ḥilyā*, vol. I, pp. 151–6; Khazrajī, *Khulāṣa*, p. 148.
47 For Salmān al-Fārisī (d. 36/651), see *SEI*: s.v. 'Salmān al-Fārisī'; Abū Nuʿaym, *Ḥilyā*, vol. I, pp. 185–208; *Ṣifāt al-ṣafwa*, vol. I, p. 210; Khazrajī, *Khulāṣa*, p. 125.
48 Abū Nuʿaym, *Ḥilya*, vol. I, pp. 337–386.
49 On the Emigrants, see *SEI*: s.v. 'Muhādjirūn'.
50 Muḥammad b. Ismāʿīl al-Bukhārī (d. 256/870), author of the *Ṣaḥīḥ*, one of the most authoritative compilations of *ḥadīth*s, or traditions of the Prophet; on him, see *SEI*: s.v. 'al-Bukhārī'.
51 Bukhārī, *Ṣaḥīḥ*, 'al-Riqāq', p. 96; Tirmidhī, *Sunan*, 'qiyāmat', p. 36; Abū Nuʿaym, *Ḥilya*, vol. I, p. 377.
52 Qushayrī, pp. 216–7. See also Shihāb al-Dīn al-Suhrawardī, *ʿAwārif al-maʿārif*, vol. V, in Ghazālī, *Iḥyā'*, pp. 64 *ff.*
53 Qushayrī, pp. 216–7.
54 Ibid.

Chapter Two

1 See Ghazālī, *Iḥyā'*, vol. III, pp. 2–48: chapter 'On the meaning of the spirit (*rūḥ*), the soul (*nafs*), the intellect (*ʿaql*) and the heart (*qalb*)'.
2 Tirmidhī, *Sunan*, 'qadar', p. 5; Muslim, *Ṣaḥīḥ*, 'qadar', pp. 23 and 46.
3 Ismāʿīl b. Muḥammad al- ʿAjlūnī, *Kashf al-khafā' wa-muzīl al-ilbās ʿammā ishtahara min al-aḥādīth ʿalā alsinat al-nās*, 2 vols (Beirut: Dār al-Kutub al-ʿIlmiyya, 1988), vol. I, p. 216. Ṭanjī references a similar tradition to Muslim, in which it is said, 'O My slaves, it is only your actions that I count for you, and then reward for you.' Ṭanjī, *Shifā'*, p. 21.
4 ʿAbd Allāh b. ʿAbbās (d. 68/687) was one of the Companions of the Prophet; see *Iṣāba*, vol. II, pp. 322–6; *IA*: s.v. 'Abdullah b. Abbas'.
5 Here I did not use the translation by Arthur Arberry, *The Koran Interpreted* (London: George Allen and Unwin Ltd., 1964): 'I have not created jinn and mankind except to serve Me'; I have used Marmaduke Pickthall's, *The Meaning*

of the Glorious Koran (New York/Toronto: Alfred A. Knopf, 1992). Pickthall translated the verb *yaʿbudūn* as 'worship' rather than the verb 'serve', as in Arberry. The reference to his explanation of the Qur'ānic verse is found in Qushayrī, p. 6.

6 In popular Sufi cosmology, there are three worlds: *al-Jabarūt* ('the world of absolute Immensity or Sovereignty, or Domination, which is that of the Spirit', and the 'highest'), *al-Malakūt* ('the World of the Realm or the Dominion; the psychic world', and the 'intermediate' of the three worlds) and *al-Mulk* ('the World of the Kingdom; the physical world of existence', and the 'lowest'). See the notes of Victor Danner in Ibn ʿAṭā'illāh, *Ṣūfī Aphorisms*, p. 71.

7 Bukhārī, *Ṣaḥīḥ*, 'taʿbīr', p. 4.

8 Ibn Ḥanbal, *Musnad*, vol. II, pp. 219 and 232–3.

9 Bukhārī, *Ṣaḥīḥ*, 'waḥy', p. 3; Muslim, *Ṣaḥīḥ*, 'īmān', p. 202.

10 Ghazālī, *Iḥyā'*, vol. III, p. 22.

11 'Aflātūn wa-huwa kabīr al-ḥukamā' wa-kabīr al-mutaṣṣawwifa', in Ms.A, p. 10, and Ms.B, p. 83; and 'wa-huwa kabīr al-mutaṣawwifa al-aqdamīn', in Ṭanjī, *Shifā'*, p. 24.

12 This verse is translated by Arberry as, '*O believers, if you fear God, He will assign you a salvation.*' I chose to quote Pickthall's translation here.

13 Tirmidhī, *Sunan*, 'daʿawāt', p. 82; see also Ghazālī, *Iḥyā'*, vol. III, p. 24.

14 Ghazālī, *Iḥyā'*, vol. I, p. 71; Zabīdī, vol. I, p. 403; Abū Nuʿaym, *Ḥilya*, vol. x, p. 15. Ṭanjī notes that Abū Nuʿaym declared the tradition to be 'weak' (*ḍaʿīf*), and ʿIrāqī did likewise; Ṭanjī, *Shifā'*, p. 25.

15 Zabīdī, vol. x, p. 45; Abū Nuʿaym, *Ḥilya*, vol. x, p. 15. Ṭanjī notes that Ibn al-Jawzī included this tradition in his *Mawḍūʿāt* [Ḥadīth Forgeries]; Ṭanjī, *Shifā'*, p. 25.

16 Abū Nuʿaym, *Ḥilya*, vol. x, pp. 281–2; *Ṣifāt al-ṣafwa*, vol. II, p. 239. Ṭanjī notes that Tirmidhī narrated this tradition and declared it to be 'fair' (*ḥasan*); Ṭanjī, *Shifā'*, p. 25.

17 Ghazālī, *Iḥyā'*, vol. III, p. 24; Ibn al-Jawzī, *Tārīkh ʿUmar*, p. 34. Ṭanjī notes that Bukhārī narrated this tradition; Ṭanjī, *Shifā'*, p. 26.

18 For Abū Yazīd Tayfūr al-Bisṭāmī (d. 260/874), see *SEI*: s.v. 'al-Bistāmī'; Louis Massignon, *Essai sur les Origines du Lexique Technique de la Mystique Musulmane* (Paris: Librairie Philosophique J. Vrin, 1954), pp. 273–90. Quote in Ghazālī, *Iḥyā'*, vol. III, p. 24.

19 For Abū Bakr al-Ṣiddīq (d. 13/634), see *SEI*: s.v. 'Abū Bakr'; Abū Nuʿaym, *Ḥilya*, vol. I, pp. 28–38. When Abū Bakr told his daughter ʿĀ'isha that her heirs will be her two brothers, they were not born yet and ʿĀ'isha had only one sister at the time. Ms.A, p. 11, and Ms.B, p. 84, only quote part of the tradition. Ghazālī, *Iḥyā'*, vol. III, p. 24–5

20 Sāriya b. ʿAbd Allāh al-Kannānī (d. 30/650–51) was leading the Muslim army in Persia and was warned by ʿUmar b. al-Khaṭṭāb, who was in Medina, that the enemy was coming down towards the army from behind the mountains. *IA*: s.v.

'Sāriye b. Zuneym'; quote in Ghazālī, *Iḥyā'*, vol. III, p. 25; Zabīdī, vol. VII, p. 260.

21 Ghazālī, *Iḥyā'*, vol. IV, pp. 296–7.

22 Ibid., pp. 207 *ff.*

23 Zabīdī: vol. IX, pp. 572–3.

24 Ghazālī, *Iḥyā'*, vol. IV, p. 309; Zabīdī, vol. IX, p. 574. Ṭanjī notes that Bukhārī and Muslim, amongst others, narrate this tradition; Ṭanjī, *Shifā'*, p. 27.

25 Ghazālī, *Iḥyā'*, vol. IV, pp. 312 *ff.*

26 Ibid.

27 Ibid., vol. IV, p. 314. Ṭanjī notes a similar tradition narrated by Muslim: 'Every slave will be raised in the state he died upon'; Ṭanjī, *Shifā'*, p. 29.

28 Ghazālī, *Iḥyā'*, vol. IV, p. 313; *Ṣifāt al-ṣafwa*, vol. I, p. 88. Ṭanjī notes that ʿAlī Qārī cited this tradition in his *Mawḍūʿāt*; Ṭanjī, *Shifā'*, p. 29.

29 Ghazālī, *Iḥyā'*, vol. IV, p. 313; Zabīdī, vol. IX, p. 582; *Ṣifāt al-ṣafwa*, vol. IV, p. 16. Ṭanjī notes that ʿIrāqī mentioned that this is not established as a *ḥadīth*, but is known as a statement of Bakr b. ʿAbd Allāh al-Muzanī; Ṭanjī, *Shifā'*, p. 29.

30 For Abū ʿAbd Allāh al-Thawrī (d. 161/777), see Abū Nu ʿaym, *Ḥilya*, vol. VI, pp. 387–93.

31 For Rābiʿa bint Ismāʿīl al-ʿAdawiyya (d. 185/801), see *SEI*: s.v. 'Rābiʿa al-ʿAdawiyya'; *Ṣifāt al-ṣafwa*, vol. IV, p. 17; ʿAbd al-Raḥmān Badawī, *Rābiʿa al-ʿAdawiyya* (Kuwait: Wakālat al-Matbūʿāt, 1978); Massignon, *Lexique*, pp. 215–9; Margaret Smith, *Rābiʿa the Mystic and her Fellow-Saints in Islam* (Cambridge: Cambridge University Press, 1928); Jean Annestay, *Une femme Soufie en Islam—Rabiʿa al-ʿAdawiyya* (Paris: Entrelacs, 2009) .

32 Ghazālī, *Iḥyā'*, vol. III, p. 310.

33 Ibid., p. 313.

34 'Wa'l-ḥikāyāt ʿanhum fī hādhā'l-bāb kathīra', in Ms.A, p. 12; sentence missing in Ms.B, p. 13, and in Ṭanjī, *Shifā'*, p. 29.

35 Qushayrī, p. 67.

36 Ibid.

37 Zabīdī, vol. IX, p. 674.

38 For Bahlūl, see *Ṣifāt al-ṣafwa*, vol. II, p. 290; *IA*: s.v. 'Behlūl'.

39 Qushayrī, p. 67; Zabīdī, vol. II, pp. 72–3. There is a similar tradition narrated by Muslim in which the Prophet (may God bless him and grant him peace) said, 'His veil is light'—'or fire'—'If He was to remove it, the sublimity of His Face would burn whatever He would glance at from His creation.' For the Arabic text, and an alternative translation, see Abū al-Ḥusayn Muslim, *English Translation of Ṣaḥīḥ Muslim*, translated by Nāṣiruddīn, al-Khaṭṭāb (Riyadh: Darussalam Publications, 2007), vol. I, p. 286.

40 Qushayrī, p. 69.

41 Ibid., p. 68.

42 For Abū ʿAlī Ḥasan al-Jūzajānī or al-Jawzajānī (4th/10th century), see Abū Nuʿaym, *Ḥilya*, vol. X, p. 350. Quote in Qushayrī, p. 161.

43 Ibn ʿArabī, 'Risālat al-anwār', in *Rasā'il* (Beirut: Iḥyā' al-Turāth al-ʿArabī, 1968), p. 4.
44 Ibid.
45 'Intahā kalāmuhu.' Ms.A, p. 14 and Ms.B, p. 16; this sentence is missing in Ṭanjī, *Shifā'*, p. 33

Chapter Three

1 Qushayrī, quoting Ibn ʿAtā'Allāh al-Iskandarī, p. 88.
2 Ibn Ḥanbal, *Musnad*, vol. IV, p. 287, p. 217; Nawawī, *Riyāḍ*, p. 204. A famous tradition with very similar wording is found narrated by Bukhārī and Muslim, and is *ḥadīth* number 6 in Nawawī's famous *Arbaʿūn* [*Forty Ḥadīth*].
3 Bukhārī, *Ṣaḥīḥ*, 'buyūʿ', p. 3; Ibn Ḥanbal, *Musnad*, vol. II, p. 152; Nawawī, *Riyāḍ*, p. 205.
4 For ʿAbd Allāh b. ʿUmar b. al-Khaṭṭāb (d. 72/691) see Abū Nuʿaym, *Ḥilya*, vol. II, p. 7; *Iṣāba*, vol. III, p. 135, and vol. II, pp. 338–341; *Ṣifāt al-ṣafwa*, vol. I, p. 228; Ghazālī, *Iḥyā'*, vol. I, p. 19. First quote in *Hilyā*, vol. VIII, p. 264; second quote in Zarrūq, *Qawāʿid al-taṣawwuf*, p. 23.
5 Qushayrī, p. 90.
6 Ms.A, p. 15, and Ms.B, p. 17, read 'Qirā'at umm al-Qur'ān'; the mistake is corrected in Ṭanjī, *Shifā'*, p. 35: 'Qirā'at fātiḥat al-Qur'ān.'
7 Qushayrī, p. 160. Ibn Māja, *Sunan*, vol. I, p. 61.
8 Qushayrī, p. 161.
9 Ibid.; Abū Nuʿaym, *Ḥilya*, vol. IV, p. 350; Ghazālī, *Iḥyā'*, vol. III, p. 64.
10 For ʿĀ'isha bint Abī Bakr (d. 58/678), see *SEI*: s.v. 'Aisha'; Ibn Saʿd, *Ṭabaqāt*, vol. II, p. 374; Tāj al-Dīn al-Subkī, *Ṭabaqāt al-Shāfiʿiyya al-kubrā*, 10 vols (Cairo: Matbaʿat ʿĪsā al-Bābī al-Ḥalabī, 1964–76), vol. I, pp. 166–7. The reference for the tradition is in Muslim, *Ṣaḥīḥ*, 'musāfirīn', p. 139; Zabīdī, vol. VII, p. 92.
11 Ghazālī, *Iḥyā'*, vol. III, p. 55; Zabīdī, vol. VII, p. 92. A similar tradition is narrated by Mālik, except the word *ḥusn* is used instead of *makārim*, with no substantial change to the meaning; see http://www.sunnah.com/malik/47 (last accessed 25 October 2016).
12 Qushayrī, p. 157. In the translation, I have used the words 'will' and 'willer' (instead of 'wayfarer') to try to reflect the etymological links between the Arabic words *irāda* and *murīd*.
13 Ibid.
14 Muslim, *Ṣaḥīḥ*, 'nikāḥ', p. 271; Nawawī, *Riyāḍ*, p. 62.
15 Zabīdī, vol. IX, p. 41; *Ṣifāt al-ṣafwa*, vol. I, p. 79.
16 ʿAjlūnī, *Kashf al-khafā'*, vol. II, p. 52; Ibn Māja, *Sunan*, vol. II, p. 290. See a similarly worded tradition in Bukhārī; http://sunnah.com/bukhari/81/53 (last accessed 29 October 2016).
17 Ibn Māja, *Sunan*, vol. II, p. 290.
18 Ms.B, p. 21, reads 'wa-huwa ikhmād al-ṣifāt al-bashariyya wa-khalʿ al-ṣifāt

al-badaniyya bi-manzilat mā yaqaʿu li'l-badan bi'l-mawt.' Ms.A, p. 16, reads 'wa-huwa maḥu al-ṣifāt al-bashariyya wa-taʿaṭṭul al-qiwā al-badaniyya bi'l-riyāḍa wa'l-mujāhada hatta yaḥṣilu li'l-rūh mā yaqaʿu baʿda'l-mawt.' I opted for the latter.

19 For Abū Muḥammad b. Ḥusayn al-Jarīrī (d. 311/923), see Qushayrī, p. 39; Sulamī, *Ṭabaqāt*, pp. 259–64; *Ṣifāt al-ṣafwa*, vol. II, p. 252. Quote in Qushayrī, p. 40.

20 For Abū Bakr Muḥammad b. Mūsā al-Wāṣiṭī (d. 120/932), see Qushayrī, p. 40; Sulamī, *Ṭabaqāt*, pp. 320 *ff.* Quote in Qushayrī, p. 161.

21 Ghazālī, *Iḥyā'*, vol. III, p. 76; Zabīdī, vol. VII, p. 371.

22 Statement by Sahl al-Tustarī found in Qushayrī, p. 129.

23 Ghazālī, *Iḥyā'*, vol. III, p. 176; Zabīdī, vol. VII, p. 371.

24 Ibid.

25 ʿAjlūnī, *Kashf al-khafā'*, vol. II, p. 291. Ṭanjī notes that ʿAlī al-Qārī cited this tradition in his *Mawḍūʿāt*; Ṭanjī, *Shifā'*, p. 42.

26 For Abū Bakr al-Shiblī (d. 334/945), see Qushayrī, p. 43; *Ṣifāt al-ṣafwa*, vol. II, p. 258; Sulamī, *Ṭabaqāt*, pp. 337–48.

27 For Abū al-Ḥasan ʿAlī b. Ibrāhīm al-Ḥuṣarī (d. 371/982), see Qushayrī, p. 51. Quote in Ghazālī, *Iḥyā'*, vol. III, p. 77; Zabīdī, vol. VII, p. 374.

28 Qushayrī, p. 51.

29 Qushayrī, p. 51.

30 Ghazālī, *Iḥyā'*, vol. III, pp. 77–9; Zabīdī, vol. VII, pp. 375 *ff.*

31 Qushayrī, pp. 79–80.

32 Zabīdī, vol. VIII, p. 508; Abū Nuʿaym, *Ḥilya*, vol. I, p. 149. Ṭanjī refers this tradition to Muslim; Ṭanjī, *Shifā'*, p. 46.

33 Qushayrī, p. 91.

34 Ghazālī, *Iḥyā'*, vol. IV, p. 311.

35 Ibid.

36 Qushayrī, p. 217.

37 Muḥammad b. ʿAlī al-Qassāb Abū Jaʿfar al-Baghdādī (d. 275/888) was al-Junayd's shaykh; see Sulamī, *Ṭabaqāt*, p. 155. Quote in Qushayrī, p. 217.

38 Qushayrī, p. 217.

39 For Ruwaym b. Aḥmad b. Yazīd al-Baghdādī (d. 303/915), see Qushayrī, p. 34; *Ṣifāt al- ṣafwa*, vol. II, p. 249. Quote in Qushayrī, p. 217.

40 For Abū al-Ḥasan Samnūn b. Ḥamza (d. 'after Junayd al-Baghdādī', according to Sulamī, *Ṭabaqāt*, pp. 195 *ff.*), see Qushayrī, pp. 36–7. Quote in Qushayrī, p. 217. In *ʿAwārif al-maʿārif*, p. 62, this statement is attributed to Junayd.

41 For Abū Ḥamza Muḥammad b. Ibrāhīm al-Baghdādī (d. 289/951), see Qushayrī, p. 41. Quote in Qushayrī, p. 217.

42 Ibid., pp. 217–8; *ʿAwārif al-maʿārif*, p. 62.

43 For Muḥammad b. ʿAlī b. Jaʿfar al-Kattānī (d. 322/933 or 328/939), see Qushayrī, p. 218. Quote in Qushayrī, p. 218.

44 Ibid., pp. 26 and 57.

45 For Abū Muḥammad b. ʿAtiyya ʿAbd al-Ḥaqq b. Ghālib al-Gharnāṭī (d. 542/1147 or 546/1151), see *IA*: s.v. 'Ibn Atiye el-Endelusi'; Khalaf Ibn Bashkuwāl, *al-Ṣila fī tārikh a'immat al-Andalus* (Cairo: Al-Dār al-Miṣriyya, 1966), vol. II, pp. 386–7. Quote in Ibn ʿAtiyya's *al-Muḥarrar al-wajīz*, as seen in Ṭanjī, *Shifā'*, p. 50, note 6.

46 Muslim, *Ṣaḥīḥ*, 'nikāḥ', p. 271; Nawawī, *Riyāḍ*, p. 62.

47 For ʿAbd Allāh b. ʿAmr b. al-ʿĀṣ (d. 42/663 or 43/664), see *EI*²: s.v. 'Amr'; *IA*: s.v. 'Amr b. As'; Abū Nuʿaym, *Ḥilya*, vol. I, p. 283; Ibn Saʿd, *Ṭabaqāt*, vol. I, p. 270, and vol. VII, p. 493, note 4. Quote in Bukhārī, *Ṣaḥīḥ*, 'sawm', p. 56; Muslim, *Ṣaḥīḥ*, 'ṣiyām', p. 181; Nawawī, *Riyāḍ*, pp. 341–2.

48 For ʿUthmān b. Maẓʿūn (d. 41/662), see Abū Nuʿaym, *Ḥilyā*, vol. I, p. 102; Ghazālī, *Iḥyā'*, vol. III, p. 42; *Ṣifāt al-ṣafwa*, vol. I, p. 178. Quote in Abū Nuʿaym, *Ḥilya*, vol. I, p. 106.

49 Abū Nuʿaym, *Ḥilya*, vol. V, p. 168; Ibn Māja, *Sunan*, vol. II, p. 285; Nawawī, *Riyāḍ*, p. 62.

50 Bukhārī, *Ṣaḥīḥ*, 'ṣawm', p. 52; Muslim, *Ṣaḥīḥ*, 'ṣiyām', pp. 175 and 179.

51 Bukhārī, 'tamannī', p. 9, and 'ṣawm', p. 20. This was the Prophet's answer to the Companion's who objected saying that he himself practised the *wiṣāl* or uninterrupted fasting.

Chapter Four

1 See Ghazālī, *Iḥyā'*, vol. I, pp. 19 *ff.*

2 For Abū Yazīd al-Bisṭāmī, see *SEI*: s.v. 'Bistāmī'; *IA*: s.v. 'Bāyezīd-i Bistāmī'. On Abū Yazīd's *shaṭaḥāt*, see Massignon, *Lexique*, pp. 273–386. Quote in *ʿAwārif al-maʿārif*, p. 72; Zabīdī, vol. I, pp. 251–2.

3 There is no other reference to this saying besides in Ibn Khaldūn's *Shifā'*; see Badawī's reference to the *Shifā'* in *Rābiʿa al-ʿAdawiyya*, p. 192.

4 The next two pages in Ṭanjī, *Shifā'*, pp. 56–58, and Ms.B, pp. 26–28, are missing in Ms.A, p. 24.

5 Ghazālī, *Iḥyā'*, vol. IV, pp. 416 *ff.*; Zabīdī, vol. X, p. 157; Qushayrī, p. 90. Nawawī, *Riyāḍ*, p. 37; Ibn Māja, *Sunan*, vol. I, p. 247.

6 ʿAjlūnī, *Kashf al-khafā'*, vol. II, p. 285.

7 Ibn ʿArabī, *Tafsīr al-Qur'ān al-karīm*, 2 vols. (Beirut: Dār al-Yaqẓa al-ʿArabiyya, 1968), vol. I, pp. 39, 59 and 779.

8 Ibn Khaldūn's discussion of the two Sufi groups, *aṣḥāb al-tajallī* and *aṣḥāb al-waḥda*, is very similar to that of Ibn al-Khaṭīb in *Rawḍa*, pp. 582–612. For Chodkiewicz, the concise listing of Ibn Khaldūn is more subtle than that of other polemists. At least—he says—Ibn Khaldūn divides the Sufis he disapproves of in two groups: the people of the theophany and the people who upheld unicity; or, in other words, the Akbari school and the school of Ibn Sabʿīn; see Michel Chodkiewicz, *Un Océan sans Rivage. Ibn ʿArabi, le Livre et la Loi* (Paris: Editions du Seuil, 1992), pp. 293–4 and *Awhad al-dīn Baylāni, Epître sur l'Unicité Absolue* (Paris: Les Deux Océans, 1982), pp. 37–38.

9 For Ibn al-Fāriḍ Abū Ḥafṣ Sharaf al-Dīn ʿUmar (d. 632/1235), see *IA*: s.v. 'İbnü'l-Fārız'.

10 See above.

11 See above.

12 For Aḥmad b. ʿAlī al-Būnī (d. 622/1225), see *EI*: s.v. 'Buni'; *IA*: s.v. 'Būnī, Ahmed b. Alī'.

13 For Muḥyī al-Dīn b. ʿArabī al-Ḥātimī al-Ṭa'ī (d. 638/1240), see *IA*: s.v. 'İbnü'l-Arabī'; and William C. Chittick, *Ibn ʿArabi's Metaphysics of Imagination: The Sufi Path of Knowledge* (New York: State University of New York Press, 1989) and *The Self-Disclosure of God: Principles of Ibn al-ʿArabi's Cosmology* (New York: State University of New York Press, 1998).

14 Ibn Sawdakīn (d. 646/1248) was a close disciple of Ibn ʿArabī. See Veysel Akkaya, 'Bir Ibn Arabi Takipçisi İsmail b. Sevdekin', in *Tasavvuf İlmi ve Akademik Dergisi* (Istanbul: Türk Araştırma Merkezi, 2010), pp. 251–9.

15 ʿAjlūnī, *Kashf al-khafā'*, vol. II, p. 132. Ṭanjī notes that ʿAlī al-Qārī cited this tradition in his *Mawḍūʿāt*, but supported the truthfulness of its meaning with recourse to the verse of the Qur'ān, '*I created the jinn and humankind only that they might worship Me*' (Q.LI.56); Ṭanjī, *Shifā'*, p. 60.

16 Ibn Dahhāq al-Awsi (d. 611/1214–15) was the disciple of Abū ʿAbd Allāh Sūdhī.

17 That is, ʿAbd al-Ḥaqq b. Sabʿīn. For the quote, see Ibn al-Khaṭīb, *Rawḍa*, p. 606.

18 'Rather through spiritual exercise, fasting, retreats...'. See Būnī, *Shams al-maʿārif al-kubrā* (Beirut: n.p., n.d.), p. 395.

19 Note that the sentence 'huwa li'l-nafsi'l-insāniyya [wa'l-himami'l-bashariyya li-anna al-nafs al-insāniyya]...muḥīṭatun bi'l-ṭabīʿa...' is missing in Ms.B, p. 43, but not in Ms.A, p. 26.

20 *ʿAmā* is 'a thin cloud surrounded by air', as defined by Ibn ʿArabi; see Chittick, *The Sufi Path of Knowledge*, pp. 125–9.

21 Abū al-Qāsim Maslama al-Majrīṭī al-Andalusī (d. 395/1004) was the author of *Ghāyat al-ḥakīm*; see Ibn Abī Usaybiʿa, *ʿUyūn al-anbā' fī ṭabaqāt al-aṭṭibā'*, 2 vols. (Cairo: n.p., 1882), vol. II, p. 39.

22 Reference to the tradition, 'O God, I take refuge in Thee against weakness and laziness...' Ghazālī, *Iḥyā'*, vol. I, p. 186. This traditon is narrated by Bukhārī; see http://www.sunnah.com/bukhari/80/64 (last accessed 31 October 2016).

23 Abū al-Mugīth al-Ḥusayn b. Manṣūr al-Ḥallāj (d. 308/921 or 309/922) was executed on an order of the Baghdad *qāḍī*s; *SEI*: s.v. 'al-Hallāj'; *IA*: s.v. 'Hallāc-ı Mansūr'; Sulamī, *Ṭabaqāt*, pp. 350 *ff.* See also Louis Massignon, *La Passion d'al-Hallāj, Martyre Mystique de l'Islam*, 4 vols. (Paris: Gallimard, 1975).

24 About conformism or *taqlīd,* see Ibn ʿAbbād, *Letters on the Sufi Path*, pp. 146 *ff.*; see also Nwyia, *Ibn ʿAbbād*, pp. 182 *ff.*

25 That is, Abū Yazīd al-Bisṭāmī.

26 Qushayrī, p. 23.

Chapter Five

1 Missing sentence in Ṭanjī, *Shifā'*, p. 71, that reads as follows in Ms.A, p. 28, and Ms.B, pp. 46–47: 'fa-hiya mujāhadat al-istiqāma, wa-inn al-bāʿith kān al-maʿrifat bi-rafʿ al-ḥijāb wa'l-mushāhada fī ḥayāt al-dunyā…'

2 Qushayri, pp. 314–5.

3 Bukhārī, *Ṣaḥīḥ*, 'mawāqīt al-ṣalāt', p. 1.

4 Muslim, *Ṣaḥīḥ*, 'īmān', p. 23; Bukhārī, *Ṣaḥīḥ*, 'mawāqīt al-ṣalāt', p. 2.

5 Ibid.

6 'Fa-muḥtāja…baʿḍ al-shay'…ilā al-shaykh al-muʿallim' or 'the seeker may need… to a certain extant…a spiritual guide…'; missing in Ṭanjī, *Shifā'*, p. 73; see Ms.A, p. 29, and Ms.B, p. 48.

7 Ghazālī, *Iḥyā'*, vol. III, p. 67.

8 Ms.A, p. 30, reads 'al-aḥwāl al-ghayr al-maqdūra ʿalā al-aʿmāl al-maqdūra'; Ms.B, p. 51, and Ṭanjī, *Shifā'*, p. 76 reads 'al-aḥwāl al-maqdūra ʿalā al-aʿmāl al-maqdūra'. I chose to follow Ms.A.

9 A Sūfī saying considered by some compilers to be a non-established tradition; see ʿAlī al-Qārī, *al-Asrār al-marfūʿa fī al-akhbār al-mawḍūʿa* (Beirut: Muḥammad Luṭfī al-Ṣabbāgh, 1986), p. 348; Muḥammad ʿAbd al-Raḥmān al-Sakhāwī, *al-Maqāṣid al-ḥasana fī bayān kathīr min al-aḥādith al-mushtahira ʿalā al-alsina*, edited by ʿAbd Allāh Muḥammad al-Ṣiddīq (Egypt: Dār al-Adab al-ʿArabī, 1956), p. 436; ʿAjlūnī, *Kashf al-khafā'*, vol. II, p. 291.

10 Qushayrī, p. 52.

Chapter Six

1 Ibn Khaldūn refers to one 'shaykh-denier' and uses the plural when quoting the 'shaykh-partisans'. For the sake of clarity, I have decided to refer to both parties in the singular.

2 For Uways al-Qaranī (d. 35/656), see *Iṣāba*, vol. III, pp. 122–5; *Ṣifāt al-ṣafwa*, vol. I, p. 228. The story to which Ibn Khaldūn is referring is told in *Ṣifāt al-ṣafwa*, vol. III, pp. 22–30. ʿUmar b. al-Khaṭṭāb came to ʿUways for advice.

3 For Shībān al-Rāʿī (death date unknown), see Abū Nuʿaym, *Ḥilya*, vol. VIII, p. 317; Zabīdī, vol. I, p. 170.

4 For Abū ʿAbd Allāh Muḥammad b. Idrīs al-Shāfiʿī (d. 204/820), see *SEI*: s.v. 'al-Shāfiʿ'; Subkī, *Ṭabaqāt al-Shāfiʿiyya*, vol. I, pp. 100–3; *Muqaddima*, vol. III, pp. 3–12. The story Ibn Khaldūn is referring to is related in Qushayrī, p. 314; Zabīdī, vol. I, p. 170. Although Shībān the shepherd was illiterate, he showed more knowledge in spiritual questions than the great Imam and legist, founder of one of the major schools of Islamic law, Shāfiʿī.

5 For Aḥmad b. Muḥammad b. Ḥanbal (d. 241/855), see *SEI*: s.v. 'Aḥmad'; *IA*: s.v. 'Ahmed b. Hanbel'.

6 For 'sicknesses', see 'zalal' in Ms.A, p. 33, and 'ʿilal' in Ms.B, p. 109.

7 'Aw kād' is missing in Ṭanjī, *Shifā'*, p. 85, line 12; see Ms.A, p. 34, and Ms.B, p. 58.
8 'ᶜAmal' in Ms.A, p. 34, as opposed to 'amal' in Ms.B, p. 59, and Ṭanjī, *Shifā'*, p. 87.
9 The name of this group is derived from *ḥulūl*, translated as 'in-dwelling' or 'substantial union'; see *SEI*: s.v. 'ḥulūl'; *IA*: s.v. 'Hulūl'.
10 Zindīq/Zanādiqa means 'heretic(s)'; see *SEI*: s.v. 'Zindīq'.
11 'Ibāḥīs' means 'freethinkers'; see *SEI*: s.v. 'Taṣawwuf'; *IA*: s.v. 'İbāhiyye'.
12 The name of this group is derived from *tanāsukh* or 'metempsychosis or transmigration'; see *SEI*: s.v. 'tanāsukh'.
13 The name of this group is derived from *jabr* or 'the compulsion' of God; see *SEI*: s.v. 'djabriya'.
14 The last sentence is missing in Ṭanjī, *Shifā'*, p. 90, and in Ms.B, p. 62; but reads as following in Ms.A, p. 36: 'Wa-kalāmuka al-ladhī yukhrijuhum ᶜan dhālika, bāṭil bi'l-ijmāᶜ', and is added in Pérez, p. 224.
15 Here Ibn Khaldūn is referring to *Qūt al-qulūb fī muᶜāmalat al-maḥbūb* by Abū Ṭālib al-Makkī (d. 386/998); see *EI*: s.v. 'al-Makkī'.
16 Ms.A, p. 37, and Ms.B, p. 65, show the word 'ṣaᶜb' or 'arduous'; but Ṭanjī, *Shifā'*, p. 93, chose to correct it as 'ṣalb' or 'pillar', which we decided to choose too. Pérez, p. 228, in his translation preferred to keep the word as it appeared in manuscripts A and B.
17 Ms.B, p. 66 reads as follows: 'al-shaykh dūn al-shaykh', as does Ṭanjī, *Shifā'*, p. 94. However, Ms.A, p. 37, reads 'al-shaykh dūn al-kutub'. Pérez chose to follow the latter in his translation, p. 229; see also comment in Pérez, p. 284, note 193. We decided to follow Ms.A since the meaning corresponded to the idea of the debater.
18 The five rules of behaviour are: *ḥarām* ('unlawful'), *makrūh* ('reprehensible'), *mubāḥ* ('indifferent'), *wājib* or *farḍ* ('incumbent or obligatory duty') and *mandūb* ('recommended').
19 'Mā lā yaᶜrifūn' in Ms.A, p. 39, and 'mā yaᶜrifūn' in Ṭanjī, *Shifā'*, p. 97.
20 Ms.A, p. 39, and Ms.B, p. 69, show the word 'nāqil' rather than 'naql'; see Ṭanjī, *Shifā'*, p. 98.
21 The three terms used here are common in Mālikī legal works. The *ᶜariyya* (pl. *ᶜarāyā*) is 'a palm tree which its owner assigns to another, who is in need for him to eat its fruit during a year'; see E. W. Lane, *An Arabic English Lexicon*, 2 vols. (Cambridge: Islamic Texts Society, 1984), s.v. '*ᶜariyya*'. The *qirāḍ* or 'making a loan' is the giving of capital to a third party who will administer it for an undetermined gain; Lane, s.v. '*qirāḍ*'. The *musāqāt* is a 'man's employing a man to take upon himself, or manage, the culture (or watering) or palm trees or grapevines (or the like) on the condition of his having a certain share of their produce'; Lane, s.v. '*musāqāt*'. The three examples given by Ibn Khaldūn refer to contingent aleatory contracts and therefore exceptional in view of the general legal rules.
22 Khuzayma b. Thābit (d. 36/656), also called *dhū al-shahādatayn* ('The Possessor

of Two Testimonies'), testified having seen the Prophet pay for a horse he had bought, although he was not present, for he knew his Prophet could only speak the truth; his testimony was declared by the Prophet to be as valid as the testimonies of two Muslim men; see *Iṣāba*, vol. I, p. 425.

23 Abū Burda b. Niyār (d. 45/665) sacrificed his lamb before the Prophet had sacrificed his, and so was asked to repeat the sacrifice. Abū Burda could, then, only find a lamb he liked very much and asked the Prophet if he could be excused from the task. The Prophet agreed and made this an exception too; see *Iṣāba*, vol. IV, pp. 25–6.

24 ʿAjlūnī, *Kashf al-khafā'*, vol. I, p. 64. The wording of this tradition in Ṭanjī, *Shifā'*, p. 99, is the same as that found in Tirmidhī; and a similar tradition is narrated by Ibn Māja, with the addition of the pronoun 'them' (*hum*); see http://www.sunnah.com/search/?q=ibn+maja%2C+scholars+heirs+of+prophets (last accessed 3 November 2016).

25 As in the case of the celebrated Shaykh Abū al-Hasan al-Kharaqānī (d. 425/1034), who was guided by the *rūḥāniyya* or spirit of Abū Yazīd al-Bistāmī, a way followed by the Uwaysīs who are educated by a master remote in time, space or both.

26 'Wa ilhām' is missing in Ṭanjī, *Shifā'*, p. 101; see Ms.A, p. 40, and Ms.B, p. 72.

27 For Khālid b. al-Walīd al-Mughīra al-Makhzūmī (d. 21/641–2), see EI^2: s.v. 'Khālid'; *IA*: s.v. 'Hālid b. Velīd'; Ibn Saʿd, *Ṭabaqāt*, vol. II, pp. 393-8; *Iṣāba*: vol. I, pp. 412-5.

28 'Fī nafī' is missing in Ṭanjī, *Shifā'*, p. 102; see Ms.A, p. 41, and Ms.B, p. 73.

29 'Bi-iʿtibārihā' is missing in Ṭanjī, *Shifā'*, p. 102, and Ms.B, p. 72; see Ms.A, p. 41.

30 Bukhārī, *Ṣaḥīḥ*, 'waḥy ', p. 7.

31 In Ṭanjī, *Shifā'*, p. 103, 'ḥāmil' is misread as 'ḥal'; see Ms.A, p. 41, and Ms.B, p. 74.

Conclusion and Ascertainment

1 'Lam yakun min al-īmān min shay''. The words 'min al-īmān' are missing in Ms.B, p. 88, and Ṭanjī, *Shifā'*, p. 108, but not in Ms.A, p. 43.

2 That is, 13 June 1485.

BIBLIOGRAPHY

Abd el-Kader, Emir. *Ecrits Spirituels*, translated and presented by Michel Chodkiewicz. Paris: Le Seuil, 1982.

Abdesselam, Ahmed. *Ibn Khaldūn et ses Lecteurs*. Paris: Presses Universitaires de France, 1983.

Abun-Nasr, Jamil. *A History of the Maghrib in the Islamic Period*. Cambridge: Cambridge University Press, 1987.

Abū Nuʿaym. *Ḥilyat al-awliyā' wa-ṭabaqāt al-aṣfiyā'*, 10 vols. Cairo: Matbaʿat al-Saʿāda, 1971.

ʿAjlūnī, Ismāʿīl b. Muḥammad, al-. *Kashf al-khafā' wa-muzīl al-ilbās ʿammā ishtahara min al-aḥādīth ʿalā alsinat al-nās*, 2 vols. Beirut: Dār al-Kutub al-ʿIlmiyya, 1988.

Akkaya, Veysel. 'Bir Ibn Arabi takipçisi İsmail b. Sevdekin', *Tasavvuf İlmi ve Akademik Dergisi*: 2010.

Al-Azmeh, Aziz. *Ibn Khaldūn: An Essay in Reinterpretation*. London: Frank Cass, 1982.

———*Ibn Khaldūn in Modern Scholarship: A Study in Orientalism*. London: Third World Center for Research and Publication, 1981.

Anawati, M. and Gardet, L. 'La Place du Kalam d'après Ibn Khaldūn', in *Introduction à la Théologie Musulmane*. Paris: Librairie Philosophique J. Vrin, 1948.

———*Mystique Musulmane*. Paris: Librairie Philosophique J. Vrin, 1961.

André, Pierre-Jean. *Confréries Religieuses Musulmanes*. Algiers: Editions la Maison des Livres, 1956.

Annestay, Jean. *Une Femme Soufie en Islam: Rabiʿa al-ʿAdawiyya*. Paris: Entrelacs, 2009.

Anṣārī, ʿAbd Allāh, al-. *Les Etapes des Itinérants vers Dieu*, edited by S. De Laugier de Beaurecueil. Cairo: Imprimerie de l'Institut Français d'Archéologie Orientale, IFAO, 1962.

Arberry, Arthur. J. *Revelation and Reason in Islam*. London: George Allen and Unwin Ltd., 1956.

———*Sufism*. London: George Allen and Unwin Ltd., 1956.

———*The Koran Interpreted*. London: George Allen and Unwin Ltd., 1964.

Arnold, T. and Guillaume, A. *The Legacy of Islam*. Oxford: Clarendon Press, 1931.

Arslan, Ahmet. 'Ibn Haldun ve Tarih', in *Tarih Lacelemeleri Dergisi*, vol. I: 1983.

ʿAsqalāni, Ibn Ḥajar, al-. *Al-Iṣāba fī tamyīz al-ṣaḥāba*, 4 vols. Cairo: al-Maktaba al-Tijāriyya al-Kubrā, 1939.

———*Al-Durar al-kāmina fī aʿyān al-mā'a al-thāmina*, 6 vols. Cairo: Dār al-Kutub al-Ḥadīth, 1966.

Baali, Fuad and Wardi, Ali. *A Study in Reinterpretation: Ibn Khaldun and Islamic Thought Styles: A Social Perspective*. Boston: G. K. Hall and Co., 1981.

Bābā, Aḥmad. *Nayl al-ibtihāj bi-ṭaṭrīz al-dībāj*, in Ibn Farḥūn, *al-Dībāj al-mudhahhab fī maʿrifat aʿyān al-madhhab*. Cairo: n.p., 1932–3.

Badawī, ʿAbd al-Raḥmān, al-. *Mu'allafāt Ibn Khaldūn*. Cairo: Dār al-Maʿārif, 1962.

———*Rābiʿa al-ʿAdawiyya*. Kuwait: Wakālat al-Matbūʿāt, 1978.

———*Tārīkh al-taṣawwuf al-Islāmī min al-bidāya ḥattā nihāyat al-qarn al-thānī*. Kuwait: Wakālat al-Matbūʿāt, 1975.

Badīsī, ʿAbd al-Ḥaqq, al-. '*Al-Maqṣad*, Vie des Saints du Rif', translated by G. S. Colin, in *Archives Marocaines*: 1926.

Barnes, H. E. *Contemporary Sociological Theory*. New York: Appleton Century Co., 1940.

Basset and Levi-Provencal. 'Chella une Necropose Merinide', *Archives Berbères et Bulletin des Hautes Etudes Marocaines, Hespéris*, vol. II: 1922.

Bel, Alfred. *La Religion Musulmane en Berbérie*. Paris: Librairie Orientaliste Paul Geuthner, 1938.

———'Le Soufisme en Occident Musulman', *Annales de l'Institut des Etudes Orientales*: 1934–5.

———'Sidi Bou Medyan et son Maître ed-Deqqaq a Fez', in *Mélanges*: 1923.

Ben Cheneb, Muḥammad. 'Etudes sur les Personnages Mentionnés dans l'Idjaza du Cheikh ʿAbd al-Qādir al-Fāsī', in *Actes du XIV Congrès International des Orientalistes*. Algiers: n.p., 1978.

Bercque, Jacques. *L'Intérieur du Maghreb: XV–XIX Siècle*. Paris: Gallimard, 1978.

Blachère, Régis. 'Quelques Détails sur la Vie Privée du Sultan Mérinide Abū'l-Ḥasan', vol. I, in *Mémorial d'Henri Basset*, 2 vols. Paris: Librairie Orientaliste Paul Geuthner, 1928.

Bosworth, C. E. *The Islamic Dynasties*. Edinburgh: Edinburgh University Press, 1981.

Bourouiba, Rachid. *Ibn Tumart*. Algiers: Societé Nationale d'Edition et de Diffusion, 1974.

Bousquet, Georges Henri. *L'Islam Magrébin*. Algiers: La Maison des Livres, 1954.

Bouthoul, G. *Ibn Khaldūn, Sa Philosophie Sociale*. Paris: Librairie Orientaliste Paul Geuthner, 1930.

Brockelmann, C. *Geschishte der Arabishen Litteratur*, 2 vols. Leiden: E. J. Brill, 1943.

Brosselard, 'Les Inscriptions Arabes de Tlemcen', in *Revue Africaine*: 1860.

Brunschwig, Robert. *La Berbérie Orientale sous les Hafsides des Origines à la Fin du XV Siècle*, 2 vols. Paris: Adrien Maisonneuve, 1940–47.

Brunschwig, Robert and Pérès, H. 'Ibn Khaldūn: Sa Vie et son Œuvre', *Bulletin des Etudes Arabes*: 1943.

Bukhārī, Abū ʿAbd Allāh Muḥammad b. Ismāʿīl, al-. *Al-Ṣaḥīḥ*. Leiden: E. J. Brill, 1962–8.

———*Al-Ṣaḥīḥ*, in *Mawṣūʿat al-Sunna ʿalā al-kutub al-sitta wa-sharḥihā*. Istanbul: Çağrı Yayınları Dâru Sahnūn, 1992.

Būnī, al-. *Shams al-maʿārif al-kubrā*. Beirut: n.p., n.d.

Busch, Briton Cooper. 'Divine Intervention in the "Muqaddimah" of Ibn Khaldūn', in *History of Religions*, vol. VII. Chicago: The University of Chicago Press, 1968.

Bustānī, Butrus, al-. *Muḥīt al-muḥīt*. Beirut: Dā'irat al-Maʿārif, 1983.

Casewit, Yousef. 'The Forgotten Mystic: Ibn Barrajān (d. 536/1141) and the Andalusian Muʿtabirūn.' PhD thesis, Yale University, 2014.

———*The Mystics of al-Andalus: Ibn Barrajān and Islamic Thought in the Twelfth Century*. Cambridge: Cambridge University Press, 2017.

Chaumont, Eric. 'Notes et Remarques autour d'un texte de la Muqaddima', *Studia Islamica*, vol. CXI: 1986.

Chittick, William C. *Ibn ʿArabi's Metaphysics of Imagination: The Sufi Path of Knowledge*. New York: State University of New York Press, 1989.

———*The Self-Disclosure of God: Principles of Ibn al-ʿArabi's Cosmology*. New York: State University of New York Press, 1998.

Chodkiewicz, Michel. *Awhad al-dīn Baylāni, Epître sur l'Unicité Absolue*. Paris: Les Deux Océans, 1982.

———'Ibn Khaldūn and Islamic Ideology; Ibn Khaldūn, an Essay in Reinterpretation', *Studia Islamica*, vol. LXII: 1985.

———'Ibn Khaldūn in Modern Scholarship', *Studia Islamica*, vol. LXI: 1985.

———'Ibn Khaldūn, La Voie et la Loi', *Studia Islamica*, vol. LXXVII: 1993.

———'Maîtres Spirituels en Islam', *Connaissance des Religions*: 1998.
———*Un Océan sans Rivage. Ibn ʿArabi, le Livre et la Loi*. Paris: Editions du Seuil, 1992.
Cornell, Vincent J. *Realm of the Saint, Power and Authority in Moroccan Sufism*. Texas: University of Texas Press, 1998.
———'Understanding Is the Mother of Ability: Responsibility and Action in the Doctrine of Ibn Tūmart', *Studia Islamica*, vol. LXVI: 1988.
Cuoq, J. 'La Religion et les Religions selon Ibn Khaldūn', *Islamochristiana*: 1984.
De Boer, T. J. *The History of Philosophy in Islam*. London: Luzac and Co., 1933.
Demeerseman, A. 'Ce que Ibn Khaldun pense d'Al-Ghazzali', *Revue de l'Institut des Belles-Lettres*, vol. LXXII: 1958.
———'Le Magreb a-t-il une Marque Ghazalienne?', *Revue de l'Institut des Belles-Lettres*, vol. LXXII: 1958.
Depont-Coppolani. *Confréries Religieuses Musulmanes*. Algiers: A. Jourdan, 1897.
Dermenghem, Emile. *Le Culte des Saints dans L'Islam Maghrébin*. Paris: Gallimard, 1954.
Dozy, R. *Supplément aux Dictionnaires Arabes*, 2 vols. Paris: Maisonneuve et Larose, 1967.
Drague, G. 'Esquisse d'Histoire Religieuse du Maroc, Confréries et Zaouias', *Cahiers de l'Afrique et l'Asie*: 1951.
Encyclopedia of Islam (first edition). Leiden: E. J. Brill, 1931–6.
Encyclopedia of Islam (second edition). Leiden: E. J. Brill, 1971.
Farghānī, Saʿīd, al-. *Muntahā al-madārik*, 2 vols. Cairo: Matbaʿat al-Ṣanāʾiʿ, 1974.
Fāsī, ʿAbd al-Raḥmān, al-. 'Qiṣṣat makhṭūṭ Ibn Khaldūn', *Risālat al-Maghrib*, vol. x: 1948.
Fındıkoğlu, Z. 'İstanbul Kütüphanelerinde yazma Ibn Haldun Nushalarından biri Hakkında', *Zeki Velidi Toğana Armağanı*. Istanbul: Maārif Basımevi, 1950.
———'Les Théories de la Connaissance et de l'Histoire chez Ibn Haldun', in *Proceedings for the 10th International Congress of Philosophy* I. Amsterdam: North-Holland, 1949.
———'Türkiyede Ibn Haldunizm', *Fuad Köprülü Armağanı*. Istanbul: Osman Yalçın Matbaası, 1953.

Fishel, W. J. *Ibn Khaldūn in Egypt, His Public Functions and His Historical Research (1832–1406)*. Berkeley: University of California Press, 1967.

———'Selected Bibliography', in *Ibn Khaldūn, Muqaddimah,* translated by F. Rosenthal, vol. III. Princeton: Princeton University Press, 1980.

Frank, H. *Beitrag zur Erkenntnis des Sufismus nach Ibn Haldun*. Leipzipg: Dragulin, 1884.

Geoffroy, Eric. *Le Soufisme en Egypte et en Syrie*. Damas: Institut Français d'Etudes Arabes de Damas, 1995.

Ghazālī, Abū Ḥāmid, al-. 'Al-Risāla al-laduniyya', in *al-Quṣūr al-ʿawālī*. Cairo: Maktabat al-Jundī, 1970.

———*Faḍā'iḥ al-bāṭiniyya*, edited by A. R. Badawi. Cairo: n.p., 1964.

———*Iḥyā' ʿulūm al-dīn*, 5 vols. Beirut: n.p., n.d.

Gibb, Sir Hamilton. 'The Islamic Background of Ibn Khaldūn's Political Theory', *Bulletin of the School of Oriental Studies*, vol. VII: 1933–5.

Ḥaddād, Gibrīl Fouād. *The Four Imams and their Schools*. Muslim Academic Trust, n.d.

Hitti, Philip. *History of the Arabs*. New York: Summit Books, 1981.

Hujwirī, ʿAlī. *Kashf al-maḥjūb*, translated by R. A. Nicholson. Lahore: Luzac and Co., 1976.

Ḥusayn, ʿAlī Ṣāfī. *Al-Adab al-ṣūfī fī Misr*. Cairo: Dār al-Maʿārif, 1964.

Ḥusayn, Ṭaha. *Etude Analytique et Critique de la Philosophie Sociale d'Ibn Khaldūn*. Paris: A. Pedone, 1917.

Ibn ʿAbbād. *Al-Rasā'il al-kubrā*. Fez: Matbaʿat al-ʿArabī al-Arzaq, 1903

———*Ibn ʿAbbād of Ronda: Letters on the Sufi Path*, translated by John Renard. New Jersey: Paulist Press, 1986.

———*Lettres de Direction Spirituelle, al-Rasā'il al-sughrā*, edited by Paul Nwyia. Beirut: Dār al-Mashriq, 1974.

Ibn Abī Usaybiʿa. *ʿUyūn al-anbā' fī ṭabaqāt al-aṭṭibā'*, 2 vols. Cairo: n.p., 1882.

Ibn ʿAjība. *Īqāẓ al-himam fī sharḥ al-Ḥikam wa'l-futūḥāt al-ilāhiyya fī sharḥ al-Mabāḥith al-aṣliyya*. Cairo: Matbaʿat Aḥmad Ḥanafī, n.d.

Ibn al-ʿArīf. *Maḥāsin al-majālis*, edited by Asin Palacios. Paris: Librairie Orientaliste Paul Geuthner, 1933.

Ibn al-Fāriḍ. *The Poem of the Way*, translated by Arberry, London: Emery Walker, 1952–6.

Ibn al-ʿImād. *Shadharāt al-dhahab fī akhbār man dhahab*, 8 vols. Beirut: al-Maktab al-Tijārī li'l-Tibāʿa wa'l-Nashr wa'l-Tawzīʿ, n.d.

Ibn al-Jawzī. *Ṣifāt al-ṣafwa*, 4 vols. India: Matbaʿat Dā'irat al-Maʿārif, 1968.

———*Talbīs Iblīs*. Cairo: Matbaʿat al-Manār, 1928.

———*Tārīkh ʿUmar b. al-Khaṭṭāb*. Damascus: Dār Ihyā' ʿUlūm al-Dīn, n.d.

Ibn al-Khaṭīb. *Al-Iḥāṭa fī tārīkh Gharnāta*, 3 vols., edited by M. A. Inan. Cairo: Dār al-Kutub al-Miṣriyya, 1974.

———*Rawḍat al-taʿrīf bi'l-ḥubb al-sharīf*. Cairo: Dār al-Fikr al-ʿArabi, 1968.

Ibn al-Qāḍī. *Durrat al-ḥijal fī ghurrat asmā' al-rijāl*, 2 vols. Cairo: Dār al-Turāth, 1971.

———*Jadhwat al-iqtibās*. N.l.: n.p., 1892.

Ibn al-Zayyāt. *Al-Tashawwuf fī maʿrifat rijāl al-taṣawwuf*. Rabat: Matbūʿāt Ifrīqiyya al-Shimāliyya al-Fanniyya, 1958.

Ibn ʿArabī. *Al-Futūḥāt al-Makkiyya*, 4 vols. Beirut: Dār Ṣādir, n.d.

———*Al-Rasā'il*. Beirut: Iḥyā' al-Turāth al-ʿArabī, 1968.

———*Tafsir al-Qur'ān al-karīm*, 2 vols. Beirut: Dār al-Yaqẓa al-ʿArabiyya, 1968.

Ibn ʿAṭā'illāh. *Ṣūfī Aphorisms (Kitāb al-Ḥikam)*, translated by Victor Danner. Leiden: E. J. Brill, 1984.

Ibn ʿAṭiyya. *Al-Muḥarrir al-wajīz fī tafsīr al-kitāb al-ʿazīz*. Cairo: n.p., 1974.

Ibn Bashkuwāl. *Al-Ṣila fī tārikh a'immat al-Andalus*. Cairo: Al-Dār al-Misriyya, 1966.

Ibn Baṭṭūta. *Al-Riḥla*. Beirut: Dār Ṣādir li'l-Tibāʿat, 1960.

Ibn Farḥūn. *Al-Dībāj al-mudhahhab fī maʿrifat aʿyān al-madhab*. Cairo: Maktabat Dār al-Turāth, 1974.

Ibn Ḥanbal. *Al-Musnad*. Cairo: Muḥammad Zuhrī al-Ghamrāwī, 1313/1896.

Ibn ʿIdhārī. *Al-Bayān al-mughrib fī akhbār al-Andalus wa'l-Maghrib*, 3 vols. Beirut: Dār al-Thaqāfa, 1967.

Ibn Khaldūn, ʿAbd al-Rahmān. *Al-Muqaddima*. Beirut: Dār Ihyā' al-Turāth al-ʿArabī, 1900.

———*Al-Taʿrīf bi-Ibn Khaldūn wa-riḥlatihi sharqan wa-gharban*, edited by Muḥammed b. Tāwīt al-Ṭanjī. Cairo: Matbaʿat Lajnat al-Ta'līf wa'l-Tarjama wa'l-Nashr, 1951.

———*Discours sur l'Histoire Universelle*, 3 vols., translated by Vincent Monteil. Beirut: Unesco Commission Internationale pour la Traduction des Chefs d'Oeuvres, 1967.

———*Histoire des Bérbères et des Dynasties de l'Afrique Septentrionale*, edited by M. de Slane. Algiers: Imprimerie du Gouvernement, 1847–1951.

———*Kitāb al-ʿibar*. Beirut: al-Matbaʿa al-Adabiyya, 1900.

———*Shifā' al-sā'il li-tahdhīb al-masā'il*, edited by Muḥammad b. Tāwīt al-Ṭanjī. Istanbul: Osman Yalçın Matbaası, 1957.

———*Shifā' us-sā'il litehzīb-il-masā'il, Apaisement a Qui Cherche Comment Clarifier les Problèmes*, edited by Ignace Khalifé. Beirut: al-Matbaʿa al-Katūlikiyya, 1959.

———*Shifā' al-sā'il li-tahdhib al-masā'il*, edited by Muḥammad Muṭīʿ al-Ḥāfiẓ. Damascus: Dār al-Fikr al-Muʿāṣir, 1997.

———*Tasavvufun mahiyeti, Şifaü's-Sa'il*, translated by Süleyman Uludağ. Istanbul: Dergah Yayınları, 1984.

———*The Muqaddimah: An Introduction to History*, 3 vols., translated by Franz Rosenthal. Princeton: Princeton University Press, 1980.

Ibn Khaldūn, Yaḥyā. *Histoire des Beni ʿAbd al-Wād, Rois de Tlemcen*, 2 vols., edited and translated by A. Bel. Algiers: Imprimerie Orientale Fontana Frères and Cie, 1911.

Ibn Māja. *Al-Sunan*. Cairo: al-Matbaʿa al-ʿIlmiyya, 1896.

Ibn Maryam. 'Al-Bustān fī dhikr al-awliyā' wa'l ʿulamā' bi-Tilimsān', summarized by A. Delpech in *Revue Africaine*: 1883–4.

Ibn Marzūq. *Al-Musnad al-ṣaḥīḥ al-ḥasan fī ma'āthir wa-maḥāsin mawlānā Abī al-Ḥasan*, translated into Spanish by Maria Viguera. Madrid: Instituto Hispano Arabe de Cultura, 1977.

Ibn Qunfudh. *Uns al-faqīr wa-ʿizz al-ḥaqīr*. Rabat: Editions Techiniques Nord Africaines, 1965.

Ibn Saʿd. *Al-Ṭabaqāt al-kubrā*, 8 vols. Beirut: Dār Ṣādir, 1958.

Ibn Taghribirdī. *Al-Nujūm al-zāhira fī mulūk Misr wa'l-Qāhira*, 16 vols. Cairo: Al-Hayʿa al-Miṣriyya al-ʿĀmma li'l-Kitāb, 1972.

Ibrahim E. and Johnson-Davies D. *An-Nawawī's Forty Hadith*. Cambridge: The Islamic Texts Society, 1997.

ʿInān, Muḥammad ʿAbd Allāh. *Ibn Khaldūn, ḥayātuhu wa-tārikh fikrihi*. Cairo: Matbaʿat Lajnat al-Ta'līf wa'l-Tarjama wa'l-Nashr, 1965.

Issawi, C. *An Arab Philosophy of History*. London: John Murray, 1950.

Jīlī, ʿAbd al-Karīm, al-. *Marātib al-wujūd wa-ḥaqīqat kulli mawjūd*, in *al-Kahf wa'l-raqīm*, edited by ʿĀṣim Ibrahīm al-Kayyālī. Lebanon: n.p., 2008.

Kalabādhī, al-. *Al-Taʿrīf li-madhhab ahl al-taṣawwuf*. Cairo: Dār Ihyā' al-Kutub al-ʿArabiyya, 1960.

Kempfner, G. 'Rationalisme et Mystique à propos d'al-Ghazālī', *Revue de l'Institut des Belles-Lettres*, vol. XXI: 1958.

Khazrajī, Aḥmad, al-. *Khulāṣat tadhhib al-kamāl fī asmā' al-rijāl*, 3 vols. Cairo: al-Matbaʿa al-Khayriyya, 1904.

Labica, Georges. 'Esquisse d'une Sociologie de la Religion chez Ibn Khaldoun', *La Pensée*, vol. CXXIII: 1965.

Lacoste, Yves. *Ibn Khaldoun, Naissance de l'Histoire, Passé du Tiers Monde*. Paris: Maspero, 1985.

Lakhsassi, Abderrahmane. 'Ibn Khaldūn', in *History of Islamic Philosophy*, edited by Seyyed Hossein Nasr and Oliver Leaman. London and New York: Routledge, 2001.

Lane, E. *Arabic-English Lexicon*, 2 vols. Cambridge: Islamic Texts Society, 1984.

Laroui, ʿAbd Allah. *L'Histoire du Maghrib*, 2 vols. Paris: Librairie François Maspero, 1975.

Loubignac, Victor. 'Un Saint Berbère, Moulay Bou Azza, Histoire et Légende', *Archives Berbères et Bulletin des Hautes Etudes Marocaines, Hespéris*, vol. xxxi: 1944.

Mackeen, A. M. Mohamed. 'The Early History of Sufism in the Maghrib Prior to al-Shādhilī', *Journal of the American Oriental Society*, vol. xci: 1971.

———'The Rise of al-Shādhilī', *Journal of the American Oriental Society*, vol. xci: 1971.

Mahdi, Muhsin. 'The Book and the Master as Poles of Cultural Change in Islam', in *Islam and Cultural Change in the Middle Ages,* edited by Speros Bryonis. Wiesbaden: University of California Los Angeles, 1975.

———*Ibn Khaldūn's Philosophy of History*. Chicago: The University of Chicago Press, 1964.

Makkī, ʿAbd al-Razzāq, al-. *Al-Fikr al-Islāmī ʿinda Ibn Khaldūn*. Alexandria: n.p., 1970.

Makkī, Abū Ṭālib, al-. *Qūt al-qulūb*. Cairo: Matbaʿat al-Muyammaniyya, 1961.

Maqqarī, Ahmad b. Muhammad, al-. *Nafḥ al-ṭīb min ghuṣn al-Andalus al-raṭīb wa-dhikr wazīriha Lisān al-Dīn b. al-Khaṭīb*, 10 vols. Beirut: Dār al-Kutub al-ʿArabī, 1949.

Maqrīzī, Aḥmad Taqī al-Dīn, al-. *Al-Mawāʿiz wa'l-iʿtibār fī dhikr al-khiṭaṭ wa'l-āthār*. Baghdad: n.p., n.d.

———*Kitāb al-sulūk li-maʿrifat duwal al-mulūk*. Cairo: Matbaʿat Dār al-Kutub, 1970.

Marçais, Georges. *La Berbérie Musulmane et L'Orient au Moyen Age*. Paris: n.p., 1946.

Massignon, Louis. *Essai sur les Origines du Lexique Technique de la Mystique Musulmane*. Paris: Librairie Philosophique J. Vrin, 1954.

———*La Passion d'al-Hallāj, Martyre Mystique de l'Islam*, 4 vols. Paris: Gallimard, 1975.

Māziyān, ʿAbd al-Madjīd. *Al-Naẓariyya al-iqtiṣādiyya ʿinda Ibn Khaldūn wa-usūsuha min al-fikr al-Islāmī wa'l-wāqiʿ al-mujtamaʿī*. Manshurāt al-Ikhtilāf, Algeria: n.p., 2002.

Meuleman, Johann. 'La Causalité dans la 'Muqaddimah' d'Ibn Khaldūn', *Studia Islamica*, vol. LXXIV: 1991.

Michaux-Bellaire, Edouard. 'Essai sur l'Histoire des Confréries Marocaines', *Archives Berbères et Bulletin des Hautes Etudes Marocaines, Hespéris*, vol. I: 1921.

———'Les Confréries Religieuses au Maroc', *Archives Marocaines*, vol. XXVII: 1927.

Michon, Jean Louis. *Le Soufi Marocain Ahmad Ibn ʿAjība*. Paris: Librairie Philosophique J. Vrin, 1973.

Morris, James W. 'Religion and Philosophy in Ibn Khaldūn's critique of Sufism', unpublished paper at the International Conference on Islamic Intellectual History, Harvard University, May 1988.

Muḥāsibī, al-Ḥārith, al-. *Al-Riʿāya lī-ḥuqūq Allāh*. Cairo: Dār al-Kutub al-Ḥadītha, 1970.

Muslim, Abū al-Ḥusayn. *Al-Ṣaḥīḥ*. Cairo: n.p., 1374/1955.

———*English Translation of Ṣaḥīḥ Muslim*, translated by Nāṣiruddīn al-Khaṭṭāb. Riyadh: Darussalam Publications, 2007.

Nāṣirī, Ahmad b. Khālid, al-. *Kitāb al-istiqṣā li-akhbār duwal al-Maghrib al-aqṣā*, vol. II, translated by G. S. Collin, *Archives Marocaines*, vol. XXXI: 1925; vol. III, translated by Ismail Hamid, *Archives Marocaines*, vol. XXXII: 1927; vol. IV, translated by Ismail Hamid, *Archives Marocaines*, vol. XXXIII: 1934.

Nassar, Nassif. *La Pensée Réaliste d'Ibn Khaldoun*. Paris: Presse Universitaire de France, 1957.

———'Le Maître d'Ibn Khaldoun al-Ābilī', *Studia Islamica*, vol. XX: 1965.

Nawawī, Abū Zakariyyā Yaḥyā. *Riyāḍ al-ṣāliḥīn*. Beirut: Dār Iḥyā' al-Turāth al-ʿArabī, 1399/1979.

Nwyia, Paul. *Ibn Abbād de Ronda*. Beirut: Imprimerie Catholique, 1961.

———*Ibn Atā Allāh et la Naissance de la Confrérie Shādhilite*. Beirut: Dār al-Mashriq, 1972.

———'Notes sur quelques Fragments Inédits de la Correspondance d'Ibn Arīf avec Ibn Barrajān', *Archives Berbères et Bulletin des Hautes Etudes Marocaines, Hespéris*, vol. XLIII: 1956.

Ortega y Gasset, Jose. 'Abenjaldūn Nos Revela el Secreto', *Pensamientos sobre Africa Menor*, vol. VIII: 1961.

Oumlil, Ali. *L'Histoire et son Discours*. Rabat: Publications de la Faculté des Lettres et des Sciences Humaines, 1974.

———'Ibn Khaldoun, Sens d'une Bibiliographie', *Studia Islamica*, vol. XLIX: 1979.

Pérès, Henri. 'Essai de Bibliographie d'Ibn Khaldoun', *Studi Orientalistici in Onore di Giorgio Levi Della Vida II*: 1956.

Pérez, René. *Ibn Khaldūn, La Voie et la Loi, ou le Maître et le Juriste*, Paris: Sindbad, 1991.

———*La Rawḍat al-taʿrīf bi al-ḥubb al-sharīf* (*Le Jardin de la Connaissance du Noble Amour*). PhD diss., Universite de Lyon II, 1981.

Perlman, Moshe. 'Ibn Khaldūn on Sufism', *Biblotheca Orientalis*: 1960.

Pickthall, Marmaduke. *The Meaning of the Glorious Koran*. New York/ Toronto: Alfred A. Knopf, 1992.

Qalqashandī, Aḥmad, al-. *Ṣubḥ al-aʿshā*. Cairo: Dār al-Kutub al-Miṣriyya, 1922.

Qārī, ʿAlī, al-. *al-Asrār al-marfūʿa fī al-akhbār al-mawḍūʿa*. Beirut: Muḥammad Luṭfī al-Ṣabbāgh, 1986.

Qāshānī, ʿAbd al-Razzāq, al-. *Iṣtilāḥāt al-ṣūfiyya*. Cairo: n.p., 1981.

Qunawī, Ṣadr al-Dīn Muḥammad b. Isḥāq, al-. *Sharḥ al-Arbaʿīn*. Istanbul: n.p., 1990.

Qushayrī, Abū al-Qāsim, al-. *Al-Risāla*. Cairo: n.p., 1900.

Razi, Najm al-Din. *The Path of God's Bondsmen, from Origin to Return,* translated by Hamid Algar. New Jersey: Islamic Publications International, 1982.

Renaud, Henri. 'Divination et Histoire Nord Africaines aux Temps d'Ibn Khaldoun', *Archives Berbères et Bulletin des Hautes Etudes Marocaines, Hespéris*, vol. XXX: 1943.

———'Ibn al-Bannā de Marrakech, Sufi et Mathematicien', *Archives Berbères et Bulletin des Hautes Etudes Marocaines, Hespéris*, vol. XXV: 1938.

Rinn, Louis. *Marabouts et Khouans, Carte de l'Algerie*. Algiers: Adolphe Jourdan, 1884.

Ritter, Hellmut. 'Irrational Solidarity Groups: A Socio-Psychological Study in Connection with Ibn Khaldūn', *Oriens*, vol. 1, no. 1 (Jun. 1, 1948), pp. 1-44.

Rūmi, Jalāl al-Dīn. *The Mathnawī of Jalālu'ddin Rūmī*, 3 vols., edited and translated by Reynold A. Nicholson. London: Luzac and co., 1977.

Saadé, Ignacio. *El Pensamiento Religioso de Ibn Jaldun*. Madrid: Imprenta de Aldecoa, 1974.

Sakhāwī, Shams al-Dīn Muḥammad, al-. *Al-Ḍaw' al-lāmiʿ li-ahl al-qarn al-tāsiʿ*, 12 vols. Beirut: Dār Maktabat al-Ḥayāt, 1966.

———*Al-Maqāṣid al-ḥasana fī bayān kathīr min al-aḥādith al-mushtahira ʿalā al-alsina*, edited by ʿAbd Allah Muḥammad al-Ṣiddīq. Egypt: Dār al-Adab al-ʿArabī, 1956.

Schimmel, Annemarie. *Mystical Dimensions of Islam*. North Carolina: The University of North Carolina Press, 1986.

———'Reason and Mystical Experience in Sufism', in *Intellectual Traditions in Islam*, edited by Farhad Daftary. London: IB Tauris and the Institute of Ismaili Studies, 2000.

Schmidt, Nathaniel. *Ibn Khaldūn: Historian, Sociologist and Philosopher*. New York: Columbia University Press, 1930.

———'The Manuscripts of Ibn Khaldūn', *Journal of the American Oriental Society*, vols. x–vi: 1926.

Shaʿrānī, ʿAbd al-Wahhāb, al-. *Al-Ṭabaqāt al-kubrā*, 2 vols. Cairo: n.p., n.d.

Shehadi, Fadlou. 'Theism, Mysticism and Scientific History in Ibn Khaldūn', in *Islamic Philosophy*, edited by Michael E. Marmura. Albany: State University of New York Press, 1984.

Shorter Encyclopaedia of Islam, edited by H. A. R. Gibb and J. J. Kramers. Leiden: E. J. Brill, 1974.

Silvers-Alario, Laury. 'The Teaching Relationship in Early Sufism: A Reassessment of Fritz Meier's Definition of the *shaykh al-tarbiya* and the *shaykh al-taʿlim*', *The Muslim World*, vol. xciii: 2003.

Smith, Margaret. *Rābiʿa the Mystic and her Fellow-Saints in Islam*. Cambridge: Cambridge University Press, 1928.

Subkī, Tāj al-Dīn, al-. *Ṭabaqāt al-Shāfiʿiyya al-kubrā*, 10 vols. Cairo: Matbaʿat ʿĪsā al-Bābī al-Ḥalabī, 1964–76.

Suhrawardī, Shihāb al-Dīn, al-. *ʿAwārif al-maʿārif*, vol. v, in Ghazālī, *Iḥyā' ulūm al-dīn*. Beirut: Tabʿ al-Istiqāma, n.d..

Sulamī, Abū ʿAbd al-Rahmān, al-. *Ṭabaqāt al-ṣūfiyya*. Cairo: Dār al-Kitāb al-ʿArabī, 1953.

Syrier, Miya. 'Ibn Khaldūn and Islamic Mysticism', *Islamic Culture*, vol. xxi: 1947.

Tahānawī, Muḥammad ʿAlī, al-. *Kashshāf iṣtilāhāt al-funūn*, 2 vols. Calcutta: n.p., 1854–62.

Talbī, Mohamed. *Ibn Khaldūn et l'Histoire*. Tunis: Maison Tunisienne de l'Edition, 1973.

Terrasse, Henri. *Histoire du Maroc*, 5 vols. Casablanca: Editions Atlantide, 1930.

Tirmidhī, Muḥmmad, al-. *Al-Jāmiʿal-mukhtaṣar min al-sunan*, 4 vols. Cairo: n.p., 1292/1875.

Toynbee, Arnold Joseph. 'The Relativity of Ibn Khaldūn's Historical Thought', in *A Study of History*, vols. III and V. London: n.p., 1934–54.

Trimingham, Spencer. *The Sufi Orders in Islam*. Oxford: Oxford University Press, 1971.

Wāfī, Alī ʿAbd al-Wāhid, al-. *ʿAbqariyyāt Ibn Khaldūn*. Cairo: Dār ʿAlīm al-Kitāb, 1975.

———*Ibn Khaldūn, al-Muqaddima*. Cairo: Lajnat al-Bayān al-ʿArabi, 1957–1962.

Wansharīsī, Aḥmad, al-. *Al-Miʿyār al-mughrib wa'l-jāmiʿ al-muʿrib*, 12 vols., as consulted by Ibn Tāwīt al-Ṭanjī, *Shifā' al-sā'il li-tahdhīb al-masā'il*. Istanbul: Osman Yalçın Matbaası, 1957.

Wardī, ʿAlī. *Mantiq Ibn Khaldūn fī ḍaw' ḥaḍāratihi wa-siyāsatihi, muqaddima li-dirāsat al-manṭiq al-ijtimāʿī*. Cairo: n.p., 1962.

Wehr, Hans. *A Dictionary of Modern Written Arabic*. Ithaca: Spoken Language Services, Inc., 1979.

Wensick, A. J. *A Handbook of Early Muḥammadan Traditions*, 8 vols. Leiden: E. J. Brill, 1936.

White, Hayden V. 'Ibn Khaldūn in World Philosophy of History: Review Article', *Comparative Studies in Society and History*, vol. II. Cambridge: Cambridge University Press, 1959.

Wolfson, H. A. 'Ibn Khaldūn on Attributes and Predestination', *Speculum*, vol. XXXIV: 1959.

Xicluna, M. 'Quelques Legendes Relatives a Moulay ʿAbd al-Salam Ibn Mashish', *Archives Marocaines*, vol. III: 1905.

Zabīdī, Murtaḍā, al-. *Kitāb itḥāf al-sādah al-muttaqīn bi-sharḥ asrār Iḥyā' ʿulūm al-dīn li'l-Ghazālī*, 10 vols. Cairo: Matbaʿat al-Muyammaniyya, 1894.

Zarrūq, Aḥmad. *Al-Naṣīḥa al-kāfiya*. Lith. edition, n.p., n.d.

———*ʿIddat al-murīd*. Lith. edition, 1943, as consulted by Ibn Tāwīt al-Ṭanjī, *Shifā' al-sā'il li-tahdhīb al-masā'il*. Istanbul: Osman Yalçın Matbaası, 1957.

———*Qawāʿid al-taṣawwuf*. Cairo: n.p., 1976.

———*The Principles of Sufism* [*Qawāʿid al-taṣawwuf*], translated by Zaineb Istrabadi. ProQuest/UMI: 2002.

INDEX

Aaron, 38
ʿAbd Allāh b. ʿAmr b. al-ʿĀṣ, 52
ʿAbd al-Mu'min, xi
ʿAbd al-Salām b. Mashīsh, xi, xiv
abiding in God (*baqā'*), 45, 46
al-Ābilī, Abū ʿAbd Allāh Muḥammad b. Ibrāhīm, xviii–xix, xxiv
Abraham, 101
Abū Bakr b. al-ʿArabī, Qāḍī, x, xi
Abū Bakr al-Ṣiddīq, 27, 30, 36
Abū Burda b. Niyār, 99
Abū Dharr al-Ghifārī, 17
Abū al-Ḥasan ʿAlī b. ʿUthmān, xii
Abū Hurayra al-Dawsī, 17, 18
Abū ʿInān Fāris, Sultan, xii, xix, xxi
Abū Madyan of Tlemcen, xi–xii, xiv, xviii, xxi
Abū Muḥammad b. ʿAṭiyya, Qāḍī, 52
Abū Yazīd Tayfūr al-Bisṭāmī, 27, 33, 57, 69
ādāb, see conduct/proper conduct
Adam, 59, 61
ʿādāt, see customs
aḥadiyya, see Unity
aḥkām, see principles of behaviour
ʿĀ'isha, wife of the Prophet, 16, 24, 27, 38, 52
ʿālam al-amr, see World of Divine Command
ʿālam al-ghayb, see Unseen World
ʿālam al-rūḥāniyyāt, see World of Spiritual Entities
alchemy, 65; philosophical stone, 65
Algeria, x, xiv
ʿAlī b. Yūsuf b. Tashufīn, x
Almohads, x, xi–xii
Almoravids, x, xi–xii; legalism, xi
aʿmāl, see deed
Andalusia, xi, xvii, xix–xxii, xxviii, xxxv; intellectual life, xix–xx
Andalusian debate (books or shaykh?), ix, xli, 2–3, 79–107; customs, 98, 100, 101; dangers of the spiritual Path, 84, 87, 88, 106, 107; divine unity, 87, 89; essence of the Path itself, 98, 100, 101; exception, 99, 101; expert legist, 104, 106; following the Path without a shaykh at all, 98–9, 106; Ibn ʿAbbād, al-Rundī, letter by, xxxv, xxxvi–xxxvii; Ibn Khaldūn, *Shifā'*, ix, xix, xxvi, xxvii, xxviii, xxx, xxxv, xxxvii–xl, 2–3; inherited tradition/*manqūl*, 2; Law, 80, 98, 99, 100, 101–102, 106; method of spiritual travelling varies with each wayfarer, 87, 89, 91; mystical tasting, 90, 92, 94, 97, 100; al-Qabbāb, Aḥmad, *fatwā* by, xxviii, xxxv–xxxvi; Qur'ān, 79–80, 99, 102; rational reasoning/*maʿqūl*, 2; science of Sufism, 96; seeker attracted by God/*majdhūb*, 104, 105, 106, 107, 109–10; spiritual realities go beyond limits of conventional language, 81, 90, 92, 93, 94, 97; struggle for God-wariness, xxxviii, 80–1, 90, 91–2, 94, 97, 99, 103; struggle for unveiling and witnessing, xxxviii–xl, 80, 81,

90, 92, 93, 94–5, 97, 102, 103–104, 106; struggle for walking on the straight Path, xxxviii, 80–1, 90, 91–2, 94, 97, 103; Sunna, 79–80; wayfarer to God/*sālik*, 104–105, 106; see also Andalusian debate, on books; Andalusian debate, on the need of a shaykh; book; knowledge, transmission of; shaykh; spiritual struggle; spiritual struggle and the need of a shaykh
Andalusian debate, on books, 79–80, 83–6, 90–2, 96–7, 98, 106, 107; books alone are sufficient, 82, 83–4, 88, 90–1, 94, 102; books can mislead, 85–6, 90, 96, 97; need of explanation from a master, 92, 93; occasion when books must not be consulted, 105; uselessness of, 91, 93, 107; see also book; Andalusian debate
Andalusian debate, on the need of a shaykh, 80, 81–2, 84–5, 86–8, 91, 93, 98–106; shaykh's discernment, 82–3, 86–7, 88, 89, 94, 96, 97; shaykh's experience from travelling the Path, 79–80, 81–2, 90, 91, 92, 93, 94; shaykh's presence does perfect the struggles, 102; shaykh's sources of knowledge, 94–6; see also Andalusian debate; spiritual struggle and the need of a shaykh
angel, 23, 46, 55
annihilation (*fanā'*), 33, 34, 45, 46
al-Anṣārī, ʿAbd Allāh, xxi; *Manāzil al-sā'irīn*, xx
ʿaql, see intellect
ʿārif, see gnostic
ʿarsh, see the Throne
ascetic discipline (*riyāḍa*), 36, 38, 87; ascetic training, 39; the great ascetic discipline/*al-riyāḍa al-kubrā*, 66; spiritual struggle (third), 40, 54, 55, 76, 77; use of the Divine Names and, 66
asceticism (*zuhd*), 17, 42–3, 47, 48
Ashʿarī theology, x
al-Ashqar, Sharaf al-Dīn, xxiii
associationism (*shirk*), 9
atbāʿ al-tābiʿīn, see the Followers of the Followers
atheist, 42
austerity (*taqallul*), 17
ʿAyyād, Kāmil, xvi
Ayyubids, xiv

Baali, Fuad, xvi
al-Badawī, ʿAbd al-Raḥmān, xxv, xxviii, xxix
al-Badawī, Aḥmad, xiv
the Badawiyya (Aḥmadiyya), xiv
al-Baghdādī, Abū Ḥamza Muḥammad b. Ibrāhīm, 50
Bahlūl, 33, 107
baqā', see abiding in God
baṣīra, see insight
al-bāṭin, see the inward
Bāṭinīs, 15, 59, 87–8
Baybars II, Sultan, xxiii
beauty, 28–9, 34
bidʿa (pl. *bidaʿ*), see innovation
Bilāl al-Ḥabashī, 17
the blameworthy (*madhmūm*), 6, 7, 9, 12, 37, 39, 52, 67, 74; annihilation and obliteration, 46
body, xxxiv, 19, 20–1, 25, 61; corporeal forces, 40, 49, 54, 76; death, xxxviii, 29, 40; perception, 29; subtle reality and, 19, 20, 22, 55
book (*kitāb*), xix, xxxvii, xxxviii, xxxix, xl, 2, 77, 83; Ibn ʿAbbād, al-Rundī, xxxvii; knowledge from unveiling should not be registered in books, 56, 57, 67–8,

70; misleading the disciple, xxxvi, 85–6, 90, 96, 97; mystical tasting and, 92; science of unveiling, 56, 57, 67–8, 70; struggle for God-wariness, guidance from books in, 71, 90, 91–2, 94, 102; struggle for unveiling and witnessing, uselessness of books, 78, 93; struggle for walking on the straight Path, guidance from books in, 90, 91–2, 94, 102; Sufi books, ix, 48, 51, 56, 73, 83–6, 90–3 (are useless unless imparted by the masters, 91, 92; purpose and usefulness of, 92–3); uselessness of, 78, 90, 91, 93; see also Andalusian debate; Andalusian debate, on books
Bouthoul, Gaston, xvi
al-Bukhārī, Abū ʿAbd Allāh Muḥammad: *Al-Ṣaḥīḥ*, 18, 72
al-Būnī, Aḥmad b. ʿAlī, 60, 63, 65; *Al-Anmāṭ*, 66, 67
al-Būshanjī, ʿAli b. Aḥmad, xxxii

celibacy, 52
certainty (*yaqīn*), 26, 45, 48, 55; science of certainty/*ʿilm al-yaqīn*, xl, 45, 47; truth of certainty/*al-ḥaqq al-yaqīn*, xl, 45, 47; vision of certainty/*ʿayn al-yaqīn*, xl, 45, 47; will, a state of absolute certainty, 38
charismatic acts (*karāma*), 34, 44, 55, 86, 101, 106; charismatic gifts, 83, 101
Companions of the Prophet, xxx, xxxv, 8, 10, 17–18, 72, 103
conduct/proper conduct (*ādāb*), 32, 33, 56, 68
created universe (*kawn*), 25, 61, 62
creation (process of), 24–5; first creation, 63; God created instincts and forces within the heart, 6–9; mankind, 19, 22; Qur'ān, 25; subtle reality, 20, 25; the Tablet, 25
customs (*ʿādāt*), 5, 11, 17, 98, 100, 101
al-Daqqāq, Abū ʿAbd Allāh, xi
al-Dasūqī, Ibrāhīm, xiv
the Dasūqiyya (Burhāniyya), xiv
David, Prophet, 52
death, xxxviii; body, xxxviii, 29, 40; 'Die before you die', 43, 76; 'Man dies in keeping with how he lived…', 30; perception and knowledge after death, 29–30; perfection after death, 29; pleasure after death, 30; third spiritual struggle, premeditated death, 43, 76; unveiling after death, 29–30, 74; vision after death, 29–30, 76; witnessing after death, 34; witnessing and Self-disclosure, 33, 34
deed (*aʿmāl*), 8, 74–5; effect on the subtle reality, 20–1; evil deed, 21; good deed, 21; see also inward deed; outward deed
dervish, xv, xxii
devil/Devil, 23, 39, 43, 46, 83, 85, 86; Satan, 84
dhawq, see mystical tasting
dhikr, see remembrance
discernment: discernment of intimate findings, 100–101; God-wariness, 98, 99–100, 102; shaykh, 44, 75, 78, 82–3, 86–7, 88, 89, 94, 96, 97
disciple (*murīd*), 2; being a corpse in the hands of the mortician (shaykh), 42, 74; each wayfarer deserves an education that corresponds to his nature, 87; lack of sincere disciples, xxxvii; seeker attracted by God/*majdhūb*, 104, 105, 106, 107 (exemption from religious duties, 109); wayfarer to God/*sālik*, 104–105, 106; see also novice; Sufi-aspirant

discursive thinking (*fikr*), 6–7, 22, 24, 25, 43, 62; see also reason
dissemblance (*riyā'*), 9, 85
Divine Attributes, 20, 25, 28, 54, 58, 61, 70; unveiling and, 31; witnessing and, 32; see also God
divine graces, descent of (*munāzala*), 45, 47
Divine Names, 60, 61, 65; Allāh, 43; the Creator/*al-Bārī*, 6–7, 20, 25, 28, 29, 62; loci of manifestation, 63; Most Beautiful Names of God/*al-asmā' al-ḥusnā*, 63, 66; the One/*al-Wāḥid*, 62; perfection related to, 60, 61, 63, 67; power of, 65, 66–7; the Unseen/*al-Ghayb*, 31; witnessing, 67; see also God
divine unity (*tawḥīd*), xxi, 45, 77, 87, 89, 107; heart's focus on divine unity/*al-tawḥīd bi'l-qalb*, 13; self-realization of divine unity, 87; tasting of, 2; *tawḥīd-waḥda* doctrine, xxi; see also Oneness; Unicity; Unity
Dominion (*malakūt*), 22, 24, 28, 59, 68, 73; disclosure of knowledge of the Dominion, 57–8; secrets of the Dominion, 59, 68; understanding the Dominion, 68; witnessing and, 32
doubt, 31, 54, 85
the doubtful/uncertain, 35–6, 48

Egypt, x, xiii–xiv, xxii, xxiii; Alexandria, xiv; Cairo, xiv–xv, xvii, xxiii, xxviii; Sufism, xiv–xv
Emigrants, 18; People of the Veranda/*ahl al-ṣuffa*, 17–18
essence/Essence: essence/*dhāt*, 25, 30, 62; Divine Essence/*dhāt Allāh*, 54; Essence/*huwiyya*, 62; Essence of His Essence/*ʿayn ʿaynihi*, 63; the Most Sanctified Essence to Itself, 60; subtle reality, 25 (reaching the subtle reality's essence through itself, 25–6, 55); the Unique Essence/*al-dhāt al-aḥadiyya*, 61
excellence (*iḥsān*), 15, 99–100; harmony between the inward and the outward, 15
extinction, 31; *ikhmād*, xxxviii
Eve, 59

faith (*īmān*), 5, 8, 58; station of faith, 15, 99–100; subtle reality, 21
fanā', see annihilation
faqīh, see legist
faqr, see poverty
al-Fāsī, ʿAbd al-Qādir, ix, xxvi
al-Fāsī, Abū al-ʿAbbās Aḥmad, xxvii
al-Fāsī, Aḥmad b. al-Mallīḥ, xxix
fasting, 30, 40, 42, 52–3
felicity, 7, 9, 14, 16, 20, 80; corporeal felicity, 30; eternal felicity, 21; faith, 8; felicity of the heart: the vision of God's Face, 30, 32; gnosis, 76; Hereafter, 30, 32; knowledge, 27–31, 32; Law, 74; levels of, 28–9, 32, 51; meaning of, 27; Sufi, 110; ultimate felicity, 32, 45, 56, 74, 80
fikr, see discursive thinking
fiqh, see law
al-Fishtālī, Qāḍī xii, xxxvi
fiṭra, see primordial nature
Followers (*tābiʿūn*), 10, 27
Followers of the Followers (*atbāʿ al-tābiʿīn*), 10, 27
Footstool (*kursī*), 54, 59, 62
free choice, 9–10, 50, 73, 74–5, 80, 81, 82, 90

Gabriel, 72
Gabrieli, Francesco, xvi

al-Ghazālī, Abū Ḥāmid, x, xi, xii, 15, 19, 84, 90, 96; auto-da-fé, x–xi; different sources of knowledge for the soul, 24; *Iḥyā' ʿulūm al-dīn*, x, xi, xiii, xxxvi, 2, 12, 56, 83–4, 88, 92; Law/Sufi Path reconciliation, xiii, xviii, xxxiv; legist/Sufi-aspirant comparison, 12–13
Gibraltar, xxxv
gnosis (*maʿrifa*), 2, 6, 23, 45, 68, 83, 107; felicity, 76; gnosis of Oneness, 63; heart, 46; it leads to direct vision and witnessing, 30; union with God, 47; unveiling, 46
gnostic (*ʿārif*), xx, 30, 34, 47, 48, 57, 68; realization, 63
God: Divine Essence/*dhāt Allāh*, 54; divine gifts, 46, 53; forgiveness, 16; God created instincts and forces within the heart, 6–9; 'God has seventy veils of light', 33; knowledge of, 6–7, 11, 28, 32; love for God, 30–1, 43; mercy, 14, 16; nearness to, 55; vision of God's Face, 30, 32, 49; see also Divine Attributes; Divine Names
God-wariness (*taqwā*), 13; Andalusian debate, xxxviii, 80–1, 90, 91–2, 94, 97, 99, 103; books, guidance from, 71, 90, 91–2, 94, 102; discernment, 98, 99–100, 102; an individual obligation, 51, 71, 91; Law, 80–1, 102, 103; meaning, 35–6; outward and inward God-wariness, 35, 49; Prophets, following and imitating them, 103; Qur'ān, 26, 71, 80–1; salvation, 40, 49, 55–6, 70, 80, 93, 103; shaykh, need of, 71–3, 81; struggle for, xxxviii, 35–6, 40, 45, 47, 49, 55–6, 70, 77, 91; Sunna, 26, 71; unveiling and, 26, 40–1, 54, 56; worship, 40; see also moral care; spiritual struggle
goodness, 7, 21, 50, 80
Granada, xx, xxii, xl; Granada debate, ix, xxxvi–xxxvii, xli; Ibn Khaldūn, x, xxi, xxxiii, xxxi; see also Andalusia; Andalusian debate
gratitude (*shukr*), 45, 48
guidance: directly from God, 101, 105; Qur'ān, 98; right guidance, 16; wayfarer as guide, 44; see also shaykh

ḥāl, see state/spiritual state
al-Ḥallāj, al-Ḥusayn b. Manṣūr, xxvi, 68
Ḥalwī, Abū ʿAbd Allāh Shūdhī, xii
ḥaqīqa, see Truth
al-ḥaqīqa al-Muḥammadiyya, see Muḥammadan Reality
al-Ḥazmīrī, Abū Yaʿzzā, xi
heart, xxxi; colourations of, 12, 73, 76; corrupted spiritual state and, 75–6; deeds of the heart, xxxiv, xxxvii, 12, 17, 18, 35; expansion of the chest, 26; eye of the heart, 95; felicity of the heart: the vision of God's Face, 30, 32; focus on divine unity/*al-tawḥīd bi'l-qalb*, 13; God created instincts and forces within the heart, 6–9; going straight, 41–2; the innermost secret, 46; inspired knowledge, 23–4; Islam, 13; knowledge of the heart/*fiqh al-qulūb*, 11; knowledge of the inward/*fiqh al-bāṭin*, 11; pleasure of, 28; Prophet Muḥammad, 5–6, 7, 8, 9, 14; purification, 55; qualities of, 5; soul, 46; spherical shape and perfection of, 41; spirit, 46; spiritual state, xl–xli, 75; subtle reality, 19; Sufism and, xxxiv, 10–11, 18; three facets of, 46; unveiling, 41–2, 54–5; walking

on the straight Path, 41–2; will is the awakening of the heart to the quest for the Truth, 39; witnessing, 46; wounds of, 13
Hellfire, 14, 15, 30
Hereafter, 7, 13, 54; felicity, 30, 32; knowledge of the Hereafter/*fiqh al-ākhira*, 11; Sufism and, xxxiv, 12, 13; witnessing, 44
heresy (*zandaqa*), x, xii, xiii, xxii, xxv, xxxi, 2, 59, 75, 83; he who studies Sufism and does not study the Law is a heretic, xxxv
Ḥudhayfa b. al-Yamān, 8
Ḥulūlīs, 87–8
ḥurūf, see letters
al-Ḥuṣarī, Abū al-Ḥasan ʿAlī b. Ibrāhīm, 43
Ḥusayn, Ṭāhā, xvi
hypocrisy (*nifāq*), 8–9

ʿibāda, see worship
Ibāḥīs, 87–8
Ibn ʿAbbād al-Rundī, ix, xii, xiii, xviii, xix, xxvi, xxviii, xxxiv, xxxviii; letter by, xxxv, xxxvi–xxxvii
Ibn ʿAbbās, 22
Ibn ʿAjība, Aḥmad, ix, xxvii
Ibn ʿArabī, Muḥyī al-Dīn Muḥammad, 60, 63
Ibn al-ʿArīf, xi
Ibn ʿĀshir of Salé, xii, xiii, xix, xxi, xxxv
Ibn ʿAṭāʾ Allāh, xiii, xiv, 12, 35, 90, 92
Ibn al-Bannā, xviii; *Al-Mabāḥith al-aṣliyya*, xxvii
Ibn Barrajān, xi, 60
Ibn Baṭṭūṭa, xiv–xv
Ibn Dahhāq al-Awsi, 62
Ibn al-Fāriḍ, 60
Ibn al-Furāt, xxiii
Ibn Ḥanbal, Aḥmad, 81
Ibn Ḥirzihim, ʿAlī, x, xi
Ibn Khaldūn, Abū Bakr Muḥammad b. Khaldūn al-Ḥaḍramī (Ibn Khaldūn's father), xxv, xxvii, 1
Ibn Khaldūn, Abū Zayd ʿAbd al-Raḥmān, ix–x, xvii, xl–xli, 1; Andalusia, xvii, xix–xxii; death, xxiv; early training, xvii–xix; Egypt, xxii–xxiv; epistemology, xxxii–xxxiii; Fez, xxviii; head of Khanaqa al-Baybarsiyya, Cairo, xv, xvii, xxiii–xxiv; historian, xvi–xvii, xxv, xxxii, xli; judge and legist, xv, xvii, xxiii, xxxiii, xxxvii, xl, xli; the Maghrib, xiii, xvii–xix; the Mashriq, xiii, xvii, xxiii–xxiv; pilgrimage, xxiii; political life, x, xxi, xxii; religion, xvi, xvii, xxiv; spiritual life, x, xxii, xxxii, xxxvii; withdrawal from the world, xxi, xxii; see also the entries below for Ibn Khaldūn, Abū Zayd
Ibn Khaldūn, Abū Zayd: Sufism, xiii, xv–xxiv, xxxiii, xli; absolute complementarity between the inward and the outward, xxxiv; criticism and rejection of Sufism, xv–xvii, xxxiii–xxxiv; 'Sufism' and the 'Science of Sufism', xxxi–xxxii
Ibn Khaldūn, Abū Zayd: works, xxiv, xli; *Kitāb al-ʿIbar*, xxv; *Lubāb al-muḥassal*, xxv; minor works, xxv; *Al-Muqaddima*, x, xvi, xx, xxv, xxix (sixth chapter 'On Sufism', xvii); *Al-Taʿrīf bi-Ibn Khaldūn wa-riḥlatihi sharqan wa-gharban*, xvii, xxiv, xxix; see also *Shifāʾ al-sāʾil li-tahdhīb al-masāʾil*
Ibn Khaldūn, Muḥammad (Ibn Khaldūn's brother), xxvii

Ibn al-Khaṭīb, Lisān al-Dīn, xvii, xx, xxi–xxii, xxiii; imprisonment, torture and death, xxii, xxv; Sufism, xx; *Rawḍat al-taʿrīf bi'l-ḥubb al-sharīf*, xx, xxiii, xxv, xxvii–xxviii
Ibn Marzūq: *Musnad*, xii
Ibn Qasī, xi, 60
Ibn Qunfudh, al-Qusṭanṭīnī, xii; *Uns al-faqīr wa-ʿizz al-ḥaqīr*, xii
Ibn Sabʿīn, ʿAbd al-Ḥaqq, xxvii, 62, 63
Ibn Sawdakīn, 60
Ibn Sīnā, xviii; *Kitāb al-ishārāt*, xviii; *Kitāb al-shifāʾ*, xviii
Ibn Taghribirdī, Jamāl al-Dīn Yūsuf b., xiv
Ibn Tūmart, al-Mahdī, xi, xii
Ibn ʿUmar, ʿAbd Allāh, 36
Ibn al-Zayyāt, Abū Mahdī ʿIsā, xx–xxi; *Kitāb al-maqāmāt*, xx
Ibrāhīm b. al-Adham, prince of Balkh, xxi–xxii
idleness, 16, 68
iḥsān, see excellence
ikhlāṣ, see sincerity
ilhām, see inspiration
ʿilm, see knowledge/learning
ʿilm al-taṣawwuf, see science of Sufism
imagination, 22, 25, 29, 30, 43
īmān, see faith
imitation (*taqlīd*), xl, 68, 71
initiatic chain (*silsila*), xiv, xl, 87, 100, 106
innovation (*bidʿa*, pl. *bidaʿ*), 2, 11, 69, 74, 83
insight (*baṣīra*), xxxv
inspiration (*ilhām*), 23; see also inspired knowledge
inspired knowledge (*ʿilm al-ilhāmī*), xxxii, 26, 28, 95; acquired knowledge/inspired knowledge distinction, 26, 28; God-given knowledge, 26–7, 28, 49; heart, 23–4; intimate finding/*wijdānī*, xxxii, 2, 59, 69, 77, 90, 97, 102; purification, 40; saints and Sufis, xxxii, 23, 24, 32, 95–6; spiritual perception, 31; subtle reality, 23, 31, 40; unveiling, 31; walking on the straight path, 42; see also knowledge/learning
intellect (*ʿaql*), 77, 109; instinct of, 6, 7; love of perfection, 6; subtle reality, 19
interaction, 10, 12; interaction with God/*muʿāmala*, 45, 47, 55; science of interaction/*ʿilm al-muʿāmala*, 45, 54, 55–6
intention (*niyya*), 10, 16, 35; as the principle of all actions, 9–10; sincerity of intention, 43; worship, 10
the inward (*al-bāṭin*), 15, 33; ascetic training, 39; disregard of, 10; God-wariness, 35, 49; harmony between the inward and the outward, xxxiv, 14, 15; hypocrisy as contradiction between the outward and the inward, 9; importance of, 9; the inward always rules the outward, 5; knowledge of the inward/*fiqh al-bāṭin*, xxxiv, 11–12, 14, 34; science of the inward, 56; wisdom of legists and Sufis should be all-inclusive, xxxv; see also Sufism
inward deed, 5, 8, 12, 14, 15; deeds of the heart, xxxiv, xxxvii, 12, 17, 18, 35
irāda, see will
Islam, xvii, 13; Sufism, xxxv; see also religion
islām, see submission
iṭṭilāʿ, see spiritual perception

Jabarīs, 88
al-Jarīrī, Abū Muḥammad b. Ḥusayn, 40–1, 50

jinn, 22
Judgement Day, 21, 30
al-Junayd, Abū al-Qāsim, 17, 31, 37, 50
al-Jūzajānī, Abū ʿAlī, 34

karāma, see charismatic acts
kasal, see laziness
kashf, see unveiling
al-Kattānī, Muḥammad b. ʿAlī b. Jaʿfar, 50
kawn, see created universe
Khālid b. al-Walīd, 101
Khalifé, Ignace-Abdo, xxix, xxx
khanaqa (Sufi lodge), xiv–xv, xvii, xxiv
Khanaqa al-Baybarsiyya, Cairo, xxiii; Saʿīd al-Suʿadāʾ, xxiii
Khārijīs, 11
Khuzayma b. Thābit, 99
kitāb, see book
knowledge/learning (*ʿilm*), 6; acquired knowledge/*ʿilm al-kasbī*, xxxii, 22, 23, 26, 82; acquired knowledge/inspired knowledge distinction, 26, 28; degrees of, 30, 31, 32, 47; felicity and, 27–31, 32; the forbidden, 58; al-Ghazālī, different sources of knowledge for the soul, 24; hierarchical view of, xxxii–xxxiii, 22–4; the highest, most perfect, clearest and pleasurable knowledge, 28; knowledge is a seed to the vision that will turn into unveiling, 30, 32; knowledge of God, 6–7, 11, 28, 32; knowledge of the heart, 11; knowledge of the inward, xxxiv, 11–12, 34; knowledge of the ultimate Truth as object of Sufism, xxxii; mystical tasting, xxxv; perception and knowledge after death, 29–30; perfection, 6–7, 41; the permissible, 58; pleasure from knowledge obtained through unveiling, 31–4; Prophets, xxxii; realization and, 94, 95–6; scholars, xxxii; subtle reality, 20–1, 25, 30, 32; revelation, xxxii; 'to worship means to know', 22; see also inspired knowledge
knowledge, transmission of, xix, 11, 63, 72; by a conveyed report, xl, 72, 81; by example and direct observation, 72–3, 76; by masters, ix, xix, xxxv; disclosure of knowledge of the Dominion, 57–8; excessive systematization of learning, xix; legist, 72–3; oral transmission, xl, 10, 72, 100; written transmission, xl, 2, 72, 79, 81–2, 90, 107; secret between the servant and his Lord, xxvi; see also Andalusian debate; book
kufr, see misbelief
kursī, see Footstool

Lacoste, Yves, xvi–xvii
laṭīfa rabbāniyya, see subtle reality
Law (*sharīʿa*), xviii, 7; Andalusian debate, 80, 98, 99, 100, 101–102, 106; division into two branches, 11–17; felicity, 74; he who studies Sufism and does not study the Law is a heretic, xxxv; knowledge of the inward, 11–12, 14; knowledge of the outward, 11–12, 14, 15; Law/Sufi Path reconciliation, xiii, xviii, xxxiv; proper conduct, 33, 69; salvation, xxxiv, 14, 74; seeker attracted by God, 109; shaykh, 94, 95; struggle for God-wariness, 80–1, 102, 103; struggle for walking on the straight path, 80, 102; studying the Law is safer than unveiling divine secrets, 58, 59–60; Sufism and, xiii, xviii–xix, xxxi, 69; three levels at which the

Law can be kept, 14–15; unveiling, 95; at variance with the Law, 69; wayfarer to God/*sālik*, 104
law (substantive law/*fiqh*), xv, xvii, xxxv, 11, 12, 98; knowledge of the outward/*fiqh al-ẓāhir*, 11
the lawful, 13, 36, 48; it is evident, 35; third spiritual struggle, lawfulness of, xxxix, 51–2, 92, 93, 103, 105
lawḥ, see Tablet/Preserved Tablet
laylat al-qadr, see Night of Destiny
laziness (*kasal*), 16, 44, 68, 75
legist (*faqīh*), x, xiii, xxxi, 12, 81; expert legist/*al-faqīh al-muftī*, 15, 104, 106; Ibn Khaldūn on, xxxiv; knowledge of the outward/*fiqh al-ẓāhir*, 11; legist/Sufi-aspirant comparison, xxxiv, xl, 12–13; legist/Sufi close relationship, xiii, xviii; legist/Sufi dichotomy, x, xxxiii, xxxiv, xxxvii; state legist, x, xi; substantive law, 11, 12; transmission of knowledge, 72–3; wisdom of legists and Sufis should be all-inclusive, xxxv; worship, 10; see also the outward
letters (*ḥurūf*), 63–5
light, 26, 70, 96, 107, 109; bewildered by the light of Self-disclosure and witnessing, 33; discerning light/*al-nūr al-furqānī*, 98, 100, 102; disclosure of the lights, 46, 80; lifting of the veil, 46; light of God, 26; light of witnessing/*nūr al-mushāhada*, 48
litany (*wird*), xxi, 43, 48
love, xl; *ʿishq*, xl; love for God, 30–1, 43; love of perfection, 6; *maḥabba*, 45

madhmūm, see the blameworthy
madness, 33, 68, 85; seeker attracted by God, 107, 109
madrasa, xiv, xvii; opposition to the building of, xix; state-controlled *madrasa*, xii
the Maghrib (the West), ix–xiii, xiv, xviii, xxx, xli; legist/Sufi close relationship, xiii, xviii; religious and doctrinal unity of, x; saints in, xii; spiritual life, xi–xii; Sufism in, xii, xv, xviii–xix, xxv
magic, 65–7, 68; magical squares, 64, 66; magical sciences, 42
maḥabba, see love
maḥmūd, see the praiseworthy
maḥū, see obliteration
al-Makkī, Abū Ṭālib: *Qūt al-qulūb fī muʿāmalat al-maḥbūb*, 92
malakūt, see the Dominion
Mālik b. Anas, xxxv; *Muwaṭṭa'*, xvii
Mālikī school, x, xi, xiii, xxxiii, xxxv, xli
Mamluks, xiv, xv, xxiii
manifestation (*ẓuhūr*): degrees of, 60
mankind, 22, 26, 38, 51, 60, 109; creation of, 19; trust, 19–20; see also body; subtle reality
maqām, see station/spiritual station
al-Maqqarī, Abū ʿAbd Allāh, xviii, xix, xx
al-Maqrīzī, Aḥmad Taqī al-Dīn, xxiii
maʿrifa, see gnosis
Marinids, xii–xiii, xiv, xix
martyr, 40, 49, 51
the Mashriq (the East), x, xiii–xiv, xvii, xviii, xli; Law/Sufi Path reconciliation, xiii, xviii; saints in, xiv; Sufism, xiv
Maslama al-Majrīṭī, Abū al-Qāsim: *Ghāyat al-ḥakīm*, 67
al-Masnāwī, Abū ʿAbd Allāh, ix, xxvi–xxvii; *Juhd al-muqill al-qāṣir*, xxvi
master, see shaykh
misbelief (*kufr*), 8, 69
al-Miṣrī, Dhū al-Nūn, xiv, 47

moderation, 36, 37, 39, 42
monasticism (*rahbāniyya*), 40, 51–2, 74
moral care (*wara*ʿ), 11, 12, 35, 45, 47, 49, 71, 91; see also God-wariness
Moroccan Royal Library, Rabat, xxviii
Morocco, x, xii, xiii, xiv, xxi, xxix; Fez, x, xi, xii, xviii, xxviii, xxxv, 1–2
Moses, 38
mosque, 17, 18, 69
Mother of the Book, 20
muʿallim, see teacher
muḥāḍara, see presence with God
Muḥammadan Reality (*al-ḥaqīqa al-Muḥammadiyya*), 61
al-Muḥāsibī, al-Ḥārith b. Asad, 81, 90; *Kitāb al-riʿāya*, xix, 2, 12, 56, 92
mujāhada, see spiritual struggle
mukāshafa, see unveiling
multiplicity, 60, 61, 62
munāzala, see divine graces, descent of
murīd, see disciple
al-Mursī, Abū al-ʿAbbās, xiv
mushāhada, see witnessing
mutaṣawwif, see Sufi-aspirant
Muʿtazila, 11
Muṭīʿ al-Ḥāfiẓ, Muḥammad, xxx
muwāṣala, see union with God
mystical/ecstatic experience, xxxvi, 47, 56–7, 86, 87, 88; only those who have attained mystical experiences can understand them, 91
mystical tasting (*dhawq*), xxxv, xxxviii, 28, 45, 65, 77; Andalusian debate, 90, 92, 94, 97, 100; books and, 92; legal principles and, 95, 97, 109–10; of divine unity, 2; of the spiritual states, xl; Self-disclosure, 47
mysticism, see Sufism
nafs, see soul
najāt, see salvation
nifāq, see hypocrisy
Night of Destiny (*laylat al-qadr*), 54–5
niyya, see intention
North Africa, xi, xii, xiii, xix–xx
novice, xxxvi, xxxviii, 3, 60; see also disciple; Sufi-aspirant

obliteration (*maḥū*), 23, 31, 33, 40, 43, 45, 46
Oneness (*waḥda*), xx, xxvii, xxxiv, 60, 61, 62–3, 68; gnosis of Oneness/*maʿrifat al-waḥda*, 63; *tawḥīd-waḥda* doctrine, xxi; see also divine unity; Unicity; Unity
opinion: *ra'y*, 60; *ẓann*, 26
the outward (*al-ẓāhir*), 5, 33; ascetic training, 39; God-wariness, 35, 49; harmony between the inward and the outward, xxxiv, 14, 15; hypocrisy as contradiction between the outward and the inward, 9; knowledge of the outward/*fiqh al-ẓāhir*, xxxiv, 11–12, 14, 15; wisdom of legists and Sufis should be all-inclusive, xxxv; see also legist
outward deed, 5, 8, 34; free choice and, 9–10; station of faith, 15; station of submission, 15

Paradise, 30–1, 34
path/straight path, 7, 16, 34; see also walking on the straight Path
patience (*ṣabr*), 5, 45, 46, 48
Pen (*qalam*), 25, 54, 61
perception, 82; faculties of, 27; levels of, 29; perception after death, 29; perception of Beauty in the presence of the Lord, 28–9; perfection of, 41; rational perception, 77; sensorial perception, 73, 77; subtle reality, 22–6, 27–8; see also spiritual perception
perfection, 14, 27, 52, 73, 99; after

death, 29; Divine Names, 60, 61, 63, 67; heart, spherical shape and perfection of, 41; the highest perfection/*al-kamāl al-aʿlā*, 6–7; intellect, love of perfection, 6; knowledge, 6–7, 41; Prophet Muḥammad, 38; Self-disclosure contains perfection, 61; spiritual perfection, xxxv; subtle reality, 20–1, 22–3, 25; virtue, 21, 41
Pérez, René: *La Voie et la Loi ou le Maître et le Juriste*, xxx
philosophy, xxxiii, 60, 62, 68, 90
pilgrimage, xv, xxiii, 58–9, 72
Plato, xxvi, 26
pleasure: after death, 30; the highest pleasure, 28–9; the most pleasurable knowledge, 28; related to corporeal instincts, 28; related to the heart, 28
Portugal, xi
positivism, xvi, xxxii
poverty (*faqr*), 17, 40, 50, 96
the praiseworthy (*maḥmūd*), 6, 7, 12
prayer, 9, 30; Gabriel, 72; Prophet Muḥammad, 13, 26, 52, 72; ritual/obligatory prayer, 13, 36, 43, 48, 77; supplication, 7; teaching of, 72; see also worship
Predecessors (*salaf*), 18, 80, 103
presence with God (*muḥāḍara*), 31, 45, 47
Presences, 61; Nebulous Presence/*al-ḥaḍra al-ʿamāʾiyya*, 61, 62; Presence of Fine Dust/*al-ḥaḍra al-habāʾiyya*, 62
primordial nature (*fiṭra*), 20, 53, 57
principles of behaviour (*aḥkām*), 5, 10, 96, 103; mystical tasting and, 95, 97, 109–10
Prophet Muḥammad, xxxi, 53, 96, 99; ascension of/*miʿrāj*, 55; fasting, 40, 52–3; following the Sunna, 40, 52; heart, 5–6, 7, 8, 9, 14; initiatic chain, 87, 100; perfection of noble character traits, 38; prayer, 13, 26, 52, 72; Qur'ān, 38, 99, 102 ('His nature was the Qur'ān', 38); revelation to, 24, 55; three statuses, 102–103 (guidance of the people, 102; personal spiritual struggle, 102; spiritual perception through meditation, 102–103); unveiling, 102–103
prophethood, 23, 54, 58, 80; vision, 24
Prophets, 14, 36, 38, 49, 55, 61, 63, 99; God-wariness, 103; knowledge, xxxii; knowledge of the Dominion, 57–8; primordial nature of, 53, 57; revelation, 23; unveiling and witnessing, masters of, 57; walking on the straight Path, 49, 73, 91, 93, 103, 107
purification (*taṣfiya*): ascetic training, 39; degrees of, 31; heart, 55; inspired knowledge, 40; self-purification, xiii; soul, 24, 31, 37; subtle reality, 21, 22, 23, 31; Sufi, 32; unveiling, 25, 31, 42, 74
purity (*ṣafāʾ*), 18; purity of deeds and states, 75

al-Qabbāb, Abū al-ʿAbbās, ix, xxviii, xxxv; *fatwā*, xxviii, xxxv–xxxvi
qalam, see Pen
al-Qalqashandī, Aḥmad, xv
al-Qassāb, Muḥammad b. ʿAlī, 50
Qur'ān, xi, xvii, xviii, xxxviii, 36, 40, 70, 74; Andalusian debate, 79–80, 99, 102; creation, 25; as foundation of the wayfaring, 79, 80; guidance, 98; memorization, xvii, 27; Prophet Muḥammad, 38; Qur'ānic recitation, 43, 48; shaykh, xxxix, 94, 95, 99; struggle for God-

wariness, 26, 71, 80–1; struggle for walking on the straight path, 36, 38, 40, 49, 73, 80–1, 91, 93, 107; Sūrat al-Fātiḥa, 36; Sūrat Hūd, 37; worship, 22
al-Qushayrī, Abū al-Qāsim, 11, 31, 33, 38–9, 71, 74, 78, 92; *Al-Risāla*, xxxvi, xxxviii, 56, 71

Rābiʿa al-ʿAdawīyya, 30–1, 57
Rāfiḍīs, 11
rahbāniyya, see monasticism
ra'y, see opinion
al-Rāzī, Najm al-Dīn, xxxix
realities (*ḥaqā'iq*), 25, 41, 42, 54, 61; Muḥammadan Reality, 61
realization (*taḥqīq*), xl, 63, 71, 95; knowledge and, 94, 95–6; levels of, xl, 63; self-realization, 2, 84, 87, 90
reason, xviii; limited role of, xxxiii; rational reasoning/*maʿqūl*, 2; see also discursive thinking
rectitude, 9, 36, 37, 39–40
religion, xvi–xvii; revelation, 23; see also Islam
remembrance (*dhikr*), xxi, 31, 43–4, 48, 80; formula of, 43
renunciation (*zuhd*), 45
repentance (*tawba*), 35, 45, 47–8
Resurrection, 55, 58
retreat/spiritual retreat, xxi, 42, 43–4, 48, 77, 80; aim of, 48
revelation (*waḥy*), xxxii, 23, 24, 55; religion, 23
the righteous, 40, 49, 51
Ritter, Hellmut, xvi
riyā', see dissemblance
riyāḍa, see ascetic discipline
rūḥ, see spirit
al-Rūmī, Jalāl al-Dīn, xl
Ruwaym al-Baghdādī, 50
ru'yā, see vision
ṣabr, see patience
ṣafā', see purity
saint, xi, xx, xxi, 55, 57, 63, 95; *abdāl*, 2; *awliyā'*, 23; the Maghrib, xii; the Mashriq, xiv; Muḥammadan saints, 61; *walī*, 55
sainthood (*walāya*), 109
salaf, see Predecessors
Salé, xii, xiii, xix, xxi, xxxv, 99
Salmān al-Fārisī, 17
salvation (*najāt*), 12, 13, 14, 15, 51, 58; God-wariness, 40, 49, 55–6, 70, 80, 93, 103; Law, xxxiv, 14, 74; Sufism, 18, 34
Samnūn, Abū al-Ḥasan, 50
science of Sufism (*ʿilm al-taṣawwuf*), xxxi, xxxii, xxxvi, 49, 96
secret, 46, 54, 63, 69, 77; Divine Names, 66; keeping divine mysteries hidden, 56, 57–8, 59, 68, 70; letters, 63, 64–5; secrets of the Dominion, 59, 68; Sufism, xxiv, xxvi, 18, 56, 59, 68, 70, 77, 78, 91, 95
Self-disclosure (*tajallī*), xxxiv, xxxix, 29–30, 32, 46, 60; bewildered by the light of, 33; dangers, 33, 44; death, 33; degrees of, 30; mystical tasting, 47; Self-disclosure contains perfection, 61; see also witnessing
senses, 22, 23, 24, 25, 77, 107; external senses, 23, 24; reliance on, 72, 73
al-Shādhilī, Abū al-Ḥasan, xi, xiv
the Shādhiliyya, xi, xiii; origins, xiv
al-Shāfiʿī, Muḥammad b. Idrīs, 81
sharīʿa, see Law
al-Sharīshī, Abū Bakr Muḥammad b. Aḥmad: *Al-Rā'iyya fī al-sulūk*, xxvii
al-Shāṭibī, Abū Isḥāq, ix, xxviii
shaykh (Sufi master), xiii, xxxvi, xl, 81;

alive or dead, 100; dangers of excessive systematization of learning, xix; difficulty in finding a shaykh, xxxvii, 104, 105–106; discernment and understanding of higher realities, 44, 75, 78, 82–3, 86–7, 88, 89, 94, 96, 97; easing the way of the wayfarer to his Lord, 39; emulation of, 42, 56, 85–6; excessive need for, xxxvii; experience from travelling the Path, 42, 43–4, 74, 75, 78, 79–80, 81–2, 90, 91, 92, 93, 94; following one master only, 98; Law, 94, 95; need for a living master, xxxvi; Qur'ān, xxxix, 94, 95, 99; *shaykh al-murabbī*/educating shaykh, 76, 80; *shaykh al-taʿlīm*/teaching shaykh, xxxvi–xxxvii, xxxviii; *shaykh al-taʿlīm*/*shaykh al-tarbiya* comparison, xl; *shaykh al-tarbiya*/educating shaykh, xxxvi, xxxvii, xxxix; spiritual essence of, xxxix; spiritual guide, xxiv–xxv, xxxvi–xxxvii, xxxix, xl; spiritual state, 85–6; Sunna, 94, 95; Sunni shaykh, 85; types of, xxxvi; see also Andalusian debate; Andalusian debate, on the need of a shaykh; spiritual struggle and the need of a shaykh
Shībān al-Rāʿī, 81
al-Shiblī, Abū Bakr, 43
Shifāʾ al-sāʾil li-tahdhīb al-masāʾil, x, xxiv–xxxi; Andalusian debate, ix, xix, xxvi, xxvii, xxviii, xxx, xxxv, xxxvii–xl, 2–3; appendix, xxxix; authorship, xxv–xxvii; date of composition, xxvii–xxviii; devoted to Sufism, xvii; Fez, xxviii; Ibn Khaldūn's silence on, xxiv–xxv; love, xl; manuscripts, xxvi, xxviii–xxix, xxx; nature and purpose of, xxx–xxxi; one of Ibn Khaldūn's early works, xxiv; origins of, ix; printed editions and translations, xxix–xxx; see also Ibn Khaldūn, Abū Zayd ʿAbd al-Raḥmān
shirk, see associationism
shukr, see gratitude
al-Shushtarī, Abū al-Ḥasan, xxvi–xxvii, 62; *Al-Qaṣīda al-nūniyya*, xxvi
ṣiddīqūn, see sincere believers
silsila, see initiatic chain
sincere believers (*ṣiddīqūn*), 23, 36, 45, 51, 93, 95, 107
sincerity (*ikhlāṣ*), 35, 37, 45, 58, 110; lack of sincere disciples, xxxvii; sincerity of intention, 43
sleep, 40, 42, 52, 53
soul (*nafs*), 7; curing and healing the character traits of, 36–7, 39–40, 49, 73, 91; guide on the straight path, 8; heart, 46; power of, 65, 66; purification, 24, 31, 37; spiritual struggle, 24, 31, 36–40; subtle reality, 19; subtle soul/*laṭīfa rūḥāniyya*, 109; walking on the straight path, 36–7, 39–40, 49, 73, 91
Spain, x, xx; see also Andalusia; Granada
sphere: celestial spheres/*aflāk*, 62, 63, 65, 66; heart, spherical shape and perfection of, 41
spirit (*rūḥ*), xxxviii, 10; heart, 46; Spirit, 57–8; subtle reality, 19
spiritual guide, see shaykh
spiritual perception (*iṭṭilāʿ*), 24, 28, 31; third spiritual struggle, 40, 42, 49, 73, 92; see also perception; unveiling
spiritual struggle (*mujāhada*), xxxviii, 24, 31, 42, 45–9, 56; divine gifts, 46; first spiritual struggle/God-wariness, xxxviii, 35–6, 40, 45,

47, 49, 55–6, 70, 77, 91; science of Sufism, 49; second spiritual struggle/walking on the straight path, xxxviii, 36–40, 45, 47, 49, 51, 56, 70, 77, 91; soul, 24, 31, 36–40; Sufi, 3, 18, 32, 44–5, 48; Sufism, 45, 49, 50–1, 56, 70–1; stations, 47–8; see also God-wariness; spiritual struggle (third); spiritual struggle and the need of a shaykh; walking on the straight Path

spiritual struggle (third), 40–4, 49, 70; Andalusian debate, xxxviii–xl, 80, 81, 90, 92, 93, 94–5, 97, 102, 103–104, 106; ascetic discipline, 40, 54, 55, 76, 77; asceticism and spiritual retreat, 42–4; books, uselessness of, 78, 93; conditions to, 40–4, 54; corporeal forces, 40, 49, 54, 76; death (premeditated), 43, 76; difference between 'walking on the straight path' and 'unveiling', 71; God-wariness, 40–1, 54, 56; lawfulness of, xxxix, 51–2, 92, 93, 103, 105; purification, 74; shaykh, xxxviii–xl, 42, 43–4, 73–8, 80; sincerity of intention, 43; spiritual perception, 40, 42, 49, 73, 92; spiritual states, 74; unveiling, xxxviii–xl, 40, 41, 45, 49, 54, 56, 70, 92; walking on the straight path, 41, 44, 54, 56; witnessing, xxxviii–xl, 40, 49, 54, 70; see also spiritual struggle; unveiling; witnessing

spiritual struggle and the need of a shaykh, 71, 73; the need for a master varies according to the struggle, 71, 106; no need of a shaykh, 71, 73, 81, 102; occasions when a shaykh is imperative, xxxviii–xl, 73–8, 106; occasions when a shaykh is strongly recommended, 73; struggle for God-wariness, 71–3, 81; struggle for unveiling and witnessing, xxxviii–xl, 42, 43–4, 73–8, 80; struggle for walking on the straight Path, 73, 81; see also Andalusian debate, on the need of a shaykh; shaykh; spiritual struggle

Spiritual World (*al-ʿālam al-rūḥānī*), xxxii, xxxviii, 2, 20, 26, 73

stars, 63, 67

state/spiritual state (*ḥāl*), xxxvi, xxxviii, xl, 2, 45; acquired virtues and, 74–5; colourations, 47; corrupted spiritual state, 75, 89; heart and, xl–xli, 75; shaykh, 85–6; state-enslaved mystic, 85, 86; state of absolute certainty/*ḥāl al-yaqīn*, 38; station of dreams/*ḥāl al-ru'yā*, 23; third spiritual struggle, 74; virtues that cannot be acquired are called 'state', 46

station/spiritual station (*maqām*), xxxvi, 23–4, 45, 56; control over, 33; spiritual struggle, 47–8; station of ultimate unification/*maqām jamʿ al-jamʿ*, 47; station of unification/*maqām jamʿ*, 47; virtues that depend on choice or acquisition are called 'station', 46

submission (*islām*), 15, 99–100

subtle reality (*laṭīfa rabbāniyya*), 19; acquired knowledge, 22, 23; body, 19, 22, 55 (effects of the body's actions on, 20); created by God, 20, 25; deed, 20–1; faith, 21; heart, 19; inspired knowledge, 23, 31, 40; knowledge/learning, 20–1, 30, 32 (learning and gnosis as the pleasure of the subtle reality, 27; perfection through knowledge, 25); perception, 22–6, 27–8; perfection, 20, 21, 22–3, 25; purification of, 21, 22, 23, 31; reaching the subtle reality's essence through itself, 25–6, 55; revelation, 23; World of Divine Command, 20, 22; see also heart; intellect; soul; spirit

Sufi: etymology of the name 'Sufi', 17–18 (People of the Veranda/*ahl al-ṣuffa*, 17–18; *ṣafā'*/purity, 18; *ṣūf*/wool, 17; *ṣuffa*, 17, 18); felicity, 110; first/earlier Sufis, xxxi, xxxv, 3, 18, 32, 49; legist/Sufi-aspirant comparison, xxxiv, xl, 12–13; legist/Sufi close relationship, xiii, xviii; legist/Sufi dichotomy, x, xxxiii, xxxiv, xxxvii; purification, 32; spiritual struggle, 3, 18, 32, 44–5, 48; the term, 11, 17; those who value actions stemming from the heart are called 'Sufis', 10–11; unveiling, 32, 80; witnessing, 32–3; see also Sufism

Sufi-aspirant (*mutaṣawwif*), xxxix, 12–13, 18; see also disciple; novice

Sufi lodge, see *khanaqa*; *zāwiya*

Sufi master, see shaykh

Sufi order, see *ṭariqa*

Sufism (*taṣawwuf*), x, 3, 18; crackdown on, x–xi; criticism, xv–xvii, xxxiii–xxxiv; definition, 18, 50–1, 70; discretion, xxv; Eastern/Western Sufism connections, xiv; frontier outposts/*ribāṭ*, xii, xiv, 1; heart, xxxiv, 10–11, 18; Hereafter, xxxiv, 12, 13; hostels/*buyūt al-fuqarā'*, xii; Islam and, xxxv; Law, xiii, xviii–xix, xxxi, 69; Law/Sufi Path reconciliation, xiii, xviii, xxxiv; knowledge of the inward, 11; knowledge of the ultimate Truth as object of Sufism, xxxii; the Maghrib, xii, xv, xviii–xix, xxv; the Mashriq, xiv; nomenclature and specific terms, 45–6, 49, 56, 68, 73, 92; rural area, xii, xiii, xiv; salvation, 18, 34; science of unveiling, 59; secret, xxiv, xxvi, 18, 56, 59, 68, 70, 77, 78, 91, 95; spiritual struggle, 45, 49, 50–1, 56, 70–1; urban area, xii, xiii; virtue, 50; Western Sufism, xi, xiv; see also the inward; science of Sufism; Sufi

Ṣuhayb al-Rūmī, 17

al-Suhrawardī, Shihāb al-Dīn: *ʿAwārif al-maʿārif*, xxxviii, 56

sulūk, see wayfaring

Sunna, xi, xxxviii, 44, 70, 74, 90; Andalusian debate, 79–80; following the Sunna, 40, 52; as foundation of wayfaring, 79, 80; shaykh, 94, 95; struggle for God-wariness, 26, 71; struggle for walking on the straight path, 40, 73

Sunnism, xii, xxxi, 11; Sunni shaykh, 85

supererogatory act of devotion, 43, 52, 77, 104

tābiʿūn, see the Followers

Tablet/Preserved Tablet (*lawḥ*), 25, 54, 61

taḥqīq, see realization

tajallī, see Self-disclosure

ṭalāṣim, see talismans

talismans (*ṭalāṣim*), 65–6, 67

Tanāsukhīs, 88

al-Ṭanjī, Muḥammad b. Tāwīt, xxv–xxvi, xxvii, xxviii, xxix, xxx

taqallul, see austerity

taqlīd, see imitation

taqwā, see God-wariness

ṭariqa (Sufi order), xii, xiv

taṣawwuf, see Sufism

taṣfiya, see purification
al-Taṭwānī, Abū Bakr, xxviii
tawakkul, see trust
tawba, see repentance
tawḥīd, see divine unity
teacher (*muᶜallim*), xxxviii, 71; educating teacher/*al-muᶜallim al-murrabī*, 73; First Teacher/*al-muᶜallim al-awwal*, 87
temporal world, 16, 17; 'Be in this world like a stranger or like a passer-by', 17; body and, 20; degrees of knowledge gathered in, 30; legist, 13
al-Thawrī, Abū ᶜAbd Allāh, 30
al-Tilimsānī, al-Sharīf, xix
Throne (*ᶜarsh*), 54, 59, 62
trust, 69, 86, 105; *amāna*, 19–20; trust in God/*tawakkul*, 45, 46, 47, 48
Truth (*ḥaqīqa*), xxxv, 55; the One is the Truth, 62; truth of certainty/ *al-ḥaqq al-yaqīni*, xl, 45, 47; will is the awakening of the heart to the quest for the Truth, 39
Tunisia, x, xiv; Tunis, ix, xvii, xviii

Uludağ, Suleyman, xxx
ᶜUmar b. al-Khaṭṭāb, 8–9, 17, 26–7, 81
Unicity (*wāḥidiyya*), 60, 61; see also divine unity; Oneness
union with God (*muwāṣala*), 45, 47
Unity (*aḥadiyya*), 60, 61; see also divine unity; Oneness
the unlawful, 13, 36, 48; it is evident, 35
Unseen World (*ᶜālam al-ghayb*), 57
unveiling (*kashf/mukāshafa*), xxxiii, xxxviii, 23, 28, 30, 31, 45, 49; after death, 29–30, 74; conveyed report on, 81; dangers of, 44, 53, 75, 80; Divine Attributes, 31; first level of, 31; fullness of, 31, 46; God-wariness and, 26, 40–1, 54, 56; heart, 41–2, 54–5; inspired knowledge, 31; knowledge, 54; knowledge is a seed to the vision that will turn into unveiling, 30, 32; knowledge resulting from unveiling should not be registered in books, 56, 57, 67–8, 70; Law, 95; levels of, 31–2; lifting of the veil/*rafᶜ al-ḥijāb*, 18, 25, 29, 33, 42, 44, 46, 54, 70, 73, 80, 92; pleasure from knowledge obtained through, 31–4; presence with God, 31; Prophet Muḥammad, 102–103; Prophets, 57; purification and, 25, 31, 42, 74; removal of the veil/*inkishāf*, 23, 29, 31, 32; science of unveiling, 54, 55, 56–9, 63, 67–8, 69, 70; spiritual perception, 40, 49, 73; Sufi, 32, 80; ultimate felicity, 45, 56, 74, 80; vision of certainty/*ᶜayn al-yaqīn*, 47; walking on the straight path, 41–2, 44, 54; witnessing as the highest level of, 31–2; see also spiritual struggle (third); veil; witnessing
ᶜUthmān b. Maẓᶜūn, 52
Uways al-Qaranī, 81
Uwaysīs, xxxix

veil, 25; 'God has seventy veils of light', 33; see also unveiling
vice, 21, 46, 39
virtue, 21, 34, 36, 41, 45–6, 90; acquired virtues, 74–5; ascetic training, 39; heart, 46; perfection of, 21, 41; praiseworthy virtues, 37, 39, 45, 46, 74; 'state', 46; 'station', 46; Sufism, 50
vision (*ru'yā*), 24, 47; after death, 29–30, 76; direct vision/*naẓar*, xl; prophethood, 24; spiritual vision, 33, 76, 80, 101, 107; true vision/ *al-ru'yā al-ṣāliḥa*, 24; vision of

certainty/ʿayn al-yaqīn, xl, 45, 47; vision of God's Face, 30, 32, 49
Von Kremer, Alfred, xvi

waḥda, see Oneness
wāḥidiyya, see Unicity
waḥy, see revelation
walāya, see sainthood
walking on the straight Path: Andalusian debate, xxxviii, 80–1, 90, 91–2, 94, 97, 103; books, guidance from, 90, 91–2, 94, 102; curing and healing the character traits of, 36–7, 39–40, 49, 73, 91; easing the way of the wayfarer to his Lord, 39, 53; felicity, 70; going straight is arduous, 36, 37; heart, 41–2; an individual obligation, 38, 92; inspired knowledge, 42; Law, 80, 102; Prophets, 49, 93 (character traits of, 73, 91, 103, 107); Qur'ān, 36, 38, 40, 49, 80–1 (character traits of, 40, 73, 91, 93, 107); shaykh, need for, 73, 81; soul as guide on the straight path, 8, 36–7, 39–40, 49, 73, 91; struggle for, xxxviii, 36–40, 45, 47, 49, 51, 56, 70, 77, 91; Sunna, 40, 73; third spiritual struggle, 41, 44, 54, 56; unveiling, 41–2, 44, 54; see also path/straight path
al-Wansharīsī, Aḥmad, ix; *Al-Miʿyār*, ix
waraʿ, see moral care
Wardi, Ali, xvi
al-Wāṣiṭī, Abū Bakr Muḥammad, 41
wayfaring (*sulūk*), xxxix, 70; dangers of, 84, 87, 88, 106, 107; gradual wayfaring/*sulūk wa-tadarruj*, 71; meanings dealing with the core of, 77–8; method of spiritual travelling varies with each wayfarer, 87, 89, 91; mystical wayfaring, xxx, xxxiii, xl, 88–9; Qur'ān, 79, 80; Sunna, 79, 80
weakness, 68, 87
will (*irāda*), 38–9, 45, 46; it is the awakening of the heart to the quest for the Truth, 39; a state of absolute certainty, 38
wird, see litany
witnessing (*mushāhada*), xxxiii, xxxviii, 30, 45, 46, 48; after death, 34; bewildered by the light of, 33; death, 33, 34; definition, 31; Divine Names, 67; 'Do not seek witnessing…', 34, 44; extinction, 31; first step towards, 33; heart, 46; Hereafter, 44; light of witnessing/*nūr al-mushāhada*, 48; the most perfect knowledge of God, 32; Prophets, 57; Sufi, 32–3; truth of certainty, 47; union with God, 47; see also Self-disclosure; spiritual struggle (third); unveiling
women, 39, 40, 52
word, 57, 77; *ʿibra*/spoken word, xxx; *qāl*/spoken word, xl; recorded word, xxx–xxxi; spiritual realities go beyond limits of conventional language, xxx, 28, 68, 78, 81, 90, 92, 93, 94, 97; technical word, xxx, 97
World of Divine Command (*ʿālam al-amr*), 20, 22
World of Spiritual Entities (*ʿālam al-rūḥāniyyāt*), 22
worship (*ʿibāda*), 3, 5, 11; God-wariness, 40; intention, 10; Qur'ān, 22; seeker attracted by God, 109; standardization of outward worship, 10; station of faith, 15; three levels of, 15; wisdom and, 26; 'to worship means to know', 22; see also prayer
wretchedness, 7, 10, 20, 21

yaqīn, see certainty
al-Yūsī, ʿAbd al-Karīm, xxviii
al-Yūsī, al-Ḥasan b. Masʿūd, xxvi, xxviii

al-ẓāhir, see the outward
al-Ẓāhir Sayf al-Dīn Barqūq, Sultan, xxiii, xxiv
Zanādiqa, 87–8
zandaqa, see heresy
ẓann, see opinion
Zarrūq, Aḥmad, ix, xxvi
zāwiya (Sufi lodge), xii, xiv, xviii, 43
Zaydān, ʿAbd al-Raḥmān, xxviii
al-Zubaydī, Abū ʿAbd Allāh, xvii
zuhd, see asceticism; renunciation
ẓuhūr, see manifestation